T0291180

The Circular Bioeconomy

Interest in issues surrounding sustainable production–consumption systems and alternatives to fossil fuels is booming. The circular bioeconomy is currently mainstreamed in policymaking, industry and academia as an important part of the solution to the climate crisis and towards the creation of more sustainable economies. Based on the university-level teaching and research experience of the four authors in Italy, Finland, and France, this textbook fills an important gap in the literature by providing an in-depth and unique guide to the circular bioeconomy. The chapters critically discuss the potential contribution of a circular bioeconomy to fostering societal and organisational transformations towards sustainability globally. This timely book joins a suite of important new titles on sustainability, environmental and ecological economics.

Piergiuseppe Morone is Full Professor of Economic Policy at Unitelma Sapienza, University of Rome, where he works on green innovation and sustainable circular bioeconomy. His work regularly appears in prestigious innovation and environmental economics journals. He is Editor-in-Chief of *Societal Impacts* and Vice-chair of the Circular Bio-based Europe Joint Undertaking (CBE JU) Scientific Committee.

Dalia D'Amato is a senior research scientist at the Finnish Environment Institute (Syke). She is also an adjunct professor at the University of Helsinki and a member of the Helsinki Institute of Sustainability Science. Her work focuses on societal and organisational sustainability transformations based on a biodiversity-positive circular bioeconomy.

Nicolas Befort is an associate professor of economics at NEOMA Business School, where he is the Director of the Chair in Bioeconomy and Sustainable Development (NEOMA BS, Greater Reims, Marne en Champagne Chamber of Commerce, Caisse d'Epargne Grand Est Europe). His research work is at the crossroads of innovation studies, ecological economics, transition studies, and organisation studies at developing an economics and management of the ecological transition.

Gülşah Yilan is a researcher at the Unitelma Sapienza, University of Rome, with a strong interest in life-cycle assessment, sustainability analysis, and circular economy. Her recent publications appeared in leading journals, including *Scientific Reports* and *Journal of Cleaner Production*. She also acts as a guest editor for *Current Opinion in Green and Sustainable Chemistry*.

The Circular Bioeconomy

Theories and Tools for Economists and Sustainability Scientists

PIERGIUSEPPE MORONE
Unitelma Sapienza University of Rome

DALIA D'AMATO
Finnish Environment Institute
and
University of Helsinki

NICOLAS BEFORT
NEOMA Business School

GÜLŞAH YILAN
Unitelma Sapienza University of Rome

Shaftesbury Road, Cambridge CB2 8EA, United Kingdom

One Liberty Plaza, 20th Floor, New York, NY 10006, USA

477 Williamstown Road, Port Melbourne, VIC 3207, Australia

314–321, 3rd Floor, Plot 3, Splendor Forum, Jasola District Centre, New Delhi – 110025, India

103 Penang Road, #05–06/07, Visioncrest Commercial, Singapore 238467

Cambridge University Press is part of Cambridge University Press & Assessment, a department of the University of Cambridge.

We share the University's mission to contribute to society through the pursuit of education, learning and research at the highest international levels of excellence.

www.cambridge.org
Information on this title: www.cambridge.org/9781009232555

DOI: 10.1017/9781009232586

First published 2023

A catalogue record for this publication is available from the British Library

Library of Congress Cataloging-in-Publication Data
Names: Morone, Piergiuseppe, author. | D'Amato, Dalia, author. | Béfort, Nicolas, author. | Yilan, Gülşah, author.
Title: The circular bioeconomy : theories and tools for economists and sustainability scientists / Piergiuseppe Morone, Unitelma Sapienza, Dalia D'Amato, Finnish Environment Institute (Suomen Ympäristökeskus – SYKE) and University of Helsinki, Nicolas Befort, NEOMA BS, Gülşah Yilan, Unitelma Sapienza University of Rome.
Description: Cambridge, United Kingdom ; New York, NY : Cambridge University Press, 2023. | Includes bibliographical references and index.
Identifiers: LCCN 2023016293 | ISBN 9781009232555 (hardback) | ISBN 9781009232586 (ebook)
Subjects: LCSH: Environmental economics. | Sustainability.
Classification: LCC HC79.E5 M666 2023 | DDC 338.9/27–dc23/eng/20230627
LC record available at https://lccn.loc.gov/2023016293

ISBN 978-1-009-23255-5 Hardback
ISBN 978-1-009-23259-3 Paperback

Contents

Figures

Tables

Preface

Why a textbook on the bioeconomy? As its name does *not* indicate, the bioeconomy has been essentially confined to a technological problem of developing new processes and defining technological roadmaps. This had the effect of initially distancing the issue of the bioeconomy from the field of social sciences. However, starting in the mid-2010s, the question of defining the bioeconomy began to emerge little by little, mainly under the impetus of critical researchers questioning the effective scope of the bioeconomy to achieve its promise of breaking with the fossil economy. This trend was accompanied and accelerated by the parallel transition from a linear to a circular economy, which complements the bioeconomy and leads to the emerging circular bioeconomy model of production and consumption.

The investment of social science scholars in the field of the bioeconomy has been carried out first in the context of science and technology studies and then in the context of transition studies. The emergence of this new meta-field of research opens the prospect of a profound transformation of economic sciences. Indeed, the interdisciplinary study of the emergence of new sustainability practices invites to cross the perspectives of social sciences and thus, for economists, to enrich and transform their tools.

This enrichment necessarily involves integrating into the analysis the questions of the institutionalisation/de-institutionalisation of new material flows, the role of prosperity narratives in structuring economic development, the role of innovation in the ecological transition, and the development of new governance institutions capable of guiding change through regulation as well as new standards and indicators capable of accounting for the complexity of transition processes and evaluating the sustainability of economic systems. Thus, the development of the bioeconomy opens up new perspectives for disciplinary crossings within and beyond the social sciences.

In this book, we outline the historical emergence and current development of the bioeconomy in the broader context of sustainability transformations, and we illustrate theoretical frameworks and tools relevant to its study and analysis. We hope this will allow students and teachers to engage conceptually with the bioeconomy and participate in its development by leveraging an interdisciplinary approach and a systemic sustainability perspective.

Box. The Whys and Hows of Teaching Sustainability and Bioeconomy

Alex Giurca, Principal Scientist, European Forest Institute (EFI), and Helga Pülzl, Assistant Director for Policy Support, European Forest Institute (EFI) and Senior Scientist, BOKU

Teaching sustainability is no easy task, and most of the time it starts with the well-known Brundtland definition. Adding a highly interdisciplinary and inter-sectoral concept such as 'bioeconomy' into the mix makes that task even more complex. Given the rising number of academic programmes on bioeconomy mushrooming all over Europe (i.e. master's programmes, graduate schools, university networks, and online seminars), it becomes paramount to take a step back and critically reflect on why and how bioeconomy and sustainability are taught in universities. Since many of these programmes are recent, little systematic knowledge is available about their objectives, teaching philosophies, approaches, and effectiveness. In a recent Pan-European study, Masiero and colleagues (2020) attempted to understand how the bioeconomy is perceived by forestry students. The authors were able to show that student awareness of the bioeconomy differs from northern to southern Europe, and from eastern to western Europe. In fact, students from those countries whose governments already had somewhat comprehensive political bioeconomy strategies seem to know more about the topic than those where this is not the case. This inequality in knowledge production and transfer is mirrored by the unequal bioeconomy-related funding distribution as Lovrić and colleagues (2020) so aptly show. What is taught in relation to bioeconomy, or under the bioeconomy label, differs considerably from one university to the next. Countries, where the forest industry plays a central role in national strategies, tend to focus more on this prerequisite, whereas other countries may highlight other areas. While Masiero's study focused only on universities with a forestry profile, it seems safe to assume that these observations also apply to universities with different profiles.

The solution to this conundrum must not be dichotomous. Yet, on the one hand, natural scientists ask for more informal STEM education to accelerate the bioeconomy (Hakovirta & Lucia 2019). Social scientists, on the other hand, argue that there are still significant gaps in bioeconomy teaching from their perspective (Sanz-Hernández et al. 2019). Going beyond the debate of 'what' to teach in relation to bioeconomy, a more important question remains about 'how' to teach it. How does one teach an ever-expanding, interdisciplinary, and highly politicised concept in the context of sustainability? And how does one avoid unintentionally legitimising political narratives in academia? Some scholars have argued that a T-shaped approach is useful. This approach calls for combining profiles with deep expertise in a certain field, with integrative abilities allowing students to move across different disciplines (Lask et al. 2017). In a similar vein, Urmetzer and colleagues (2020) argue for a transformative approach to bioeconomy education, one that includes elements from transformative knowledge, such as communication, participation, decision-making skills, and skills related to the ability to revise and reflect on one's personal values. This includes critical reading and reflection about the narratives of societies and students embedded in the so-called power/knowledge nexus. To not fall into the pitfalls of legitimising political narratives, it is crucial to uncover what is 'allowed' to be said and not said in a given bioeconomy context. Such transferable skills will likely equip future generations with adequate tools for dealing with complexity, regardless of what this complexity may entail: new political buzzwords or urgent environmental challenges.

References

Hakovirta, M., & Lucia, L. (2019). Informal STEM education will accelerate the bioeconomy. *Nature Biotechnology*, **37**, 103–104.

Lask, J., Maier, J., Tchouga, B., & Vargas-Carpintero, R. (2018). The bioeconomist. In I. Lewandowski, eds., *Bioeconomy*. Springer, Cham.

Lovrić, M., Lovrić, N., & Mavsar, R. (2020). Mapping forest-based bioeconomy research in Europe. *Forest Policy and Economics*, **110**, 101874.

Masiero, M., Secco, L., Pettenella, D., Da Re, R., Bernö, H., Carreira, A., Dobrovolsky, A., Giertlieova, B., Giurca, A., Holmgren, S., Mark-Herbert, C., Navrátilová, L., Pülzl, H., Ranacher, L., Salvalaggio, A., Sergent, A., Sopanen, J., Stelzer, C., Stetter, T., Valsta, L., Výbošťok, J., & Wallin, I. (2020). Bioeconomy perception by future stakeholders: Hearing from European forestry students. *Ambio*, **49**, 1925–1942.

Sanz-Hernández, A., Esteban, E., & Garrido, P. (2019). Transition to a bioeconomy: Perspectives from social sciences. *Journal of Cleaner Production*, **224**, 107–119.

Urmetzer, S., Lask, J., Vargas-Carpintero, R., & Pyka, A. (2020). Learning to change: Transformative knowledge for building a sustainable bioeconomy. *Ecological Economics*, **167**, 106435.

Acknowledgements

The authors would like to acknowledge the following institutions for their support:

- Academy of Finland ('OPerationalising Ecosystem services in business Sustainability: drawing from green and circular bioeconomy' – OPES, grant no. 315912)
- NordForsk and Formas, which are respectively an organisation under the Nordic Council of Ministers that funds Nordic research cooperation, and the Swedish Research Council for Sustainable Development ('Green forests policies: a comparative assessment of outcomes and trade-offs across Fenno-Scandinavia' – Green-Pole, decision no. 103443)
- Nordic Forest Research SNS ('Transdisciplinary co-production in forest policy research' – ForPol, decision no. SNS-128)
- The Nordic Forestry, Veterinary and Agricultural University Network NOVA ('The Future of the Bioeconomy: circular and ecosystem services-aware?')
- The Chair in Bioeconomy and Sustainable Development (NEOMA Business School, Greater Reims, Marne en Champagne Chamber of Commerce, Caisse d'Epargne Grand Est Europe) (Greater East Region, AGRIBIOEST project). Excerpts from chap. 2 are extracted from Befort, N., 2020. Going beyond definitions to understand tensions within the bioeconomy: The contribution of sociotechnical regimes to contested fields. Technological Forecasting and Social Change 153, 119923. https://doi.org/10.1016/j.techfore.2020.119923. with the authorization of Elsevier, 2023.

Fabio Giudice, Eleonora Staffieri, and Gelsomina Russo are also acknowledged for the support they provided during the preparation of the book.

Note on the Text

Alexandru Giurca, Executive Manager, Heidelberg Center for the Environment (HCE), and Helga Pülzl, Assistant Director for Policy Support, European Forest Institute (EFI) and Senior Scientist, BOKU, Preface. The Whys and Hows of Teaching Sustainability and Bioeconomy.

Elias Hurmekoski, Academy research fellow, University of Helsinki, Box 7.1 Assessing the net climate impacts of the forest-based bioeconomy in Finland.

Luana Ladu, Researcher, Technological University of Berlin, Box 7.2 Selection of LCA impact categories for bio-based products.

Andreas Pyka, Professor of Innovation Economics, University of Hohenheim, Box 8.1 Dedicated Innovation Systems.

Abbreviations and Notations

ADEME	French Environmental Protection Agency
AGREV	Programme Agriculture Environment Vittel
BBI-JU	Bio-based Industries Joint Undertaking
1,4 BDO	1,4 butanediol
BE	bioeconomy
BETA	Bureau of Theoretical and Applied Economics
CAC	command and control
CED	cumulative energy demand
CExD	cumulative exergy demand
CO_2	carbon dioxide
DNA	deoxyribonucleic acid
EC	European Commission
EEA	European Environmental Agency
EEC	European Economic Community
EHS	environmentally harmful subsidy
E-LCA	environmental life cycle assessment
EPR	extended producer responsibility
ETS	emission trading system
EU	European Union
FAO	Food and Agriculture Organization of the United Nations
FaST program	Framework about SusTainability
FP	Founding Programme
GDP	gross domestic product
GET	General Equilibrium Theory
GHG	greenhouse gases
GVC	global value chain
GWP	global warming potential
H2020	Horizon 2020
iLUC	indirect land use change
IMF	International Monetary Fund
INRA	Institut National de la Recherche Agronomique
IP	intellectual property
IPBES	Intergovernmental Platform on Biodiversity and Ecosystem Services
IPR	intellectual propriety rights
ISBWG	International Sustainable Bioeconomy Working Group (ISBWG)
ISO	International Organization for Standardization
KBBE	knowledge-based bio-economy

LCA	life cycle assessment
LCC	life cycle costing
LCOE	levelised cost of energy
LCSA	life cycle sustainability assessment
MB	marginal benefit
MCDA	multi-criteria decision analysis
MD	marginal damage
MLT	multi-level perspective
MRS	marginal rate of substitution
MRT	marginal rate of transformation
MSW	municipal solid waste
NASDAQ	National Association of Securities Dealers Automated Quotation
NGO	non-governmental organisation
NREL	National Renewable Energy Laboratory
OECD	Organisation for Economic Co-operation and Development
PBF	Product Biodiversity Footprint
PBS	polybutylene succinate
PET	polyethylene terephthalate
PHA	polyhydroxyalkanoates
PLA	polylactic acid
PPP, 3P or P3	public–private partnership
R&D	research and development
SDG	Sustainable Development Goals
SEEA	System of Environmental-Economic Accounting (SEEA 2022)
S-LCA	social life cycle assessment
SME	small and medium-sized enterprise
SNM	strategic niche management
SO-LCA	social organisational life cycle assessment
STEM	science, technology, engineering, and math
SUP	Single-use plastics
SUPPs	single-use plastic products
TDR	tradable development rights
TIS	technological innovation systems
TM	transition management
TNFD	Taskforce on Nature-related Financial Disclosures
UK	United Kingdom
UN	United Nations
UNEP	United Nations Environment Programme
US	United States
USA	United States of America
USD	United States dollar
WBCSD	World Business Council on Sustainable Development
WTO	World Trade Organization
WWF	World Wide Fund for Nature

Part I

1 The Historical Origins of the Bioeconomy

Learning Objectives

To understand and be able to critically discuss:

- the role of strategies for building a vision of the future for the transition towards a sustainable bioeconomy.
- the history of the bioeconomy.
- the role of collective innovation strategies for the transition towards the bioeconomy.

1.1 From Today's Bioeconomy to Those of the Past

In its 2012 paper, the European Commission defined the bioeconomy as encompassing 'the production of renewable biological resources and the transformation of these resources and waste streams into value-added products such as food, feed, bioproducts and bioenergy'.[1] It thus gave impetus to a broad movement of thinking, which took the form of the development of national strategies towards the bioeconomy (Lokko et al. 2018; Staffas et al. 2013), which reincorporated earlier exercises dealing with biorefinery.

However, this questioning is not new. We have identified two in particular that could have been moments of development of a bioeconomy. In the United States, the 1920s was a moment of crystallisation during which a social bloc was formed at the initiative of isolationists and agrarianists who joined the project of pioneer scientists, seeking to lift the Deep South out of poverty and its cotton monoculture through the non-food use of other products and co-products of agriculture. They sought to theorise and promote what they called *Chemurgy*. To do so, we have relied on the work of historians of technology (Finlay 1997, 2003) or economic policy (Pursell 1969), the very abundant historical documentation gathered by the American Soybean Information Center (Shurtleff & Aoyagi 2011), as well as documents of the American Chemistry Society.

---

[1] This document extends the Lisbon strategy adopted in 2000, which launched the 'Knowledge Based Economy' (KBE), which will be declined into a Knowledge Based Bio-Economy (KBBE) in 2007.

At the end of the 1970s, the crisis in the chemical industry, linked to the oil crisis and the saturation of its markets and the slowdown in its innovations, led to the exploration of sugar chemistry as a vector for new growth. During the foresight exercises of the time (published between 1979 and 1982), a large number of the paths explored today were mentioned, hence our interest in this particular moment of problematisation. Biotechnology was then 'chosen' as one of the two fields in which a return to growth was expected.

During these periods, actors problematised their industry (Jullien & Smith 2012). This means that economic and political actors sought to determine collectively the innovations to be developed to drive the development of their industry. Section 1.2 of this chapter explains the role of actors' expectations in driving the development of an industry and the development of innovations. Section 1.3 is devoted to the presentation of the biorefinery. Section 1.4 is devoted to chemurgy. Section 1.5 details the bioindustry movement.

1.2   Problematisation, Visions of the Future, and Promises

1.2.1   Visions of the Future as a Basis for the Problematisation of Economic Activities

The transition to a sustainable bioeconomy aims to develop an economy that is no longer based on the use of oil but on the use of renewable resources that must respect planetary limits (cf. Chapter 2). This dynamic brings into play visions of the future. That is, the opportunity for a transition to the bioeconomy relies on the need for actors to share common representations (Beckert 2013, 2016; Borup et al. 2006).

These shared representations have the function of accompanying the actors in their activities that are subject to very high uncertainty. This uncertainty is linked to the instability related to production, demand, and the ability to access the natural resources necessary for production. To counter these uncertainties, actors translate their visions of the future into narratives. These narratives are then expressed in speeches, projects, etc.

From this point of view, the transition to the bioeconomy is being played out today under the influence of the futures that the actors represent (Giurca et al. 2022). In doing so, actors act 'as if' this future were true and build their innovation strategies in this direction. Actors are then strongly invested in the definition and propagation of these visions of the future, which may be contradictory. Thus, the actors proceed with *backcasting* exercises. Unlike the scenario method, which starts from the present to identify futures, *backcasting* starts from a vision of the future to identify the transition path to be followed and the technical and economic obstacles to be overcome (Sanders et al. 2010).

1.2.2   The Role of Innovation Commons

Innovations have a role to play in the transition to the bioeconomy because the aim is to use new raw materials and develop new processes, new products, new outlets, or new forms of organisation. These innovations can aim to replace existing products (e.g. biodegradable plastics aim to replace single-use plastics) or to fulfil new functions (e.g. because of its lightness and strength, hemp can be used to produce high-speed train bodies).

We often think that innovations are the result of an individual process driven by a particularly inspired entrepreneur. However, in order to emerge, all innovation projects rely on the production of common knowledge that the actors share. These particular forms of innovation are called innovation commons (Potts 2018).

These common resources appear when actors seek to solve a common problem (here, how to industrialise the production of bio-based products). Thus, this governance tool allows actors to give themselves a common vision and to co-ordinate their activities. To do so, the actors share not only technologies and demonstrative objects but also information guiding the discovery of entrepreneurial opportunities. This collective action makes it possible to defend innovations under development from the pressures of established actors. Nevertheless, these commons are bound to disappear in the future.

1.3   A Bioeconomy Based on Biorefinery?

After the first oil crisis in 1973, the agro-industry and the paper industry put the idea of renewable-based industrial production back on the public policy agenda. The pressure of agricultural surpluses and overcapacity in the paper industry led them to define the range of products that could be produced, based on a theorisation of the biorefinery object and a strategy for disseminating its model in various areas (Cherubini et al. 2009).

By analogy with the oil refinery, the biorefinery will be conceived as the functional unit carrying out the cracking of raw materials of plant or animal origin of various natures and qualities, in order to reduce them to liquid fuels, and a small number of large chemical intermediates, allowing the preservation and continuation of carbon chemistry. Like the petroleum refinery, which generates the bulk of commodity chemistry from steam cracking in five major intermediates,[2] the prospective study conducted by the US Department of Agriculture (Werpy & Petersen 2004) proposes to target twelve major intermediates selected on the basis of expert opinion by crossing the technological expectations of rapid substitution and the size of the markets (a list reduced to a top ten by Bozell & Petersen (2010)). Although this vision is contested because of its reductive aspect or its lack of

---

[2] Ethylene, propylene, butadiene, toluene, and benzene.

attention to its sustainability, it is indeed the one that has become dominant in the bioeconomy landscape (Morone et al. 2019).

This dominant representation of the future of plant-based chemistry comes from commodity chemistry, from small light molecules such as diacids, and making it possible to reform *chemical structures identical* to those of products derived from fossil carbon. However, this is debated, as other avenues for future exploration exist. Colonna et al. (2015) identified two other paradigms: the search for molecules of renewable origin with different structures, but providing the same functions, and the search for new functionalities that can be achieved, thanks to the complex structures that living organisms have been able to produce – and which it is important not to destroy in the cracking process. Nevertheless, the bioeconomy is based on two objectives that are difficult to reconcile: increasing the use of natural resources through technical progress and ensuring the sustainable use of these resources through controlled pressure on ecosystems (Levidow et al. 2013).

1.4   The *Chemurgy*, Problematisation of a Development Path

1.4.1   Chemurgy as a Social Movement for the Use of Renewable Resources

When it emerged in the 1920s, *chemurgy* brought together very contrasting characters. G. W. Carver, son of a black slave with an uncertain birth date, sought from the 1890s to develop new agricultural production and their valorisation in order to lift the black farmers of the 'Deep South' out of its endemic poverty. Although he was excluded from federal research grants because of the racism of Alabama's laws, this did not prevent him from finding more than a hundred non-food applications for soybeans and peanuts, from seeking to valorise all waste products on the farm, from finding other ways than those of pesticides and chemical fertilisers, and from protecting soils from erosion and monoproduction. Carver's pre-World War I 'creative chemistry' (Abrams & Adair 2009) is dreamlike in its proximity to the uses expected today: the use of food co-products for the manufacture of insulating panels, paints, dyes, industrial alcohol, various types of plastic, carpets, mats and fabrics, oils, gums and waxes, etc. He became famous at the end of World War I by proposing a process for producing rubber from sweet potatoes.

In the mid-1920s, an unexpected actor emerged: the railroad companies. Stricken by the post–World War I crises of overproduction, they sought to plan a regional development likely to bring them business, based on the presence of an agro-industry 'on the farm' (Finlay 1997). The unlikely meeting between the agro-ecologist son of a slave and Henry Ford is probably because the latter was seeking to circumvent the steel cartel by producing his car bodies and some of his car parts from renewable resources. He dreamt of vertically integrating all the raw materials, processes, and components necessary for his automobile production:

In May 1935, Ford brought together over 300 leaders of agriculture, education, industry, and science in Dearborn, Michigan, for the first Dearborn Conference of Agriculture, Industry, and Science. Here the Farm Chemurgic Council was established, with Francis Garvan and the Chemical Foundation (a non-profit group dedicated to advancing the position of industrial chemistry) promising to support the group for the first year. (Permeswaran (2010), p. 97)

The Great Depression, if it strengthened the interest in *chemurgy*, was above all a moment of conflict between the isolationists and agrarians and the Roosevelt presidency because the former claimed that the 'free' development of *chemurgy* was a sufficient alternative to the interventionist measures of the New Deal; nevertheless, they ended up accepting the creation by Roosevelt in 1938 of four regional laboratories of the US Department of Agriculture dedicated to *chemurgy*. Thus, the emergence of *chemurgy* took shape through the conjunction of three phenomena: (i) the growing interest in a new industrialisation of chemistry (Galambos et al. 2007), (ii) the existence of agricultural production surpluses, and (iii) a political debate between isolationists and agrarians.

1.4.2 Promises of Chemurgy and the Constitution of Networks of Actors

The end of *chemurgy* can be explained by the cessation of large-scale projects, the victory of oil over the use of renewable resources, and the opposition to *chemurgy* by leaders of the American agricultural world, who favoured specialisation in commodity agricultural products rather than a strategy of diversification towards non-food biomass (Finlay 2003). However, two elements must be kept in mind to understand the contemporary dynamics.

On the one hand, the formation of a specific meso-economic space is a meeting place for heterogeneous actors around technical objects. Within this space, actors set up reflections on all the knowledge to be produced, the resources to be assembled, and the political alliances to be built to support the industrial effort. Through reality checks, they seek to make stable a particular regime of knowledge production and economic activities.

On the other hand, the technical and economic promises required *the production of demonstrative objects* to support the development stories. The various products proposed by Carver (often with little commercial success but always well publicised to the point that we find traces of them in major films of the time), or at Ford the prototype cars with bodies made of thermosetting plastics from renewables, fulfil this function. It is therefore interesting to focus on these promises by projecting them onto the current situation (see Table 1.1).

Table 1.1 Comparison of the techno-economic promise of chemurgy and current chemurgy

	Raw materials and targeted products	Products still targeted at present
1920–1934	– Soy milk → paints, lubricants, automotive plastics – Corn cob, pine waste, sweet potato, hemp, and various grains → raw materials – Natural alcohol (ethanol) → energy and gasoline/ethanol blends – Cellulose, starch, lignin, fructose →sugars and fibres	– Soybean oils for lubrication (e.g. biopress) – Pine waste such as bark for the production of insulating foams – Hemp-based materials and wheat for the production of PHA (high value-added biodegradable plastic) – Incorporation rate already existing, generalisation of biofuel production – Lignin (materials vs. energy), starch (materials vs. chemistry of molecules), cellulose in materials, and hygiene (e.g. toothpaste)
1935–1939	– Use of sawmill waste → production of materials and plastics – Beet sugar, artichoke waste, farm waste → butanol, acetone – Hemp, flax, rice → paper – Rice → furfural and glycerine – Sweet potato → starches – Cane sugar, sorghum, sweet potatoes → ethanol – Pines, tung → newspapers – Cellulose → synthetic fibres, automotive materials	– Reuse of sawmill waste for materials and not just energy – Bio-based butanol – Furfural – Generalisation of ethanol – Cellulosic extraction techniques
1939–1945	– American rubber sources – Molecules → pharmacy – Wheat → adhesives – Sugar cane → fat – Casein → clothing, fibres – Fermentation → production of antibiotics	– Reintroduction of natural rubber (Michelin) – Cardboard and adhesives by wheat starch (arugula) – Fermentation techniques
1945–1972	– Vegetable oils → lecithin, glycerine, plastics, adhesives, flame retardants – Fermentation using lactic, citric, gluconic acid	– Polyurethanes from vegetable oils – PLA from lactic acid fermentation

1.5   The Late 1970s: Towards a Bioindustry?

This second moment of problematisation appeared to the experts to be a deeper cri-sis than the oil shocks of 1973 and 1979 alone. In what follows, three observations that emerged from several documents published during this period will be discussed (Section 1.5.1). Then, the French foresight exercise on the bioindustry will be pre-sented (Section 1.5.2). Finally, the European position on the subject, resulting from the Framework about SusTainability (FAST) program of DG XII of the EEC, will be analysed (Section 1.5.3).

1.5.1 Three Observations at the Origin of the Reflection on the Development of Bioindustries

The first observation is the clear slowdown in the pace of innovation in the chemical industry compared to the 1950s–60s, as attested by subsequent econometric studies, such as that of Achilladelis et al. (1990).

The second observation is the saturation of large markets built through property rights monopolies and the so-called *ultimate plant* strategy, theorised by the Dupont de Nemours company. In this strategy, productivity investments allowed for a drastic reduction in production costs in order to dissuade the entry of competitors. The downside of such a strategy is the creation of structural rigidities that are ill-equipped to cope with the new instability caused by market saturation and the instability of upstream and downstream prices.

The third observation is that the United States of America, in association with the large chemical companies concerned by the crisis of the large chemical production units (and the European Commission), would have developed state-of-the-art and prospective hypotheses on the fields likely to revive growth and innovation (van Laer 2010). These states of the art are constitutive of the work that the actors carry out around technological promises, as well as the place where common resources are constituted.

1.5.2 Chemistry and 'Classical Bioindustries' at the Heart of European Reflection

During this period, several reports and journal special issues were published. With the support of policymakers, they outlined the stakes in terms of industrial exploitation of the scientific revolution of genetic engineering in a complementary way with 'classic' bioindustries. The 'classical' bioindustries and chemistry are at the heart of the development of an engineering science of continuous processes, an essential condition for achieving productivity gains in large refineries (Danielou & Broun 1981). Beyond the product innovations introduced by genetic engineering, it is the capacity to propose catalytic reactions that is the most appreciated quality of biotechnologies. Indeed, these allow us to envisage an improvement in the efficiency of processes. However, it appears that industrialists will only adopt biotechnologies when they succeed in challenging the existing process (Penasse 1981). Between the two polar situations (domination of the classical chemical process *vs.* that of a biotechnological process), the authors of the reports and journals mentioned above saw a set of technological paths qualified as *hemisynthesis* (coupling or cascade use of chemical and biotech reactions) creating a set of new economic opportunities.

The authors did not envisage the disappearance of thermochemical processes from the bioindustry landscape in favour of biotechnological processes. Thus, in order to locate themselves in the space of competing trajectories, the actors produced analytical diagrams of the main sectors. These show that the current landscape was already mapped out in 1981. For example, Chesnais (1981) already listed the raw materials under discussion today, from oil shale to biomass or waste. Biomass is transformed in processes that go either towards synthesis gases (thermochemistry) imitating petro-leum chemistry or towards fermentation processes that loop back on it from ethanol or diacids. It is the same carbon chains as those from 'king oil' that are targeted. Hence, there is confusion between bioindustries mobilising a biotechnological process and those mobilising biomasses, whatever the process.

The problematisation exercise then focuses on Schumpeterian ruptures within existing agro-industries and brings to light two elements that seem to us to be structuring today. On the one hand, innovation leads to the development of hyper-competition between biosourced raw materials as soon as scientific advances in biotechnologies can become continuous industrial processes (Zitt 1983, p. 42). On the other hand, biotechnological innovation[3] makes it possible to reconfigure the value chain to obtain control of the 'global supply chain' from intermediate products: 'Finally, this mixed process-product innovation is significant for major trends in technological evolution in the bioindustries: the development of markets for intermediate products freed from a single agricultural source, and the emer-gence of a new technical operator, "immobilised enzymes", of which the produc-tion of isoglucose is the most important industrial application to date' (Ibid., p. 42).

From this point of view, the key variable of change is economic since, in theory, most petroleum chemical products can be produced from a biotechnological process. Research in biotechs is therefore oriented in a precise direction: to challenge each exist-ing chemical or thermochemical process, in order to consider whether it is possible to envisage a substitution of these processes, with an *identical* product or final function (e.g. sweetness). This type of orientation based on a vision of the future of chemis-try hybridised with biotechnologies thus generates a particular regime of knowledge production – and of the resulting economic activities (Cohendet et al. 1987). This is dedicated to the enrichment of commons that are also specific, without the knowledge of thermochemistry targeted by the substitution disappearing for all that.

1.5.3   What Structure(s) for a Bioindustry-Based Chemistry?

The work of the Organisation for Economic Co-operation and Development (OECD) in 1978–79 and of the FAST EUR7767 program of the European Commission (DG XII), which brought together researchers and large chemical firms on the prospects for chemistry in Europe (well-known from the publications of the BETA laboratory in Strasbourg); Ancori & Cohendet (1984) had a definite influence on the development of the European chemical industry. These research programs identified four main themes around which it was proposed to articulate the innovation policy on a European scale: the chemistry of small molecules[4] (linked to the renewal of carbochemistry), the chem-istry of sugars, the chemistry of new materials, and the chemistry of function.

---

[3] Let us specify that we are talking about industrial biotechnologies that we would qualify today as classical in the sense that they involve preparing enzymes for use in industrial conditions and not 'new biotechs' based on genetic engineering manipulations.

[4] 'Small molecule chemistry' refers to the chemistry related to the production of chemical molecules with a low number of carbon atoms (one to three carbon atoms), whereas sugars contain more. This classification is structuring for the reflection on the transition of a sustainable chemistry.

However, this way of organising these themes would suggest that the bioindustry would be reserved for sugar chemistry, which is not the case, as we will show. The challenges of small molecule chemistry are discussed as those of a renaissance of coal chemistry. The core of the promise of the bioindustry core lies in the fact that one could imagine substituting for the intermediates derived from petrochemistry, an intermediate derived from gasification of the carbon chains of coal – that is, methanol – on which it is possible to base a set of technological hopes. Like the five basic petrochemical intermediates,[5] 'the downstream chemistry of methanol is very rich' (Cohendet 1982, p. 17). It allows the reformation of fuels and acetic acid, which serves as a base for plastics (PET), solvents, paints, and varnishes (Box 1.1).

However, biosourced routes for materials chemistry and functional chemistry have also been documented. It is therefore in the four themes of the report on the prospects for chemistry in Europe that we must look for traces of a problematisation of the bioindustry and not in only one, that of sugar chemistry. This observation is not surprising if we follow the work of Colombo, who was to be the founder of Novamont, a leading company in the conversion of Italian chemistry to renewables. In his 1980 article, based on a report for the OECD while he was in charge of R&D at Montedison, Colombo defended the need for a kind of technological pluralism, identifying the fields of activity where it is relevant to intervene with this or that technology, with the idea of achieving a better balance between centralised production (around the ultimate plants) and decentralised production (Colombo 1980).

Box 1.1 Acetic Acid from Ethylene (Reconstituted by us from the Article 'Acetic Acid' Ulmann's Encyclopaedia of Industrial Chemistry, vol. 1, pp. 209)

Acetic acid, produced from petroleum ethylene, methanol from coal chemistry, or by biological means (the good old vinegar), can be used as a:

- solvent: miscible with water and various organic solvents such as ethanol, diethyl ether, and glycerol, but insoluble in carbon sulphide; it is also a good solvent for gums, resins, phosphorus, sulphur, and halogenated acids;
- production of acetic anhydride, cellulose acetate, vinyl acetate monomer, and other acetates, as well as medicines, pesticides, dyes, and products of the photographic industry;
- food (production of fruit vinegars, food additive);
- textiles;
- cleaning agent (e.g. for semiconductors);
- coagulant (from natural latex);
- bacteriostatic (in solution);
- in the manufacture of plastics such as polyethylene terephthalate (PET) or cellulose acetate, useful in the production of vinyl acetate (paints, adhesives) and organic solvents; and
- additive in tobacco products (flavouring).

---

[5] Ethylene, propylene, butadiene, toluene, benzene.

1.6   Conclusion: What Lessons Can Be Learnt from the Study of the Current Bioeconomy?

This chapter focuses on the study of two moments of problematisation of the future. In these two particular moments, actors sought to construct visions of the use of renewable resources. Table 1.2 compares the characteristics of the *chemurgy*, the "bioindustry" of the 1980s and what is now called the bioeconomy. It shows the great permanence of the resources mobilised, the qualification and co-ordination mechanisms, and the underlying collective production issues. We have pointed out the dominant role of small molecule chemistry in the visions of the future of bioindustries, a result that has been found in the current bioeconomy. Indeed, this chemistry was first established in that of fossil materials, associated with large production units, providing large intermediates to the basic chemistry. This model will significantly orient biorefinery research on the small molecules of the renewable known since the chemurgy era. Today, however,

Table 1.2 The structure of the chemurgy, bioindustry, and bioeconomy innovation commons

	Chemurgy	Bioindustry	Bioeconomy
Material and immaterial resources	– Co-products of food and agriculture – Agricultural production surplus – Advances in the industrialisation of chemistry – Regional laboratories for *chemurgy*	– Government funding of prospective projects – Opportunities offered by the emergence of new processes	– Heterogeneous knowledge bases – Project financing – Biomass from agro-industrial agriculture
Knowledge production and diffusion among members of the community	– Formation of a social bloc linking isolationists and agrarians – Farm Chemurgic Council – Integration of *chemurgy* projects in large companies (Ford)	– State-of-the-art qualifying technologies – Possibility of competing with an existing process	– Definitions of the bioeconomy – Financing of projects aiming at non-food valorisation – The use of renewable resources, if possible, in a sustainable way
Common understanding of entrepreneurial opportunities	– Chemurgic Council – Development of production units – Demonstration of emblematic products	– Think tanks and foresight groups – Small molecule chemistry – Emblematic products – Centralised *vs.* decentralised production	– Biorefinery and industrial pilots – Platform molecules *vs.* new functionalities – Promise of transition carried by the bioeconomy and its products

we also find a more complex macromolecular chemistry that is more closely linked to materials science, suggesting the opportunity for a more decentralised bioeconomy – also present in the *chemurgy* or at the turn of the 1980s.

Take-Home Message

- The bioeconomy is the new name for an old dynamic.
- The development of innovations in the bioeconomy is the product of the interaction between groups of actors, the development of knowledge, and the formation of promises.
- The development of non-food uses of biomass is currently concentrated around emblematic products (e.g. biofuels, biodegradable plastics).

Learning Exercises

1. What are the periods of development of non-food uses of the biomass?
2. From the presentation of the old products, what is taken back today?
3. What are the differences between each period?

References

Abrams, D., & Adair, G. (2009). *George Washington Carver: Scientist and educator*, Infobase Publishing.

Achilladelis, B., Schwarzkopf, A., & Cines, M. (1990). The dynamics of technological innovation: The case of the chemical industry. *Research Policy*, **19**(1), 1–34.

Beckert, J. (2013). Capitalism as a system of expectations. *Politics & Society*, **41**(3), 323–350.

Beckert, J. (2016). *Imagined futures: Fictional expectations and capitalist dynamics*, Harvard University Press.

Borup, M., Brown, N., Konrad, K., & van Lente, H. (2006). The sociology of expectations in science and technology. *Technology Analysis & Strategic Management*, **18**(3–4), 285–298.

Bozell, J. J., & Petersen, G. R. (2010). Technology development for the production of biobased products from biorefinery carbohydrates – The US Department of Energy's "Top 10" revisited. *Green Chemistry*, **12**(4), 539.

Cherubini, F., Jungmeier, G., Wellisch, M., … de Jong, E. (2009). Toward a common classification approach for biorefinery systems. *Biofuels, Bioproducts and Biorefining*, **3**(5), 534–546.

Chesnais, F. (1981). Biotechnologie et modifications des structures de l'industrie chimique: quelques points de repère. *Revue d'économie Industrielle*, **18**(1), 218–230.

Cohendet, P. (1982). The European Chemical-Industry and the crisis: The necessity of technological changes. *FUTURIBLES*, (60), 13–29.

Cohendet, P., Ledoux, M. J., & Zuscovitch, E. (1987). *Les matériaux nouveaux: dynamique économique et stratégie européenne*, FAST.

Colombo, U. (1980). A viewpoint on innovation and the chemical industry. *Research Policy*, **9**(3), 203–231.

Colonna, P., Tayeb, J., & Valceschini, E. (2015). *Nouveaux usages des biomasses*. Le Déméter 2015, 275–305.

Danielou, G., & Broun, G. (1981). Bioindustrie: de la tradition artisanale à la pratique industrielle. *Revue d'économie Industrielle*, **18**(1), 14–29.

Finlay, M. R. (1997). The failure of chemurgy in the depression-era south: The case of Jesse F. Jackson and the Central of Georgia Railroad. *The Georgia Historical Quarterly*, **81**(1), 78–102.

Finlay, M. R. (2003). Old efforts at new uses: A brief history of chemurgy and the American search for biobased materials. *Journal of Industrial Ecology*, **7**(3–4), 33–46.

Galambos, L., Hikino, T., & Zamagni, V. (2007). *The global chemical industry in the age of the petrochemical revolution*, Cambridge University Press.

Giurca, A., Befort, N., & Taylor, A. (2022). Exploring transformative policy imaginaries for a sustainable Post-COVID society. *Journal of Cleaner Production*, **344**, 131053.

Jullien, B., & Smith, A. (2012). Le gouvernement d'une industrie. *Gouvernement et Action Publique*, 1(1), 103–123.

Levidow, L., Birch, K., & Papaioannou, T. (2013). Divergent paradigms of European agro-food innovation. *Science, Technology, & Human Values*, **38**(1), 94–125.

Lokko, Y., Heijde, M., Schebesta, K., Scholtès, P., van Montagu, M., & Giacca, M. (2018). Biotechnology and the bioeconomy – Towards inclusive and sustainable industrial development. *New Biotechnology*, **40**, 5–10.

Morone, P., Falcone, P. M., & Lopolito, A. (2019). How to promote a new and sustainable food consumption model: A fuzzy cognitive map study. *Journal of Cleaner Production*, **208**, 563–574.

Penasse, L. (1981). Perspectives et contraintes de la bioindustrie. *Revue d'économie Industrielle*, **18**(1), 30–37.

Permeswaran, P. (2010). Chemurgy: Using science innovatively to save American agriculture from overproduction. *The History Teacher*, **44**(1), 95–125.

Potts, J. (2018). Governing the innovation commons. *Journal of Institutional Economics*, **14**(6), 1025–1047.

Pursell, C. W. (1969). The Farm Chemurgic Council and the United States Department of Agriculture, 1935-1939. *Isis*, **60**(3), 307–317.

Sanders, J., Langevald, H., Kuikman, P., Meeusen, M., & Meijer, G. (2010). *The biobased economy: Biofuels, materials and chemicals in the post-oil era*, Routledge.

Shurtleff, W., & Aoyagi, A. (2011). *Henry Ford and his researchers – History of their work with soybeans, soyfoods and chemurgy (1928–2011): Extensively annotated bibliography and sourcebook*, Soyinfo Center.

Staffas, L., Gustavsson, M., & McCormick, K. (2013). Strategies and policies for the bioeconomy and bio-based economy: An analysis of official national approaches. *Sustainability*, **5**(6), 2751–2769.

van Laer, A. (2010). Towards a common research policy: From the silence of the EEC Treaty to the Single Act. In C. Bouneau, D. Burigana, & A. Varsori, eds., *Trends in technological innovation and the European construction: The emerging of enduring dynamics?*, P.I.E.-Peter Lang, pp. 79–100.

Werpy, T., & Petersen, G. (2004). *Top value added chemicals from biomass: Volume I – Results of screening for potential candidates from sugars and synthesis gas*, Golden, CO (United States).

Zitt, M. (1983). Un cas d'innovation: l'isoglucose. *Économie Rurale*, **158**(1), 42–50.

2 Emerging Bioeconomy Narratives

Learning Objectives

To understand and be able to critically discuss:

- the scope of each of the visions of the bioeconomy.
- the possibility of these visions to combine.
- the link between bioeconomy models and product development strategies.

2.1 Introduction

Chapter 1 presented the history of the emergence of thinking in terms of non-food uses of plants. Thus, the term 'bioeconomy' appeared to be the result of a long history, rooted in the history of industrial chemistry. This work of shaping national bioeconomy strategies has led to the emergence of academic works that aimed to describe the bioeconomy through the formation of narratives translating visions of the future and associated political projects. Similarly, the question of the relationship to growth has been addressed within this framework by attempting to link the forms of development of the bioeconomy to a pro-growth, green-growth or degrowth positioning.

This work shows the existence of the main narratives. The first is inscribed in the biotechnology paradigm and is notably defended by the Organisation for Economic Co-operation and Development (OECD). For the proponents of this vision, the emerging bioeconomy is likely to involve two elements: (1) the use of advanced knowledge of genes and complex cell processes to (2) develop new processes and products. The US government, in its Industrialization of Biology report (Friedman & Ellington 2015), provides a similar definition, based on and delineated by biotechnology. The bioeconomy is thus a Schumpeterian revolution based on biotech: an economy based on biotechnology, encompassing the health industry.

The second is articulated around the concept of biorefinery, allowing a great transition towards the non-food valuations of biomass. Thus, the European Commission (EC) defines the bioeconomy as 'encompass[ing] the production of renewable biological resources and the conversion of these resources and waste streams into value added products, such as food, feed, bio-based products and bioenergy'

(European Commission 2012, p. 9). In this economic definition, focusing on biomass processing for food and non-food applications, the use of new scientific and technological knowledge is secondary.

The approach we take here considers narratives to be intrinsically linked to the promises of the bioeconomy, to knowledge and its translation into innovation, to firms' business models and their relationships, and to institutions. The first section of this chapter outlines how the narratives of the bioeconomy form a regime. A regime describes a stable configuration over time that delimits the boundaries of the economic space under consideration.

The second section outlines three cases of emblematic molecules of the bioeconomy. First, we studied succinic acid. BASF developed an oil-based process for this product during World War II. Succinic acid appeared during the 1980s as a good candidate for industrial biotechnology, especially as incumbents in the chemical industry failed to invent new blockbusters like nylon (Bud 1991; Zeikus 1980). During the 2000s, bio-based succinic acid, produced using a biotechnology process in the biorefinery, became the model for drop-in substitution (Werpy et al. 2006). Whereas one might think that this product belongs in the biotechnology regime, industrial structure, artefacts, and relations highlight the incorporation of white biotechnologies in the bioeconomy.

Second, we studied polylactic acid (PLA). This plastic has a long history: its discovery dates back to the 1930s in Dupont laboratory. From the 1960s, it was mostly used for medical applications. During the 1980s, the development of sustainable commodity plastics became an object of interest, to avoid plastic waste, especially with the involvement of the agro-firm Cargill. Moreover, whereas succinic acid is produced from biotechnology processes, modern PLA is produced from a combination of biotechnology and chemistry processes.

Third, we studied levulinic acid. This product also has a long history: it has been produced using thermochemical and bio-based processes since the 1940s. Moreover, the process has never been oil-based; it was thus surprising that the product was selected as a top twelve product (Werpy & Petersen 2004).

2.2   The Bioeconomy and the Biotechnology as Regimes

2.2.1   Promises and Expectations of Biotechnology and the Bioeconomy

OECD countries have made great efforts to support biotech and its spread throughout the economy (OECD 2017a). The development of this sector grew from the extension of 'traditional biotechnologies' to genetic manipulations and synthetic biology (Bud 1991). Biotechnologies are expected to be key technologies for the development of a bioeconomy through scientific breakthroughs producing a new wave of Schumpeterian innovations (Levidow et al. 2012). The promise of an industrial revolution lies at the heart of biotechnology. In this view, biotechnologies are 'general-purpose technologies' that can be used in health, agriculture, and, as far as this chapter is concerned, in the manufacturing industry (mainly chemicals and materials) (Aguilar et al. 2013; McKelvey 2007). Biotechnology appears to be a technology-driven industry, since its development was initially based on advances in biology and specific institutional configurations. As a general-purpose technology, biotechnology targets many areas (OECD 2009). As an illustration, biotechnologies are classified by colours illustrating the targeted sector: red for health biotech, blue for marine biotech, gold for nanotech, and, most importantly for our case, green for agriculture and white for industry.[1]

The bioeconomy carries different promises and expectations. The EU Communication setting the European bioeconomy agenda highlights the following 'societal challenges' for the bioeconomy: ensuring food security, managing natural resources sustainably, reducing dependence on non-renewable resources, mitigating and adapting to climate change, creating jobs, and maintaining European competitiveness (European Commission 2012). These challenges may be achieved through a core artefact: the biorefinery (European Commission 2012). This concept has been produced by firms in agro-industries, chemistry, the wood sector, and biotechnology. This concept represents the transition to the use of renewable resources copying the chemical paradigm of fossil oil: cracking the input, purifying the chemicals, and reforming them into intermediate products (Kamm et al. 2006).

This artefact emerged at the beginning of the millennium at the meeting point between two dynamics. First, there was the issue of using abundantly available biomass. Since the end of the 1980s, agro-firms were searching for new outputs for their excess production. For example, firms like Cargill explored the production of bio-based plastics. Because they already knew how to produce non-food applications, agro-firms launched research programmes. Second, growing criticism of the chemical industry led to the development of 'green chemistry' based on twelve principles (Anastas & Warner 1998). Since the beginning of the millennium, the seventh principle, covering the use of renewable resources, has become preeminent, under the influence of agro-industries (Garnier & Bliard 2012). So, public and private players inventoried the top twelve – reduced to top ten – 'molecules of interest'[2] that carry strong techno-economic promise for food and non-food applications (Becker et al. 2015; Bozell & Petersen 2010; Werpy & Petersen 2004).[3] This strategy opened up two competing ways of conceiving product development. The first was a 'drop-in' strategy: replacing an oil-based molecule with exactly the same molecule, but bio-based ('drop-in substitution' in what follows). Second, some new product development strategies draw on biomass functions (biodegradation, lightness, etc.; 'novel functionality substitution' in what follows) (de Jong et al. 2012).

---

[1] OECD Key biotechnology indicators shows that most biotechnology activity is dedicated to health: www.oecd.org/sti/biotech/keybiotechnologyindicators.htm, accessed 12/10/2017.
[2] This evolution is noted here for the sake of accuracy, but according to our interviews, it did not have any influence.
[3] Some of the molecules inventoried were already well-identified research objects, and sometimes had been for more than twenty years.

The 'bioeconomy of the biorefinery' pursues two interconnected objectives: (i) to unify the transformation of renewable resources for food (human and animals) and non-food (chemistry, materials, and energy) uses in biorefineries, and (ii) to make biorefineries ecologically and economically sustainable.

2.2.2   Knowledge and Innovations of Biotechnology and the Bioeconomy

The term 'biotechnology' covers two streams of research and applications. First, it refers to the manipulation of genomes to synthesise valuable products, following on from the discovery of DNA structure in 1953 and the identification of protein synthesis and regulation in 1963, which paved the way for synthetic biology. Second, it refers to the inherent reaction capacities of microorganisms or biological agents for product development (such as yeast in the wine and brewing industries) (Bud 1991). The field of biotechnology developed through several well-documented artefacts: science-based start-ups, markets for technology, and the financialisation of start-up strategies.

In the bioeconomy, biotechnology is one of the four knowledge bases (de Jong et al. 2012), alongside thermochemistry, oil-based chemistry, and mechanical/one-pot processes. Available technological choices are constrained in several ways. First, other technologies can produce the same drop-in product, leading to competition between technological trajectories that does not exist in biotechnology (Cherubini et al. 2009). Second, biomass is enormously diverse. It can originate from dedicated crops (cereals, palm oil, beets, miscanthus, etc.), agricultural co-products (straw, bagasse), food industry waste (poultry, cooking oil, milk) or from the sea (algae or microalgae). Third, biomass and technological choices are interrelated, because technological efficiency depends on biomass choices (Kamm et al. 2006). The bioeconomy has also developed different artefacts. First, as described earlier (Section 2.2.2), the biorefinery acts as a unifying artefact, especially through the use of a second artefact: backcasting. Backcasting is a planning methodology inspired by organisation management and energy production planning (Robinson 1982; Vergragt & Quist 2011). Starting from possible futures, backcasting defines pathways to reach them, identifying technological lock-ins to solve through innovations nurtured in niches. The first use of this method for biorefinery dates back to 1999 with the 'Plant/Crop Based Renewable Resource 2020' programme. The report 'Top Value-Added Chemicals from Biomass' (Werpy & Petersen 2004) pursued this idea, identifying promising drop-in molecules (see also Bozell & Petersen 2010). The European Joint Research Centre imported this methodology in 2005 for its report 'Techno-economic Feasibility of Large-scale Production of Bio-based Polymers in Europe' and for projects such as BREW (2006) and Biorefinery Euroview/Biopol (2008). These last two projects identified players in several sectors (chemistry, pulp and paper, sugar/starch, biofuel, bioenergy, petrochemistry, etc.) that might become involved in the bioeconomy. Each project results in several biorefinery typologies with the same objective, that of imitating petrochemistry.

Following this framing, public players (regions, states, states coalitions like Nordic countries, etc.) defined strategic roadmaps to navigate towards the bioeconomy (OECD 2017b). These roadmaps act as inventories of major activities and technologies that can become part of the bioeconomy (like the wood sector in Finland) and define a vision for the future of the area covered by the roadmap, and tools to sustain the emergence of the bioeconomy (Staffas et al. 2013). Third, many academic publications define possible technological futures. These reviews (e.g. see Cherubini et al. 2009) inventory new product opportunities, together with the process, technological lock-ins, and alliances between sectors or knowledge bases required to achieve production of the molecules.

2.2.3   Business Models in Biotechnology and the Bioeconomy

From the biotech perspective, start-ups are core organisations for new knowledge production (Audretsch 2001). Such firms can be academic spinoffs or purely private entities (Mustar et al. 2008). Start-ups are associated with the heroic figure of the Schumpeterian entrepreneur making a scientific breakthrough providing techno-scientific promises, and thus gaining both private venture capital and public funding. Increased access to Intellectual Property Rights (IPR) since the Bayh–Dole Act (Mowery & Sampat 2004) and markets for technologies support the start-up model (Arora 2001). Biotechnologies use both public and private funding. The introduction of new financial regulations made possible the creation of small- and medium-sized firms specialising in basic research and in producing and selling scientific knowledge. In particular, in 1984, the so-called Alternative 2 market on the National Association of Securities Dealers Automated Quotation (NASDAQ) opened the way for a 'finance-driven model' of innovation (Coriat & Orsi 2002). This model led firms to focus on increasing their capitalisation instead of developing products to turn intellectual property (IP) into assets they can sell on technology markets (Andersson et al. 2010). Because shares are bought and sold by investors, their value has to increase continually (Hopkins et al. 2013), especially via techno-economic promises. Most biotechnology markets are in health. However, we focus here on industrial biotechnology (i.e. white biotechnology). This includes chemistry (base chemicals, speciality chemicals, and consumer chemicals), polymers and fibres, and active pharmaceutical ingredients. According to Festel et al. (2012), biotechnology sales should increase from €91.9 billion in 2010 to €515.1 billion in 2020. While in 2010, each sector had a roughly equivalent market share (between 15 per cent and 22 per cent), the proportions for polymers and fibres, consumer chemicals, and speciality chemicals are expected to be the largest in the future. This can be explained by the fact that biotechnology processes are far more expensive than oil-based processes, and speciality products are able to sustain higher production costs.

The few existing statistics show that the bioeconomy's turnover was €2.2 trillion in 2014 (Ronzon et al. 2017). In 2014, most of the turnover in the bioeconomy came from 'traditional bioeconomy sectors', that is, agro-industries (€1.52 trillion), wood and paper industries (€0.42 trillion), bio-based textiles (€0.11 trillion), and fishery and aquaculture (€0.01 trillion). In the same year, bio-based chemicals, pharmaceuticals, and rubber provided €0.13 trillion of turnover, liquid biofuels €0.03 trillion, and bio-based electricity €0.01 trillion. The bioeconomy also has different markets from biotechnology because of the issue of identifying a substitution strategy between drop-in products and products with novel functionalities. The bioeconomy model differs first in terms of actor networks. In addition to biotechnology start-ups, pulp and paper industry, agro-industries, and chemical industry are involved in the bioeconomy. Even if biotechnology start-ups carry a promise of technological breakthrough, these firms do not possess all the technological and organisational know-how to market their products or to scale their production (Mustar et al. 2008; Patrucco 2014). Therefore, knowledge production and diffusion in the bioeconomy are stimulated through calls for projects aiming at structuring interactions between actors that draw on a variety of knowledge bases.

These alliances can be research projects or joint ventures, or take the form of equity funding (Audretsch et al. 2005; Belussi 2016).[4] They may also occur in pilot and demonstration plants (Hellsmark et al. 2016). For example, Eurobioref and Biocore were two major projects that defined biorefinery business models (Dubois 2011) and demonstrated the need to develop pilot plants and technological platforms involving different players in production. Moreover, the concluding conference for these projects revealed the need for funding these shared structures. These two projects paved the way for the development of several open innovation demonstration platforms (e.g. Biovale in the UK or BioBase Europe Pilot Plant in the Netherlands and Belgium) as keys to co-ordinate knowledge production and diffusion across value chains with public funding (Fevolden et al. 2017).

To sustain the development of markets for bio-based products, industries are expecting a European program for public procurement of bio-based products, following the American example (SCAR 2015). But such a program requires a clear definition of what a bio-based product is. The United States has defined a norm that considers the product's bio-based carbon content, encouraging drop-in substitution.[5] This norm used to be controversial in Europe. Under the pressure of agro-industries, the norm has been widened to other biomass compounds, such as water or hydrogen.

2.2.4   Public Policies in Biotechnology and the Bioeconomy

Research and development policymakers have paid close attention to biotechnology and its inclusion in the bioeconomy. They have defined a policy combining

---

[4] Even if authors like Belussi (2016) identify a growing dynamic towards alliances in biotechnology, they remain in their traditional biotechnology forms: licensing or company buyouts.

[5] Drop-in substitution proponents classify molecules by the number of carbon atoms, as in modern chemistry (de Jong et al. 2012).

entrepreneurship with a strong focus on start-ups (OECD 2009), an extension of the patent system to allow broader inventions and patentees, ease of commoditised knowledge transactions (like the WIPO green technology platform), direct R&D subsidies (e.g. from the NIH in the United States), calls for research (since 1977 in Europe) and industrial projects, and the description of biotechnology as a Key Enabling Technology in Horizon 2020 program (Aguilar et al. 2013). Funded programs have encompassed science and technology development, but also initiatives to forecast the future developments of biotechnology. The goal of such programs is to develop actor–networks linking research and industry. In these networks, actors have to define 'visions for the future', especially in 'European Technology Platform'. The launch of the Lisbon Strategy in 2000 followed by the knowledge-based bio-economy (KBBE; European Commission 2005) organised these networks (Schmidt et al. 2012). Consequently, the KBBE is strongly linked to biotechnologies.

At the same time, the backcasting projects mentioned earlier (see Section 2.2.2) were launched between 1999 and 2012. They defined biorefinery models, the most promising products for the biorefinery, the knowledge bases to use and which actors should be part of the biorefinery. Then, in 2012, the European Commission first used the word 'bioeconomy', translating a combination of KBBE and biorefinery policies. The policy was no longer biotechnology driven but became 'mission driven', with the biorefinery as a core artefact.

In order to sustain the supply side of the bioeconomy, public authorities used national or European calls for projects (like FP7 or H2020), also combining public and private funding. Leading players such as the European lobby for biotechnologies EuropaBio, the Italian firm Novamont, clusters such as 'Industries & Agro-Resources Cluster', also grouped in the Bioeconomy working group of the Standing Committee on Agricultural Research, to support the development of a public–private partnership (PPP) to develop the bioeconomy (SCAR 2015).

The institutional answer to this has been the launch of a PPP, the Bio-based Industries Joint Undertaking (BBI-JU) (Carrez 2016). Launched in 2014, BBI-JU's funding is one-third public (€975 million from the EU) and two-thirds private (€2.7 billion). Bio-based Industries Joint Undertaking calls for projects are based on the definition of five value chains (SIRA 2013), for which it is possible to link a group of leading players. For each of these value chains, the goal is to fund a flagship project. Rather than simply defining a typology of value chains, BBI-JU aims to produce shared resources, for two reasons. First, as it is mainly funded by the private sector, its mechanisms are based on calls for research to develop parts of value chains. In practice, shared resources mean shared uncertainty. Second, even if BBI-JU aims to develop pilot and demonstration plants, some research topics involve pure research and small- and medium-enterprise (SME) funding. This type of funding will be used to consolidate knowledge bases grounding the value chain types. The biotechnology and the bioeconomy as sociotechnical regimes are summarised in Table 2.1.

Table 2.1 The biotechnology and the bioeconomy as sociotechnical regimes

	Biotechnology	Bioeconomy
Promises and expectations of biotechnology and the bioeconomy	– New industrial revolution – Schumpeterian entrepreneur – Technology driven – Diffusing biotechnology in health, food, industry, etc. – Industrialisation of the living	– A 'great transition' towards the sustainable use of renewable resources – Aimed at mitigating and adapting to climate change, creating rural jobs, managing sustainable resources, ensuring food security, reducing dependence on non–renewable resources, and maintaining competitiveness in Europe – Mission driven – Constraints of economic and environmental sustainability – Drop-in products (copying petrochemistry) *vs.* new function products
Knowledge and innovation	– Fermentation and synthetic biology – Patents and start-ups as core artefacts – Markets for technology	– Four knowledge bases: thermochemistry, biotechnology, oil-based chemistry, mechanical processes – Biorefinery, products, and inputs as core artefacts – Pilot and demonstration plants as co-ordination infrastructures among value chains – Backcasting as social technology to define visions for the future – National roadmaps towards bioeconomy – Review articles
Business models	– Duality between start-ups and incumbents – Development of alliances – Public–private networks – Economy of promises: investments driven by breakthrough promises	– Incumbents in agro-industries, pulp and paper, biotechnology, and chemical industries – Public–private partnership to finance scaling-up – Biotechnology start-ups – Competition between knowledge base promoters, between biomass and products (drop-in *vs.* novel functionalities strategies) – Co-operation within value chains in research programs or pilot and demonstration plants
Policy and regulations	– Technology-driven policy – Knowledge commodification and financialisation – Biotechnology as a Key Enabling Technology	– Mission-driven policy – Backcasting to identify desirable futures for bioeconomy, thanks to product identification – PPP to support scale-up of industrial processes – Call for projects to co-ordinate actors

Source: Befort 2020

2.3   Three Products in the Bioeconomy Regime

In this section, we examine the cases of succinic acid, then polylactic acid, and finally levulinic acid (summarised in Table 2.2).

2.3.1   Case 1 Succinic Acid: An Illustration of the Confusion between Biotechnology and the Bioeconomy

2.3.1.1   The Icon of White Biotechnology?

BASF developed an oil-based process in several steps to produce succinic acid during World War II. Succinic acid is mainly used to produce vaccines, cosmetics, and food and as 5 per cent of polybutylene succinate (PBS). To produce this high-value, biodegradable plastic, whose properties are close to those of polyethylene, 1.4 ButaneDiol (1.4 BDO) is needed. During the late 1970s and early 1980s, incumbent firms such as Dupont were becoming increasingly interested in biotechnologies, after failing to discover new chemical blockbusters (Bud 1991). In terms of cultural and symbolic meaning, succinic acid appeared as a symbolic product for the emerging biotechnology industry (Zeikus 1980), especially through succinic acid evolving knowledge base in the use of the bacterium *A. Succiniproducens* (Datta 1992). However, from 1992, because of low-priced agricultural inputs and the expectation of inexpensive processing using bacteria, succinic acid became the symbol of drop-in substitution, with a wide range of applications (Zeikus et al. 1999). For example, start-ups and science-based companies such as Genomatica and Bioamber claimed to be able to produce either commodity or high-value chemicals based on their patented succinic acid production processes.

Consequently, succinic acid might be considered a 'chemically pure' illustration of biotechnology: a promise of radical breakthroughs using patented living organisms and a product based on the expectations of general-purpose technology. Since succinic acid is based on a US-based biotechnology patent, the emblematic producer, Bioamber, might have been the icon of the bioeconomy of biotechnology.

2.3.1.2   Biotechnology or Bioeconomy?

When we examine the policies, guiding principles, industrial structure, and markets developed to sustain succinic acid production, differences between the two regimes appear clearly and show how biotechnological production of succinic acid is part of the bioeconomy.

First, in terms of policy, succinic acid has been listed in the 'top twelve' molecules because of its versatility in the production of other intermediary molecules (Werpy & Petersen 2004). As a versatile drop-in molecule produced from sugar extracted from corn or beet, the fall in its production cost allowed bio-based succinic acid to compete with its oil-based alternative in times of high oil prices. So, it complies with the guiding principle of drop-in substitution at the heart of the bioeconomy and can contest existing oligopolies based on former protected oil-based processes.

Second, we can differentiate between the user relations, markets and industrial structure of science-based companies and those of incumbents, both differing from biotechnology. Science-based companies are active in succinic acid. Bioamber was launched in 2008, as a joint venture between an American patent-based firm, DNP Technologies, and a French co-operative-based research firm, ARD. Characteristically for the biotechnology industry, the firm's original goal was licencing. But the firm's technological developments were supported by the construction of a pilot and demonstration plant. Instead of licencing its process or being bought by a 'big player', Bioamber first developed its production process in Sarnia (Ontario, Canada), and it is planning a new plant in Thailand (through a joint venture with PTT PLC, the Thai public petrochemical consortium). Myriant, an American science-based succinic acid firm, claims an 'open innovation' model for its processes based on the use of microorganisms. Instead of licencing the process, the firm offers formulations of its products to produce polyols[6] for firms such as Dupont Tate & Lyle and Danimer. The firm also concluded agreements to supply Showa-Denko with PBS for the production of plastic film.

Meanwhile, incumbent players outside the biotechnology field conclude joint ventures to produce succinic acid. After a period during which Roquette and DSM,[7] two incumbents, registered patents for succinic acid, they launched a joint venture called Reverdia. This company combines Roquette's expertise in starch production and preparation (as an input for succinic acid), and DSM's enzyme patents. The joint venture has concluded several contracts to market its products, including one with Proviron, to provide them with succinic acid to produce a food additive, and another with Dupont Tate & Lyle, to biosource their polyurethanes. Reverdia has also received US approval for its public procurement program. Hence, these firms, whether science-based companies or incumbent newcomers, do not enter technology markets but use contracts and agreements to secure their production and sales. Finally, Succinity – a joint venture between BASF, the major chemical company, and Corbion-Purac, a former agro-industry company that has become interested in life sciences – claims that it has been testing a succinic acid production process at a Corbion-Purac site since 2014. Hence, the joint venture can be seen as an attempt to enter the field of bio-based products through succinic acid.

2.3.2   The Case of PLA

Since the 1960s, PLA, which was already bio-based, has been used as a speciality polymer to produce prostheses and biodegradable suture thread. In 1986, Lipinsky and Sinclair (1986) theorised it as the new commodity chemical for the packaging industry, thanks to the combination of an expected increase in production, the development of new production method (especially through continuous production processes instead of batch processes) and low agricultural prices, providing economies of scale. This new plastic would have the following features: bio-based, biodegradable, nontoxic, and with equivalent properties to thermoplastics like polyethylene terephthalate

---

[6] Succinic acid is necessary in the formulation of polyol.

[7] Roquette is one of the world's leading starch producers. DSM is a historic Dutch company (created in 1902) specialising in nutrition and materials (plastics, electronics, resins, etc.).

(PET) used in plastic bottles, food packaging, or plastic cups. At the beginning of the 1990s, PLA rapidly became emblematic of commodity plastics carrying environmental promises, because of its biodegradability and use of agricultural surpluses.

Cargill, the major agro-industry player, played a predominant role. The company developed a new sugar-based production process introducing continuous PLA production, which increased PLA production while reducing its cost (Gruber et al. 1994). To achieve this innovation, the firm hybridised chemistry and biotechnology knowledge, illustrating the variety of knowledge bases in the bioeconomy. Second, the firm set up a joint venture with Dow Chemicals called Natureworks, which is now the leading producer of PLA.

The end of the 1990s and beginning of the 2000s saw several significant disappointments regarding the use of PLA as a commodity chemical because:

- It has low heat resistance, which was a problem, given that the product was expected to replace plastic cups for hot beverages.
- PLA was biodegradable only in specific industrial conditions and not in the environment.

To overcome these issues, scientists explored old PLA knowledge and uses, that is, not as a standalone plasticiser but as a blend with other plasticisers. In fact, PLA was invented in the 1930s by Carothers (1937) for the company Dupont. The team that invented PLA also invented nylon. Between this time and the 1960s, as mentioned above, PLA was used as a blend in plastics Schneider (1955). Hence, new developments arrived using a variety of co-polymers: hemp, nanocellulose from wood, or other biodegradable and bio-based plastics, such as polyhydroxyalkanoates (PHA). For example, the agro-food company Corbion, specialising in sugar and lactic acid, launched a heat-resistant PLA. Moreover, in terms of industrial structure, one should note that besides Natureworks and Corbion, the oil company Total developed two joint ventures.

In terms of markets, PLA producers face the problem of achieving acceptable production costs for commodity chemicals. This new polymer competes directly with widely used, low-cost, oil-based commodity polymers, and offers no new functions that consumers would be ready to pay for. Hence, PLA is competing with other bio-based polymers such as PHA – which is a speciality polymer – and with Novamont's Mater-Bi[8] in 'demonstration applications', such as during the Olympic Games in London for Natureworks and Novamont. This shows that players are facing issues on both the supply and demand sides. Moreover, the development of these products is clearly mission driven, to produce a biodegradable commodity plastic in economically sustainable conditions.

2.3.3   Case 3. Levulinic Acid or the Demonstration of Thermochemical Biorefinery Feasibility

From a cultural and symbolic point of view, levulinic acid is an 'old American product', as one of our respondents put it. Industrial production of levulinic acid started

---

[8] Novamont is an Italian bioeconomy company.

in the 1940s (Staley Manufacturing Company 1943). Staley is an agro-company specialising in soy and wheat. The firm developed a thermochemical process for starch (Meyer 1945). Quaker Oats, another agro-industry company, patented a different production process for levulinic acid in 1953, but also using thermochemistry (Dunlop & Wells 1957). Since then, levulinic acid has always been used as an ester for plasticisers, active chemical intermediaries, emulsifiers, pesticides and food supplements (Bozell et al. 2000; Fitzpatrick 1990; Leonard 1956). Consequently, the knowledge base (thermochemistry) and markets for levulinic acid are well identified and stabilised.

During the 1981s, when biotechnology was gaining interest, levulinic acid acquired a new status: 'a good starting point might be to re-examine some of the work on levulinic acid which was done 30-40 years ago' (Veal & Whalley 1981, p. 56). From then on, levulinic acid became a central object of interest to demonstrate the feasibility of the thermochemical biorefinery. Biofine, the main company involved, received strong institutional support from the US government. Biofine was launched in 1987, in an NREL-funded project. Whereas the laboratories were expecting great things from PLA and succinic acid, levulinic acid was already in production in the 1990s, partly funded by the New York Energy Department. But it was also a demonstration artefact. Biofine received the Green Chemistry Presidential Award for its process, and the leading chemist Bozell – who was involved in establishing the top twelve molecules list – published a paper in which he presented the levulinic acid production processes as a model.

Despite the importance now given to biotechnology processes, levulinic acid has not disappeared, and it is still produced using thermochemical processes. Moreover, it has proven the economic viability of the biorefinery based on these thermochemical processes. This case illustrates the competition between knowledge bases in the bioeconomy, here, biotechnology *versus* thermochemistry.

2.4   Conclusion

This chapter highlights the two main concepts that have driven the development of the bioeconomy: the biorefinery bioeconomy and the biotechnology bioeconomy. Analysis of these developments at the product level shows that the dominant logic is that of the biomass-use constraint rather than the biotechnology-use constraint. This notable evolution indicates the need for companies to be able to hybridise knowledge in order to develop activities in the bioeconomy.

In parallel with these developments, the question of the sustainability of the bioeconomy has also arisen, in particular through the question of the circularity of the bioeconomy and its contribution or not to the development of a green economy.

Table 2.2 Three products in the sociotechnical regime of the bioeconomy

	Succinic acid	Polylactic acid	Levulinic acid
Promises and expectations of biotechnology and the bioeconomy	– Illustration of the confusion between biotechnology and the bioeconomy – Profitable use of agricultural surpluses – Biotechnology as key for drop-in substitutions to produce high- and low-value-added products	– Transition towards a bio-based and sustainable commodity chemistry – The symbol of biodegradable plastics – Profitable use of agricultural surpluses – Economic sustainability of bio-based and biodegradable commodity plastics (cups, packaging, etc.) – Should be comparable to PET	– An old bio-based chemical product – Sustainability of thermochemistry-based biorefinery producing chemicals instead of biofuels – Thermochemistry
Knowledge and innovation	– Biotechnology – Patented processes – Pilot and demonstration plants – Top 12 list of promising bio-based products – Review papers developing the guiding principles	– Old chemical knowledge – Biotechnology principles – Top 12 list of promising bio-based products – Review paper developing the guiding principles	– Thermochemistry – Corn-based biorefinery – Review paper developing guiding principles – Top 12 list of promising bio-based products – Pilot and demonstration plant
Business models	– Start-ups industrialising processes through 1) external capabilities (infrastructures, knowledge) 2) publicised supply agreements – Joint ventures between incumbents (chemistry, agro-industries) with complementary capabilities – Joint venture to take up position – Supply agreements to secure market shares for drop-in substitution products	– Joint venture between firms from chemistry and agro-industries – Joint venture to take up position – Issues in satisfying expectations of comparability with PET – Competition between biodegradable plastics – Demonstration and marketing through visible use (e.g. Olympic Games)	– Incumbent firms – Science-based company industrialising its process – Well-identified markets and market shares
Policy and regulations	– Public procurement – Listed as a promising molecule	– Listed as a promising product – Considered non-toxic	– Green Chemistry Presidential Award – Public subsidies – Listed as a promising molecule

---

Take-Home Message

- Several competing visions of the bioeconomy have emerged in academia, business, and policymaking.
- Visions are driven by different actors who seek to take control of the development of the bioeconomy.
- These visions refer to very different ways of organising the bioeconomy.

Learning Exercises

1. What are the competing visions of the bioeconomy?
2. What are compatible visions of the bioeconomy?
3. Choose a product and identify to which vision of the bioeconomy it belongs.

References

Aguilar, A., Magnien, E., & Thomas, D. (2013). Thirty years of European biotechnology programmes: From biomolecular engineering to the bioeconomy. *New Biotechnology*, 30(5), 410–425.

Anastas, P. T., & Warner, J. C. (1998). Green chemistry. *Frontiers*, 640, 1998.

Andersson, T., Gleadle, P., Haslam, C., & Tsitsianis, N. (2010). Bio-pharma: A financialized business model. *Critical Perspectives on Accounting*, 21(7), 631–641.

Arora, A. (2001). Markets for technology and their implications for corporate strategy. *Industrial and Corporate Change*, 10(2), 419–451.

Audretsch, D. B. (2001). The role of small firms in U.S. biotechnology clusters. *Small Business Economics*, 17(1/2), 3–15.

Audretsch, D. B., Lehmann, E. E., & Warning, S. (2005). University spillovers and new firm location. *Research Policy*, 34(7), 1113–1122.

Becker, J., Lange, A., Fabarius, J., & Wittmann, C. (2015). Top value platform chemicals: Biobased production of organic acids. *Current Opinion in Biotechnology*, 36, 168–175.

Befort, N. (2020). Going beyond definitions to understand tensions within the bioeconomy: The contribution of sociotechnical regimes to contested fields. *Technological Forecasting and Social Change*, 153, 119923.

Belussi, F. (2016). The implementation of a new game strategy in biotech form. From start-up to acquisition: The case of Fidia Advanced Biopolymers (now Anika Therapeutics) of Abano Terme. In F. Belussi & L. Orsi, eds., *Innovation, alliances, and networks in high-tech environments.*, Routledge, pp. 337–352.

Bozell, J. J., Moens, L., Elliott, D. C., ... Jarnefeld, J. L. (2000). Production of levulinic acid and use as a platform chemical for derived products. *Resources, Conservation and Recycling*, 28(3–4), 227–239.

Bozell, J. J., & Petersen, G. R. (2010). Technology development for the production of biobased products from biorefinery carbohydrates – The US Department of Energy's "Top 10" revisited. *Green Chemistry*, 12(4), 539–554.

Bud, R. (1991). Biotechnology in the twentieth century. *Social Studies of Science*, 21(3), 415–457.

Carothers, W. H. (1937). Linear Condensation Process. US2071250 A., Google Patents.

Carrez, D. (2016). European strategies and policies getting towards a bioeconomy. In *Creating sustainable bioeconomies*, Routledge, pp. 229–243.

Cherubini, F., Jungmeier, G., Wellisch, M., … de Jong, E. (2009). Toward a common classification approach for biorefinery systems. *Biofuels, Bioproducts and Biorefining*, 3(5), 534–546.

Coriat, B., & Orsi, F. (2002). Establishing a new intellectual property rights regime in the United States. *Research Policy*, 31(8–9), 1491–1507.

Datta, R. (1992, September 1). Process for the production of succinic acid by anaerobic fermentation, Google Patents.

de Jong, E., Higson, A., Walsh, P., & Wellisch, M. (2012). Product developments in the bio-based chemicals arena. *Biofuels, Bioproducts and Biorefining*, 6(6), 606–624.

Dubois, J.-L. (2011). Requirements for the development of a bioeconomy for chemicals. *Current Opinion in Environmental Sustainability*, 3(1–2), 11–14.

Dunlop, A. P., & Wells, J. P. A. (1957, November 19). Process for producing levulinic acid, Google Patents.

European Commission. (2005). New perspectives on the knowledge-based bio-economy: Conference report, European Commission Brussels.

European Commission. (2012). Innovating for Sustainable Growth: A Bioeconomy for Europe (Communication from the Commission to the European Parliament, the Council, the European Economic and Social Committee and the Committee of the Regions No. SWD(2012) 11 final).

Festel, G., Detzel, C., & Maas, R. (2012). Industrial biotechnology – Markets and industry structure. *Journal of Commercial Biotechnology*, 18(1). doi:10.5912/jcb478

Fevolden, A., Coenen, L., Hansen, T., & Klitkou, A. (2017). The role of trials and demonstration projects in the development of a sustainable bioeconomy. *Sustainability*, 9(3), 419.

Fitzpatrick, S. W. (1990). Manufacture of furfural and levulinic acid by acid degradation of lignocellulosic. *World Patent*, 8910362.

Friedman, D. C., & Ellington, A. D. (2015). Industrialization of biology. *ACS Synthetic Biology*, 4(10), 1053–1055.

Garnier, E., & Bliard, C. (2012). The emergence of doubly green chemistry, a narrative approach. *European Review of Industrial Economics and Policy*, (4).

Gruber, P. R., Hall, E. S., Kolstad, J. J., Iwen, M. L., Benson, R. D., & Borchardt, R. L. (1994, October 18). Continuous process for manufacture of lactide polymers with purification by distillation, Google Patents.

Hellsmark, H., Frishammar, J., Söderholm, P., & Ylinenpää, H. (2016). The role of pilot and demonstration plants in technology development and innovation policy. *Research Policy*, 45(9), 1743–1761.

Hopkins, M. M., Crane, P. A., Nightingale, P., & Baden-Fuller, C. (2013). Buying big into biotech: Scale, financing, and the industrial dynamics of UK biotech, 1980–2009. *Industrial and Corporate Change*, 22(4), 903–952.

Kamm, B., Gruber, P. R., & Kamm, M. (2006). *Biorefineries-industrial processes and products*, Vol. 2, Wiley-VCH Weinheim.

Leonard, R. H. (1956). Levulinic acid as a basic chemical raw material. *Industrial & Engineering Chemistry*, 48(8), 1330–1341.

Levidow, L., Birch, K., & Papaioannou, T. (2012). EU agri-innovation policy: Two contending visions of the bio-economy. *Critical Policy Studies*, 6(1), 40–65.

Lipinsky, E. S., Sinclair, R. G. (1986). Is lactic acid a commodity chemical? *Chemical Engineering Progress*, 82, 26–32.

McKelvey, M. (2007). Biotechnology industry. In H. Hanusch & A. Pyka, eds., *Elgar companion to neo-schumpeterian economics*, Edward Elgar Publishing, pp. 607–620.

Meyer, W. G. (1945, August 14). *Manufacture of levulinic acid*, Google Patents.

Mowery, D. C., & Sampat, B. N. (2004). The Bayh-Dole act of 1980 and university? Industry technology transfer: A model for other OECD governments? *The Journal of Technology Transfer*, 30(1–2), 115–127.

Mustar, P., Wright, M., & Clarysse, B. (2008). University spin-off firms: Lessons from ten years of experience in Europe. *Science and Public Policy*, 35(2), 67–80.

OECD. (2009). *The bioeconomy to 2030: Designing a policy agenda*, OECD, Paris.

OECD. (2017a). Biomass for a sustainable bioeconomy: Technology and governance.

OECD. (2017b). Towards Bio-Production of Materials: Replacing the oil barrel (No. DSTI/STP/BNCT(2016)17/FINAL).

Patrucco, P. P. (2014). The evolution of knowledge organization and the emergence of a platform for innovation in the car industry. *Industry and Innovation*, 21(3), 243–266.

Robinson, J. B. (1982). Energy backcasting a proposed method of policy analysis. *Energy Policy*, 10(4), 337–344.

Ronzon, T., Piotrowski, S., M'Barek, R., & Carus, M. (2017). A systematic approach to understanding and quantifying the EU's bioeconomy. *Bio-Based and Applied Economics Journal*, 6(1050-2018-3682), 1–17.

SCAR. (2015). Sustainable agriculture, forestry and fisheries in the bioeconomy – A challenge for Europe. 4th Foresight Exercise.

Schmidt, O., Padel, S., & Levidow, L. (2012). The bio-economy concept and knowledge base in a public goods and farmer perspective. *Bio-Based and Applied Economics*, 1(1), 47–63.

Schneider, A. K. (1955, March 1). *Polymers of high melting lactide*, Google Patents.

SIRA. (2013). Bio-based and Renewable Industries for Development and Growth in Europe.

Staffas, L., Gustavsson, M., & McCormick, K. (2013). Strategies and policies for the bioeconomy and bio-based economy: An analysis of official national approaches. *Sustainability*, 5(6), 2751–2769.

Staley Manufacturing Company. (1943). Levulinic acid; a literature reference, compiled by Division of research development, A. E. Staley Manufacturing Co.

Veal, F. J., & Whalley, L. (1981). Renewable resources as chemical feedstocks. *Conservation & Recycling*, 4(1), 47–57.

Vergragt, P. J., & Quist, J. (2011). Backcasting for sustainability: Introduction to the special issue. *Technological Forecasting and Social Change*, 78(5), 747–755.

Werpy, T. A., Frye, J. G., & Holladay, J. E. (2006). Succinic Acid-A Model Building Block for Chemical Production from Renewable Resources, United States: B Kamm, PR Gruber, and M Kamm; Wiley – VCH, Weinham, Germany. Retrieved from www.osti.gov/biblio/895169.

Werpy, T., & Petersen, G. (2004). *Top value added chemicals from biomass: Volume I – Results of screening for potential candidates from sugars and synthesis gas*, Golden, CO (United States).

Zeikus, J. G. (1980). Chemical and fuel production by anaerobic bacteria. *Annual Review of Microbiology*, 34(1), 423–464.

Zeikus, J. G., Jain, M. K., & Elankovan, P. (1999). Biotechnology of succinic acid production and markets for derived industrial products. *Applied Microbiology and Biotechnology*, 51(5), 545–552.

3 The Bioeconomy, the Green Economy, and the Circular Economy

A Comparative Overview

Learning Objectives

To understand and be able to critically discuss:

- the intended societal contribution of the bioeconomy.
- the differences between the bioeconomy, the green economy, and the circular economy.
- the joint conceptualisation of the bioeconomy, the green economy, and the circular economy.

3.1 The Bioeconomy and Its Societal Contribution: An Evolving Narrative

A plurality of perspectives exists regarding the potential societal benefits of the bioeconomy due, among other reasons, to the high diversity of the bioeconomy as a concept or narrative (Box 3.1). At the moment, the politically mainstreamed bioeconomy remains strongly anchored to the goal of economic development and industrial/sectoral renewal, while a positive contribution to a variety of ecological and social goals is not self-evident (El-Chichakli et al. 2016; Holmgren et al. 2020; Kröger & Raitio 2017; Pfau et al. 2014). Concerns about the tangible societal contribution of the bioeconomy include the sustainable sourcing and use of biomass, and the regional and global distribution of resources and prosperity across people (Issa et al. 2019).

The resource-centred vision of the bioeconomy (see Chapter 2) appears to dominate policy documents and strategies so far (Meyer 2017; Priefer et al. 2017; Vivien et al. 2019). According to this vision, increasing biomass extraction would

---

Box 3.1 Definition of Sustainability Narrative

A *narrative* is defined in this chapter as a storyline used to frame one or more sustainability challenges and legitimise the need for specific sets of interventions. Such storylines are loose enough so that multiple actors with different world visions can subscribe to the same narrative (D'Amato 2021).

entail some degree of land-use intensification, resulting in negative impacts on bio-diversity and other ecological goals at the landscape level (Pedersen et al. 2020). Part of the solution to this problem is related to the efficient use of biomass resources, which was not explicitly embedded in the early definitions and framing of the bioeconomy (while it is acknowledged in the European Union (EU) Bioeconomy Strategy updated in 2018). However, the bioeconomy also appears to have a narrow focus with regard to social goals. Currently, expectations and potential benefits are largely discussed with regard to supply chains, markets, and corporate actors, as well as employment and local (rural) development, with less emphasis on citizen participation, small landowners, and small enterprises, and overall little emphasis on social justice (Holmgren et al. 2020; Mustalahti 2018; Ramcilovic-Suominen & Pülzl 2018; Sanz-Hernández et al. 2019). This calls for further understanding of whether and how compatibilities between multiple societal goals can be found in the bioeconomy.

Parallel to the bioeconomy, the green economy and the circular economy have also emerged in the past decade as policy-led narratives that describe how the existing economic system should be changed in opposition to the current status quo of the resource-intensive, fossil-based, linear economy (or 'brown economy') (Table 3.1). These three concepts are characterised by distinct sets of solutions, but all promise to reconcile the divide between increasingly prosperous economic development and progressively impoverished global environmental and social systems, against challenges such as climate change, resource scarcity, biodiversity loss and pollution, poverty, and injustice. Like the bioeconomy, the green and circular economy are subject to multiple framings and interpretations across actors in science, business, policymaking, and other societal realms. Political goals and strategies related to these concepts also differ significantly across countries and regions (Dietz et al. 2018; Ladu & Blind 2017; McDowall et al. 2017).

A few illustrative figures are proposed here to compare the economic contribution by sectors related to biomass-based activities, to environmental protection and resource management, and to recycling-repair-reuse and rental-leasing activities. While statistics explicitly referring to the green economy could not be retrieved, we made use of Eurostat data about the environmental economy (statistics about the bioeconomy and the circular economy are explicitly reported). Note that some overlaps may occur between the three domains, so the data are not to be interpreted as cumulative. In 2019, the EU27 bioeconomy was estimated to have generated €630 billion of value added and employed 17.4 million people (Ronzon et al. 2018). This amounts to around 4 per cent of the EU27 GDP and almost 9 per cent of the labour force (calculated for 2017) (Ronzon et al. 2020). Agriculture, food, and beverages (including tobacco) were recorded as key sectors in the European bioeconomy, in addition to wood products, paper and forestry, bio-based textiles, chemicals and pharmaceuticals (including rubber), fuels and electricity, and fishing and aquaculture. Eurostat defines the environmental economy as encompassing activities and products for the purpose of reducing or eliminating environmental degradation, or for the purpose of more efficiently using natural resources. This includes waste and wastewater management, renewable energy (including biofuels) and energy efficiency, water saving, and other forms of environmental protection (e.g. organic farming). The gross value added of the environmental economy (EU27) grew from 128.5 to €306.8 billion between 2000 and 2018. In 2018,

Table 3.1 An overview of sustainability-oriented narratives and proposed solutions in opposition to status quo economic systems

Narrative	Proposed solutions	In opposition to
Bioeconomy	Use of biological resources to replace or complement fossil-origin products and services, leveraging knowledge and innovation (e.g. development of innovative bio-based and biotechnology-based goods and services) (e.g. Bugge et al. 2016)	Fossil-based economy (i.e. an economic system supported by fossil energy and materials)
Green economy	Use of abiotic renewable energy (e.g. solar, wind, hydro) and leveraging of ecological functions to foster human well-being (e.g. ecosystem conservation and restoration, nature-based solutions, and green infrastructures) (Borel-Saladin & Turok 2013)	Brown economy (i.e. an economic system of environmentally unaware activities, based on fossil resources and focused on built capital)
Circular economy	Reduction of inputs/outputs in production and consumption systems by retaining material and energy flows for as long as possible within high value/functionality levels (e.g. sustainable design, material/energy efficiency, reuse, and remanufacture, recycling) (e.g. Kirchherr et al. 2017)	Linear economy (i.e. an economic system based on the extraction and use of resources, and consequent disposal of waste)

Source: D'Amato and Korhonen (2021)

the employment related to the environmental economy was estimated at 4.4 million full-time equivalents (Eurostat 2021a). In 2018, the value added at factor cost for the circular economy (EU27) was reported to be €130.8 billion with almost 3.5 million people employed. This included the recycling sector, the repair and reuse sector and the rental and leasing sector (Eurostat 2021b). The bioeconomy, the green economy, and the circular economy include conceptually overlapping elements, but overall, they have been forwarded as independent ideas. Based on these premises, this chapter provides a further comparative overview of the green economy and the circular economy, discussing their core elements and the plurality of voices and associated criticism (Sections 3.2 and 3.3, respectively). Leveraging on these notions, Section 3.4 draws considerations for the conceptual and practical development of the bioeconomy.

3.2   The Green Economy, Natural Capital, and Ecosystem Services

3.2.1   The Political Emergence of the Green Economy

While the term 'green economy' was coined before the turn of the century (Pearce et al. 2013), the green economy as a series of political strategies has been mainstreamed following the 2008 financial crisis. Such strategies have been further fostered by the

2012 United Nation Conference on Sustainable Development in Rio de Janeiro (also known as Rio+20). The process was supported by international institutions such as the Organisation for Economic Co-operation and Development (OECD), the International Monetary Fund (IMF), the World Bank, the World Trade Organization (WTO), and the World Business Council on Sustainable Development (WBCSD) (Ferguson 2015; Loiseau et al. 2016; O'Neill & Gibbs 2016). A report published by United Nations Environment Programme states that the green economy 'results in improved human well-being and social equity, while significantly reducing environmental risks and ecological scarcities. In its simplest expression, a green economy can be thought of as one which is low carbon, resource efficient and socially inclusive' (UNEP 2011, p. 1). Like the bioeconomy, the green economy remains a highly diverse concept that is the object of several interpretations and different framing by scholars and practitioners (Merino-Saum et al. 2020).

3.2.2   The Sustainability Problem Framed by the Green Economy

The green economy signals the need for a shift from an economic system currently based on fossil resources and built capital, which does not ascribe any significant role to nature, and does not consider environmental damage and social inequalities – in other words, a brown economy. The way forward highlighted by the green economy revolves mostly around two themes (Barbier 2012; Loiseau et al. 2016; Lorek & Spangenberg 2014; Robinson 2015; ten Brink et al. 2012). The first theme is the need to reconfigure energy systems, particularly by shifting from finite resources to renewable, low-carbon, and abiotic energy from solar, wind, hydroelectric, and geothermal sources. This includes the need for the efficient use of such resources, as well as the need for a more decentralised and democratic production of energy. The second theme is the role of natural capital and ecosystem services as a fundamental prerequisite underpinning human economies and well-being at the individual, organisational, and societal levels. This chapter will mainly focus on the second theme, because it is the one that most characterises and distinguishes the green economy from other narratives, such as the circular and bioeconomy.

Since the late 1990s, natural capital and ecosystem services have become increasingly central in scientific research and policymaking in the context of sustainability and resilience of social-ecological systems (Costanza et al. 2017; Droste et al. 2018). Natural capital represents the stock of renewable (e.g. forest, fisheries) and non-renewable (e.g. fossils, minerals) natural assets at a given time and place (Costanza & Daly 1992; Guerry et al. 2015). Ecosystem services are ecological processes occurring in natural and semi-natural systems which – in combination with direct or indirect human input – result in being useful or beneficial to human beings (Braat & de Groot 2012; Haines-Young & Potschin 2010; Millennium Ecosystem Assessment 2005). They are grouped into three categories: provisioning (e.g. provision of crops and wild foods, fibres, clean water, genetic resources), regulating (e.g. regulation of local and global climate, maintenance of soil and nutrient cycles, pollination, control of pests and diseases), and cultural services (spiritual, aesthetic, scientific and educational values associated with nature) (Figure 3.1).

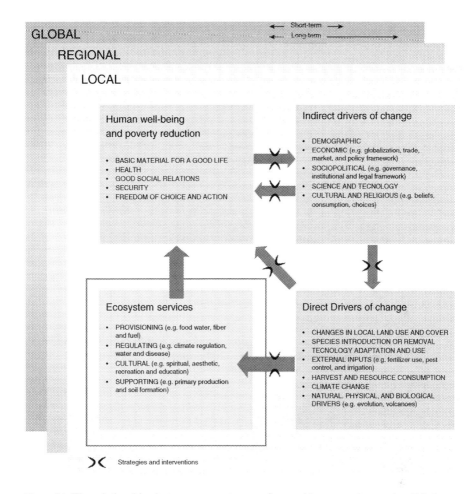

Figure 3.1 The relationships between ecosystem services and human actions and well-being. Source: Millennium Ecosystem Assessment (2005)

Ecosystem services are not to be interpreted as a universal list of items: as a human construct (in reality, nature is neither benign nor malevolent); their existence is largely determined by the geographical, ecological, social, economic, and cultural context of the observer or beneficiary. The concept of ecosystem services suggests that the biosphere provides fundamental premises for producing goods, services, and value in the society and economy.

The concept of ecosystem services suggests that the biosphere provides fundamental premises for producing goods, services, and value in society and the economy. However, the UNEP-driven Millennium Ecosystem Assessment (2005), a milestone international initiative in promoting the concept of ecosystem services, concluded that 60 per cent of global ecosystems are being degraded or used unsustainably, with important consequences for human well-being. A global assessment published by the Intergovernmental Science-Policy Platform on Biodiversity and Ecosystem Services (IPBES) further consolidated evidence that biodiversity is declining at an unprecedented rate in human history due to anthropic activities (IPBES 2018). Provisioning services such as agricultural production, fish harvest, energy, and materials have increased since 1970 at the expense of equally important regulating and cultural services (e.g. pollination, soil quality, and nature-related physical and psychological experiences) (ibid.). Several reasons lie behind these global trends. The contribution of natural capital and ecosystem services is often invisible or underappreciated by traditional measures of economic development, resulting in the erosion of natural capital in favour of other forms of human-made capital, at least until critical thresholds are reached exposing negative social and economic repercussions.

Securing the simultaneous co-existence of multiple ecosystem services in a certain place is difficult because interventions aimed at increasing the quantity or quality of some services may result in the decrease of other services in space and time (i.e. a trade-off). As a rule of thumb, the maximisation of provisioning services (e.g. intensively managed planted forests for timber production) is likely to result in a trade-off with regulating (e.g. water quality/regulation) and cultural services (e.g. wilderness-related recreation or scientific/educational opportunities) at the landscape level (Braat & de Groot 2012; Howe et al. 2014; Smith et al. 2017; UNEP 2011). Regulating and cultural services are more likely to behave in a synergic manner (i.e. with a mutual improvement of both services) (Figure 3.2). These relationships are partly physiological but can be largely influenced by endogenous and exogenous drivers, such as environmental change and policy or management interventions (Dade et al. 2019). For instance, improved land-use and management practices, such as the creation of riparian buffer zones, can mitigate or avoid existing trade-offs between timber production and water quality.

Various actors, operating at different levels, benefit from ecosystem services and/ or contribute to maintaining the flow of ecosystem services. Such actors include local

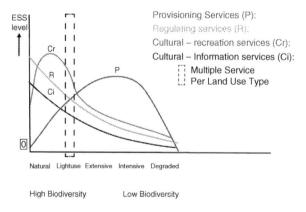

Figure 3.2 The relationship between land use and ecosystem services trade-offs.
Source: Figure modified from Braat and de Groot (2012)

communities, landowners, tourists, civil society organisations, companies, national governments, and the global community. An individual or organisation may perform several roles at the same time, for example, supplier, regulator, and beneficiary of eco-system services. However, benefits from ecosystem services and the costs of maintaining them are unequally distributed across actors. The distribution of benefits and costs depends on the biophysical availability in space and time and on institutions and power relations among social groups, countries and regions (Felipe-Lucia et al. 2015). Institutions and power relations include informal or formal conditions determining the accessibility of ecosystem services by different actors. Examples of such conditions are gender, ethnicity, social status, information asymmetry, topographic, or regional dynamics (e.g. upstream–downstream, Global North–South), land or resource rights, legislative frameworks, and treaties.

Many ecosystem services show characteristics of public goods, meaning they are non-rival (i.e. may not be possessed or physically consumed) and/or non-exclusive (i.e. access cannot be limited) (see Chapter 4). Provisioning services are more often related to tangible, physical items that are often exchanged in markets; this makes them more likely to be rival and exclusive, or in other words private goods. For instance, crops or wood are depleted after consumption, and possession/accessibility can be enforced through property rights. Regulating and cultural services or non-consumptive forms of recreation (e.g. air and water quality, hiking) tend to be non-rival and/or non-exclusive. This means that the benefits derived from such services can be freely enjoyed, with no direct maintenance costs to users. While protected areas and other public land can be managed for multiple ecosystem services in the general societal interest, private landowners are more likely to be inclined to maximise benefits from provisioning services rather than maintaining regulating and cultural services.

3.2.3   Core Solutions in the Green Economy

Key solutions under green economy strategies are meant to improve the availability of multiple ecosystem services at the landscape level. These include the conservation and restoration of natural and semi-natural ecosystems, and the development of nature-based solutions and green/blue infrastructures (especially in human-dominated environments) (Box 3.2). The practical implementation of these kinds of solutions requires identifying suppliers and users of public or quasi-public goods, or in other words, the actors bearing the costs and/or enjoying the benefits (winners/losers) of the management and use of ecosystem services. It is also important to pay attention to the transboundary nature of ecosystem services flows, including regional and global distribution of costs/benefits and power dynamics across actors. For instance, the regulation of global climate by means of carbon storage in natural systems is typically transboundary in nature, meaning that no matter where the carbon sink is located, the benefit is global. Similarly, the costs of climate change have no geographical boundaries: developed countries historically have an important responsibility where greenhouse gas emission is concerned, but the negative effects of climate change will also and perhaps more heavily affect

---

Box 3.2 Examples of Green Economy Solutions

Tree planting is at the core of the non-profit business model of Taking Root, an organisation which pays Nicaraguan farmers with the revenues of the woodcraft, coffee, and carbon credits produced by the trees they plant. Similar market mechanisms are used by other organisations worldwide to finance their biodiversity-based business models. For example, the 3Bees network brings together *beekeeping* businesses and offers citizens the opportunity to 'adopt' a beehive and receive honey as well as periodic updates about the biodiversity-positive effects of beekeeping.

Since 2006, *urban gardening projects* have been started by local associations and citizen groups in Rome (Italy) as collective, bottom-up initiatives to improve the availability and quality of green spaces in the city. Similar citizen-led initiatives also exist in other countries. For example, in Budapest, 'pocket parks' have been developed since 2010, sometimes in collaboration with a professional organisation or the local government. These are multi-functional spaces dedicated to small-scale food products, recreation, water, and local climate management, which also bring about social benefits such as community sharing and neighbourhood rehabilitation (Urban Nature Atlas 2021).

Land requalification of an unused landfill hill in the area of Vuosaari in Helsinki (Finland) has resulted in a natural area with domestic flora, which is now used for recreational, educational, and scientific purposes. The project started in 2002 as a joint project of the City of Helsinki and the Helsinki Port Authority. A similar project is being developed in Melaka (Malaysia), where there are plans to rehabilitate Krubong landfill into a public park (Urban Nature Atlas 2021).

---

areas hosting indigenous people and the world's poorest communities, who are more directly dependent on the natural environment for their livelihood (IPBES 2018).

Parallel to conservation and restoration efforts, nature-based solutions include a range of context-tailored activities leveraging (or inspired by) ecological processes, such as living roofs/walls and green indoor areas, eco-districts, urban parks and forests, community gardens, and constructed wetlands and ponds. Depending on the context, nature-based solutions may be more effective, efficient, and long-lasting in delivering multiple benefits than engineered solutions (hybrid approaches may also be considered). Nature-based solutions at the landscape level can be summed up as green infrastructure, 'a strategically planned network of natural and semi-natural areas with other environmental features designed and managed to deliver a wide range of ecosystem services' in both rural and urban settings (European Commission 2013, p. 3).

3.2.4   Financing of the Green Economy

Strategies for mobilising resources towards the green economy are context dependent. In addition to a publicly funded budget, instruments such as payments for ecosystem services, tradable permits, and offsetting/compensation schemes have been promoted at regional, national, and international levels under the green economy. These are considered to be important complements to regulatory instruments to support the conservation, restoration, and sustainable management of natural and semi-natural ecosystems (Barbier 2012; Bull & Strange 2018; Wunder et al. 2018). Such instruments are also used to direct financial resources for coupled conservation-development projects to rural areas and/or the Global South. In fact, nature conservation and restoration under the green economy narrative are often coupled with poverty alleviation/ livelihood diversification (Barbier 2012). The green economy and the related notion of ecosystem services have also emphasised the role of private sector actors through certification, private investments, company-level sustainability processes, and green financing (Hrabanski 2017). The effectiveness and legitimacy of marketising ecosystem services (e.g. payments for ecosystem services, offsetting), as well as private sector involvement in the co-governance of sustainability challenges remain objects of controversy in the scientific and practitioner community (McAfee 2012). Such neoliberal solutions are criticised by some as being insufficiently transformative in addressing the profound causes of current sustainability challenge (Borel-Saladin & Turok, 2013; Brand, 2012; Luederitz et al. 2017; Tomaselli et al. 2017).

3.3   The Circular Economy, Dematerialisation, and Sufficiency

3.3.1   The Political Emergence of the Circular Economy

Based on the tradition of industrial ecology and cleaner production (Calisto Friant et al. 2020; Chizaryfard et al. 2021; Winans et al. 2017), the circular economy has experienced a renaissance in the past decade, largely influenced by industry/ practitioner initiatives and by policy and legislative processes (Murray et al. 2017). The circular economy has become especially relevant in the EU and China, albeit with different focal areas (McDowall et al. 2017). Following the 2015 EU Circular Economy Action Plan, the 2020 updated Action Plan includes, among other things, dismissing single use; fostering longer-lasting products from non-virgin materials, which are easier to reuse, repair, and recycle; empowering customers with information on product reparability and durability; and focusing on improving the environmental footprint of resource-intensive sectors (e.g. textiles, electronics, packaging, construction, and plastics).

3.3.2   The Sustainability Problem Framed by the Circular Economy

Like the bioeconomy and the green economy, the circular economy hosts a spectrum of understandings and definitions, from conservative to radical (Calisto Friant et al. 2020; Hart & Pomponi 2021; Korhonen et al. 2018; Merli et al. 2018). A generally accepted description of the circular economy is the shift from a linear 'produce-use-dispose' economy to a closed-loop economy (Figure 3.3). The circular economy thus calls for a reduction of societal throughput (inputs and outputs) by

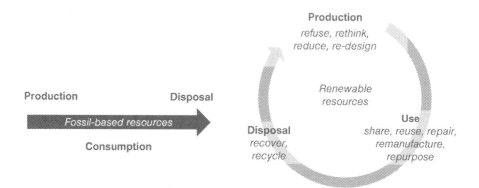

Figure 3.3 A framework depicting the circular economy.
Source: D'Amato et al. (2020c)

'slowing, closing, and narrowing material and energy loops' (Geissdoerfer et al. 2017, p. 759). Energy and material should be released to lower quality uses – and eventually to the environment – only after the full expression of their higher value potential. The Ellen MacArthur Foundation, a key non-academic actor promoting the circular economy, describes it as 'restorative and regenerative by design and aims to keep products, components, and materials at their highest utility and value at all times, distinguishing between technical and biological cycles. [...] A circular economy addresses mounting resource-related challenges for business and economies, and could generate growth, create jobs, and reduce environmental impacts, including carbon emissions' (The Ellen MacArthur Foundation 2015, p. 2).

The increase of material and energy performance of processes and products throughout a life cycle can be implemented through 'cyclical materials flows, renewable energy sources and cascading-type energy flows' (Korhonen et al. 2018, p. 39), in a system-thinking perspective (Lewandowski 2016; Sauvé et al. 2016). However, a fully closed material and energy loop is neither technically feasible nor financially and environmentally desirable. This is because recycling or otherwise reconfiguring products, materials, and energy also requires energy and generates some waste and cannot be implemented ad infinitum. Another limiting aspect is that efficiency gains from circular solutions may be lost to rebound or leakage. For example, a more efficient use of energy may lead to an increase in consumption in other sectors/regions, or in the future (Korhonen et al. 2018; Sikdar 2019). For this reason, some scholars and experts advocate the need to pursue an absolute reduction of societal material throughput, as opposed to a relative one (Reike et al. 2018).

Transformative interpretations of the circular economy have also highlighted the need for change beyond technological circularity (Hart & Pomponi 2021; Oliveira et al. 2021). Socio-cultural change is called upon to transform 'consumption and production structures based on materialism, convenience, and ownership to ones based on collaborative consumption, sharing economies and use-value' (Calisto Friant et al. 2021, p. 6). This conceptualisation of the circular economy is drawn from the notions of a sharing economy and sufficiency. The former refers to maximisation of the sharing potential of existing products/services across multiple users, possibly simultaneously (e.g. shared ownership, multi-functionality) (e.g. Frenken & Schor 2017). The latter concerns considerations of superfluous consumption, the reconnection of consumption to well-being and the satisfaction of needs, and improvements in self-sufficiency at the system level (e.g. refusing to produce or buy unnecessary goods/services, producing, and buying local goods/products) (e.g. Schäpke & Rauschmayer 2014). Consequently, there is an argument for strengthening the agency of consumers/users in the circular economy – whose role is currently expected to be largely indirect and mediated by technological solutions – towards more active participation, especially with regard to activities such as refusing and reducing superfluous consumption, as well as reselling/reusing, repairing, refurbishing, remanufacturing, and repurposing (Hobson 2016; Hobson & Lynch 2016; Reike et al. 2018; Russell et al. 2020).

In practical terms, the operationalisation of the circular economy often remains limited to efficiency, recycling, and waste management (as found in e.g. Barreiro-Gen & Lozano, 2020; Calisto Friant et al. 2020; Ghisellini & Ulgiati, 2020; Kirchherr et al. 2017). The business case for the circular economy is largely founded on reducing costs due to more efficient production and consumption processes, and stimulating innovation and improvement of existing practices by means of technological solutions (Guenster et al. 2011). Lack of consumer interest is currently deemed by experts to be an important barrier in the EU (Kirchherr et al. 2018). A holistic and transformational vision of the circular economy is still missing from EU policies (Calisto Friant et al. 2021). Academics and practitioners have also problematised the global dynamics of a circular economy, suggesting the existence of inequalities in the power relations between the Global North and the Global South with regard to value chains and waste cycles (Schröder et al. 2019). The lack of discussion on the social dimension of the circular economy has in general been identified as a problematic area (Calisto Friant et al. 2021; Clube & Tennant 2020; Kirchherr et al. 2017; Millar et al. 2019; Murray et al. 2017).

3.3.3   Core Solutions in the Circular Economy

The backbone of the circular economy concept is the R framework (Figure 3.4). This is composed of a list of relevant activities, listed in order of priority, ranging from three (3Rs: reduction, reuse, recycling) up to ten (10Rs: refuse, reduce, resell/reuse, repair, refurbish, remanufacture, repurpose, recycle, recover, re-mine) (Reike et al. 2018). Refusing consumption implies refraining from buying what is unnecessary or superfluous to prevent waste. Refusing production means refusing to employ hazardous substances, virgin materials, or waste-inducing processes. Reducing is about producing or consuming less (including using with more care and sharing). Reselling, repairing, refurbishing, and remanufacturing all have the goal of extending the former functionality of a product or to attributing to it a new function within the economy and society, while maintaining its high value. Recycling, recovering, and re-mining are about processing post-production or post-consumption waste.

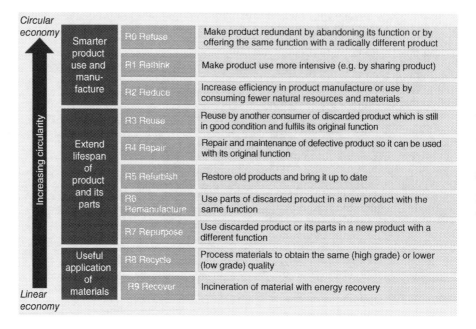

Figure 3.4 The 10R framework for the circular economy.
Source: Kirchherr et al. (2017)

The reconfiguration of the original product structure implies some loss in quality/ value. The first four activities are those in which individual consumers can operate most of their agency, while the other phases are dominated by companies and municipalities. Overall, dematerialisation is the principle underpinning each solution in the circular economy (Box 3.3).

3.3.4   Financing of the Circular Economy

While regulatory processes have been important in driving circular economy globally, the barriers outlined often include financing and market limitation (de Jesus et al. 2018; Kirchherr et al. 2017). On top of public investments, important streams of financial resources to fuel the circular economy are expected to come from the private sector. As for the bioeconomy, circular businesses are often based on innovative technological ideas that require consistent upfront financial resources for both the research and development and the marketisation phases (see Chapter 5). However, investing in highly innovative solutions is still considered a high risk by financiers. Public policy instruments, such as setting targets for material recycling and reuse, favourable taxation regimes, green public procurement and frameworks, and performance metrics for sustainable activities (e.g. the forthcoming EU taxonomy for sustainable activities) are expected to support private investments in the circular economy.

> **Box 3.3** Example of Circular Economy Solutions
>
> *Reusable and durable packaging* for takeaway food is being developed in several cities. Kamupak is a Finnish-based start-up company which has developed a system to enable customers to order takeaway food inside reusable containers, for a small deposit fee. The deposit can be redeemed as a refund or credit when the containers are returned to Kamupak. This start-up has partnered with the main Finnish supermarkets, restaurant chains, and food delivery services. Similar initiatives include the companies Eat and Back in Roubaix (France), Returnr in Australia and DeliverZero in New York (USA).
>
> *Repair cafés* are local and free meeting places where people can collaboratively repair their possessions, such as clothes, furniture, toys, or electrical appliances. The cafés leverage the skills of experienced volunteers, but it is not a repair shop as such. The ethos of the cafés is to preserve and transmit repair skills and a repairing mentality in society through a learning process, at the same time creating a sense of community. This worldwide movement began in the Netherlands in 2009 and has now expanded to over 1,000 locations in thirty-two countries. The cafés are established from the initiative of local individuals or groups, with the support of the Repair Café Foundation. Examples of other bottom-up circular economy initiatives include, for instance, local subscription and pay-per-use services for tools and appliances, collaborative household waste separation and management, and co-funded renewable energy self-production (Russell et al. 2020).
>
> *Positive Energy Districts* are urban areas that produce zero net carbon emissions and may even generate a surplus of local or regional renewable energy. This is achieved through a holistic and tailor-made approach to urban design and development, including optimisation and improved efficiency of energy consumption, use of locally available energy resources, conversion, and retrofitting of existing urban structures. Inclusiveness and quality of life are important aspects of positive energy districts. Such districts have been implemented in several European cities, such as Bilbao (Spain), Évora (Portugal), Graz (Austria), Elverum (Norway), and Limerick (Ireland) (Gollner 2020).

3.4   Towards a Complementary Understanding of the Green, Circular, and Bioeconomy

3.4.1   What Does a Green and Circular Bioeconomy Look Like?

Like the bioeconomy, the green economy and the circular economy are umbrella terms used by many societal actors to frame change, possibly towards a more sustainable economy. Their separate historical development and distinct characteristics make them independent concepts, but they share potentially overlapping areas (Figure 3.5). The bioeconomy and the circular economy are increasingly discussed as complementary concepts. Several scholars and experts now advocate the reuse and recycling of biomass resources, and the prioritisation of high-value biomass uses

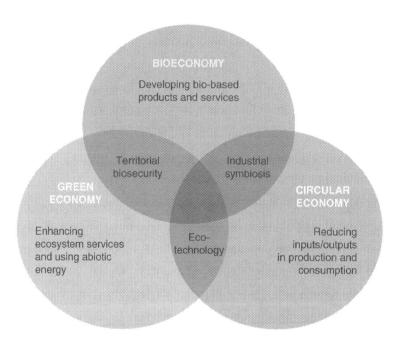

Figure 3.5 The interface of the bioeconomy, green economy, and circular economy. Inspired to: D'Amato et al. (2019)

before lower uses, such as energy production. To this end, the term 'circular bioeconomy' has emerged (D'Amato et al. 2020c; Hetemäki et al. 2017; Stegmann et al. 2020; Toppinen et al. 2020).

The bioeconomy and the green economy contribute with different solutions to the issue of biosecurity, which is about the management of environmental risk (e.g. pests, diseases, invasive species), especially in agricultural and other intensively managed systems, towards territorial adaptation and resilience. While the bioeconomy leverages biotechnologies, the green economy points to novel approaches through the application of ecological processes to production systems. Although it remains fundamentally resource-oriented, the bioeconomy literature is also beginning to absorb the notion of ecosystem services (Hetemäki et al. 2017; Neill et al. 2020). While circular solutions are considered to be part of the approach to reduce the pressure on biodiversity and ecosystems, the contribution of such solutions to biodiversity conservation remains unclear, along with the role of biodiversity in the circular economy (Buchmann-Duck & Beazley 2020). The interface between the circular economy and biodiversity, ecosystem services, and natural capital remains largely unexplored for now, but potential progress could leverage ideas such as biomimicry, ecotechnology, and nature-based solutions which combine natural and artificial systems to serve functions and solve problems in industrial and urban systems (Atanasova et al. 2021). Box 3.4 provides examples of green and circular bioeconomy solutions.

Box 3.4 Examples of Green and Circular Bioeconomy Solutions

Insect-based biorefinery is at the basis of the business model by Swedish start-up Norbite. Moths digest plastic and can then be safely used as a source of protein for food/feed, as well as a source of chemicals for medicines and skincare; the insects' excrements are used as fertilizers. Moths are thus valuable not exclusively for their biomass but also for their physiological functions, which allow them to create circularity in the economy of plastic. Another example of circular and green/bio innovation is being developed by the Finnish start-up Algonomi, which proposes *microalgae cultivation* to produce bioactive ingredients for cosmetics and food, while absorbing carbon dioxide from the industrial processes of other companies.

Bokashi is a home composting method that, through fermentation exercised by specialist anaerobic bacteria, converts food waste (including non-vegetable material, such as meat, bones, fats, dairy products) and other organic matter into soil supplements. More than a waste sorting method, making bokashi is reported to be a learning and awareness experience, where the liveliness of waste matter allows people to reform their ways of perceiving waste, from something that needs to be eliminated, to something that is part of a natural process. Microbes, plants, and insects become integrated into this urban experience.

Energy efficiency districts with blue/green infrastructure or low-carbon wooden buildings are an example of circularity, nature-based, and bio-based solutions. For example, the Honkasuo urban village in Helsinki (Finland) is being developed as a residential area of wooden houses with green infrastructure, such as stormwater-retaining vegetation and urban farming plots. The residential district of Hammarby Sjöstad, in Stockholm (Sweden), was developed to combine renewable energy (district heating from purified wastewater, combustible household waste, and biofuel), user-oriented opportunities to monitor energy and water consumption, and green and blue infrastructures.

3.4.2   The Benefits of Understanding the Three Concepts as Complementary

Recently, policy documents (e.g. the 2018 EU European Bioeconomy Strategy) and industry documents (e.g. the Global Bioeconomy Summit 2018) have acknowledged the role of circularity, as well as that of natural capital/ecosystem services in the bioeconomy. The integration of notions related to the green and circular economy can further inform the development of the bioeconomy as a concept/narrative, as well as the implementation of bioeconomy strategies. Three areas are highlighted in this chapter as relevant to this process: reconciling dominant and emerging/alternative bioeconomy visions; strengthening intra- and inter-policy coherence; and enriching tools and indicators towards a sustainable bioeconomy.

3.4.2.1   Reconciling Dominant and Emerging/Alternative Bioeconomy Visions

A dominant vision of the bioeconomy is currently anchored to an 'extractive' and technology-oriented interpretation of human–nature relations. The combined notions discussed in Chapter 2 and in this Chapter allow an exploration of the potential nuances of the bioeconomy as a multi-faceted narrative (Figure 3.6). The ecosystem services concept points to a shift in focus from natural resources to beneficial eco-system processes. This implies the recognition of multiple values co-created between the biosphere and humans, as well as the need to minimise trade-offs between provi-sioning and other ecosystem services. Both the green and circular economy literature praise the need for a stronger role for small and local societal actors in developing sustainability solutions. This opens up the portfolio of sustainability solutions from a (biomass) resource-centred logic towards a service- and human wellbeing-oriented logic. A renewed vision of the bioeconomy would thus also include lower biomass requirements, higher-value products, social innovation, and citizen participation.

3.4.2.2 Strengthening Intra- and Inter-Policy Coherence

National or regional strategies may contain an array of qualitative or quantitative goals but often miss a strategic understanding of how to reconcile tensions occurring across policies or even within the same document (Neill et al. 2020). One of the concerns regarding the bioeconomy is that there are limits to the potential intensification of terrestrial land uses (forest and agricultural biomass) against conservation goals (Ped-ersen et al. 2020). This is showcased by the potential conflicts between the EU Bioec-onomy Strategy updated in 2018, and the recently developed EU Green Deal – a plan to forward the circular economy and safeguard biodiversity in Europe, including a Biodiversity Strategy that plans to protect 30 per cent of its land and seas by 2030 and restore degraded ecosystems. Moreover, competition within the bioeconomy itself

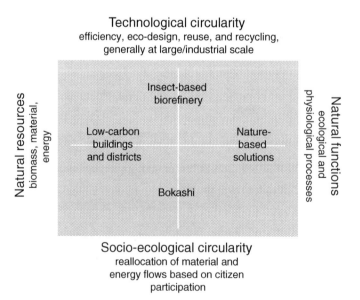

Figure 3.6 A framework mapping some examples of green and circular bioeconomy solutions.
Inspired to: D'Amato et al. (2020a)

as a strategy and the use of biomass resources may also occur between increasingly demanded biomass application types, such as food, feed, biomaterial, and bioenergy. An integrated understanding of circularity and natural capital/ecosystem services can contribute to highlighting problematic areas and possible solution paths for the bioeconomy. In addition to the deployment of sustainable land-use practices to increase productivity, and the conversion of marginal and abandoned land for biomass production, improvements in the circular use of biowaste and residues, coupled with alternative biomass sources (such as algae, fungi, which however still present technological, regulatory, and market barriers), are generally considered viable avenues to alleviate such tensions (Schoenmakere et al. 2018). Another issue is the need to regulate the use of biodegradable and bio-based plastics (possibly towards a perspective of overall reduction of plastic waste), which has also been emphasised in the new EU Circular Economy Action Plan in reference to the 2018 plastics strategy by the EU. Finally, policies must reconcile ecological goals with economic and social costs, especially safeguarding the more vulnerable regions and actors. In this regard, among other strategies, the EU Green Deal includes the Just Transition Mechanism, with the aim of legitimising the sustainability solutions needed to achieve carbon neutrality by 2050 and support its territories and people likely to be affected by such changes. Importantly, one of the aspects to consider in addition to territorial specificities and needs is that 'decisions taken at one geographical level may have repercussions at other geographical levels. In other words, while addressing specific territorial or sector-related challenges, to be "just" the transition towards a low-carbon society should also take into account the broader global framework and the connections between "multi-scalar realities"' (Sabato & Fronteddu 2020, p. 10).

3.4.2.3   Enriching Tools and Indicators towards a Sustainable and Just Society

Monitoring the progress of the bioeconomy towards sustainability requires standardised methods that can holistically assess sustainability impacts (Bastianoni et al. 2019). Zeug et al. (2020) have pointed out that integrated methods, such as the life cycle sustainability assessment (LCSA), a combination or integration of environmental LCA (E-LCA), social LCA (S-LCA), and life cycle costing (LCC), are still at an early stage of development. Available data seem to be currently concentrated on the impacts of bioenergy, especially regarding the emission of greenhouse gases (Camia et al. 2018; D'Amato et al. 2020b). Methods, tools, and data developed in the context of ecosystem services research can also feed into the efforts to measure the sustainability impacts of bioeconomy strategies, in particular in reference to the ecological boundaries of the bioeconomy and to considerations of environmental justice (Neill et al. 2020). This includes the assessment of trade-offs between ecosystem services associated with site-level and landscape-level management, and the distribution of socio-economic value and conflicts between stakeholders. Previously siloed methodologies can be integrated and further developed to capture additional dimensions of sustainability (Oliveira et al. 2021). An example of methodological integration is the assessment of ecosystem services in E-LCA (Alejandre et al. 2019; Rugani et al. 2019). For more about the topic of monitoring progress towards the circular bioeconomy, see Chapters 7 and 9.

3.5   Beyond the Green and Circular Bioeconomy

The green, circular, and bioeconomy have emerged in the past decade as independent concepts and have been largely discussed separately in the various realms of society. However, there is an increasing understanding that to strengthen potential contributions to sustainability, the diverse solutions proposed by the three concepts should be interpreted as complementary (Schoenmakere et al. 2018), even though there is a further need to evaluate synergies and (in)compatibilities towards coherent sustainability pathways.

Against the backdrop of the 2020 global health crisis due to the Covid-19 pandemic, Palahi et al. (2020) have proposed a list of action points to bring about transformations in industrial, urban, food, and health systems. Envisioned solutions leverage a participatory and more equitable biodiversity-based circular bioeconomy. Concurrently, the term 'nature-positive economy' has recently been proposed in the context of sustainable business and finance (Loorbach et al. 2020; World Economic Forum & AlphaBeta 2020) as an umbrella term linking cross-cutting solutions across human-environment systems and sectors (terrestrial and marine systems, food systems, built environment and mobility, energy, and extractives). According to those sources, the nature-positive economy aggregates a mélange of approaches, such as circularity and resource efficiency, more responsible consumption, more sustainable materials and energy, as well as leveraging the multi-functionality of natural and semi-natural ecosystems. The overall direction of such notions and solutions is towards decreasing dependence on fossil resources through a biodiversity-based and biodiversity-benign economic system, which is supposed to deliver material and immaterial benefits to people equally across space and time (D'Amato & Korhonen 2021). Even jointly, the three concepts hardly represent the full picture of worldviews and solutions to forward global net sustainability. For example, household and regional resource self-sufficiency, food security and sovereignty, equity issues, and animal rights remain largely, if not completely, unaddressed.

Remaining issues on how to pursue these avenues in practice concern the overall orchestration of changes, including the balancing of heavy expectations on corporate actors and technology versus that of smaller actors, citizens, and social innovation. Moreover, the green, circular, and bioeconomy are largely attached to a goal of economic growth, and while new production/consumption models are also envisioned by some as part of green and circular bioeconomy solutions, post-growth paradigms remain largely unexamined by these three concepts (Kovacic et al. 2021; Mastini et al. 2021). This topic is further discussed in Chapter 6.

Take-Home Message

- The bioeconomy is a multi-faceted concept, and societal actors perceive it, frame it, and use it differently according to their agendas and needs.
- The existing bioeconomy political strategies largely focus on the potential of biomass as a resource, and on biotechnology as a means to unlock new potential from biomass.

- Increasing biomass extraction is likely to require some degree of ecosystem intensification, which implies trade-offs with regulating and cultural ecosystem services.
- The regional and global distribution of resources and prosperity, as well as the participative role of citizens, small-medium enterprises, and local actors in the bioeconomy is also an important point of concern.
- The notions of circularity and ecosystem services can further promote a renewed understanding of the bioeconomy when addressing some of the existing tensions within and between sustainability dimensions.

Learning Exercises

1. What are the key criticisms of the current understanding of the bioeconomy from a sustainability perspective?
2. What are the core sets of solutions proposed by the circular and the green economy?
3. How can the notions of ecosystem services and circularity contribute to the conceptual development and practical implementation of bioeconomy solutions towards sustainability?

Online resources

Lecture 'Bioeconomy & ecosystem services' by Dr. Bartkowski, University of Helsinki. Available at: www.helsinki.fi/fi/unitube/video/b479dc7d-b6aa-453c-86ab-a6b45fef5a2a

Lecture 'Circular bioeconomy' by Prof. Hetemäki, University of Helsinki. Available at: www.helsinki.fi/fi/unitube/video/ab7b97d7-34fb-4d68-af89-e7698659a4dc

Lecture 'Ecosystem services: A quick overview' by Adj. Prof. D'Amato, University of Helsinki. Available at: www.helsinki.fi/fi/unitube/video/30b9351a-8c97-4c49-9e22-b716f601d7e5

Lecture 'Ecosystem services: Governance & policy instruments' by Adj. Prof. D'Amato, University of Helsinki. Available at: www.helsinki.fi/fi/unitube/video/9eea51f9-fb2b-4384-a47d-028e3a6d7219

Online course 'Introduction to Sustainable Bioeconomy'. Available at: www.futurelearn.com/courses/society-and-bioeconomy

Seminar 'Nature at the heart of a global circular bioeconomy', Center for International Forestry Research. Available at: www.cifor.org/event/nature-at-the-heart-of-a-global-circular-bioeconomy/?ct=t(CIFOR_ICRAF_Circular_Bioeconomy_reminder)

Urban Nature Atlas. 2021. A collection of more than 1000 inspiring nature-based solutions from European cities and beyond. Available at: https://una.city/

References

Alejandre, E. M., van Bodegom, P. M., & Guinée, J. B. (2019). Towards an Optimal Coverage of Ecosystem Services in LCA. *Journal of Cleaner Production*, 231, 714–722.

Atanasova, N., Castellar, J. A. C., Pineda-Martos, R., … Langergraber, G. (2021). Nature-Based Solutions and Circularity in Cities. *Circular Economy and Sustainability*, 1(1), 319–332.

Barbier, E. B. (2012). The Green Economy Post Rio+20. *Science*, 338(6109), 887–888.

Barreiro-Gen, M., & Lozano, R. (2020). How Circular is the Circular Economy? Analysing the Implementation of Circular Economy in Organisations. *Business Strategy and the Environment*, 29(8), 3484–3494.

Bastianoni, S., Coscieme, L., Caro, D., Marchettini, N., & Pulselli, F. M. (2019). The Needs of Sustainability: The Overarching Contribution of Systems Approach. *Ecological Indicators*, 100, 69–73.

Borel-Saladin, J. M., & Turok, I. N. (2013). The Green Economy: Incremental Change or Transformation? *Environmental Policy and Governance*, 23(4), 209–220.

Braat, L. C., & de Groot, R. (2012). The Ecosystem Services Agenda: Bridging the Worlds of Natural Science and Economics, Conservation and Development, and Public and Private Policy. *Ecosystem Services*, 1(1), 4–15.

Brand, U. (2012). Green Economy – The Next Oxymoron? No Lessons Learned from Failures of Implementing Sustainable Development. *GAIA – Ecological Perspectives for Science and Society*, 21(1), 28–32.

Buchmann-Duck, J., & Beazley, K. F. (2020). An Urgent Call for Circular Economy Advocates to Acknowledge Its Limitations in Conserving Biodiversity. *Science of The Total Environment*, 727, 138602.

Bugge, M., Hansen, T., & Klitkou, A. (2016). What Is the Bioeconomy? A Review of the Literature. *Sustainability*, 8(7), 691.

Bull, J. W., & Strange, N. (2018). The Global Extent of Biodiversity Offset Implementation Under No Net Loss Policies. *Nature Sustainability*, 1(12), 790–798.

Calisto Friant, M., Vermeulen, W. J. V., & Salomone, R. (2020). A Typology of Circular Economy Discourses: Navigating the Diverse Visions of a Contested Paradigm. *Resources, Conservation and Recycling*, 161, 104917.

Calisto Friant, M., Vermeulen, W. J. V., & Salomone, R. (2021). Analysing European Union Circular Economy Policies: Words versus Actions. *Sustainable Production and Consumption*, 27, 337–353.

Camia, A., Robert, N., Jonsson, K., … Giuntoli, J. (2018). *Biomass Production, Supply, Uses and Flows in the European Union: First Results from an Integrated Assessment*, European Commission. Retrieved from https://policycommons.net/artifacts/2163241/biomass-production-supply-uses-and-flows-in-the-european-union/

Chizaryfard, A., Trucco, P., & Nuur, C. (2021). The Transformation to a Circular Economy: Framing an Evolutionary View. *Journal of Evolutionary Economics*, 31(2), 475–504.

Clube, R. K. M., & Tennant, M. (2020). The Circular Economy and Human Needs Satisfaction: Promising the Radical, Delivering the Familiar. *Ecological Economics*, 177, 106772.

Costanza, R., & Daly, H. E. (1992). Natural Capital and Sustainable Development. *Conservation Biology*, 6(1), 37–46.

Costanza, R., de Groot, R., Braat, L., … Grasso, M. (2017). Twenty Years of Ecosystem Services: How Far Have We Come and How Far Do We Still Need to Go? *Ecosystem Services*, 28, 1–16.

Dade, M. C., Mitchell, M. G. E., McAlpine, C. A., & Rhodes, J. R. (2019). Assessing Ecosystem Service Trade-Offs and Synergies: The Need for a More Mechanistic Approach. *Ambio*, 48(10), 1116–1128.

D'Amato, D. (2021). Sustainability Narratives as Transformative Solution Pathways: Zooming in on the Circular Economy. *Circular Economy and Sustainability*, 1(1), 231–242.

D'Amato, D., Bartkowski, B., & Droste, N. (2020a). Reviewing the Interface of Bioeconomy and Ecosystem Service Research. *Ambio*, 49(12), 1878–1896. https://doi.org/10.1007/s13280-020-01374-0

D'Amato, D., Gaio, M., & Semenzin, E. (2020b). A Review of LCA Assessments of Forest-Based Bioeconomy Products and Processes Under an Ecosystem Services Perspective. *Science of The Total Environment*, 706, 135859.

D'Amato, D., & Korhonen, J. (2021). Integrating the Green Economy, Circular Economy and Bioeconomy in a Strategic Sustainability Framework. *Ecological Economics*, 188, 107143.

D'Amato, D., Korhonen, J., & Toppinen, A. (2019). Circular, Green, and Bio Economy: How Do Companies in Land-Use Intensive Sectors Align with Sustainability Concepts? *Ecological Economics*, 158, 116–133.

D'Amato, D., Veijonaho, S., & Toppinen, A. (2020c). Towards Sustainability? Forest-Based Circular Bioeconomy Business Models in Finnish SMEs. *Forest Policy and Economics*, 110, 101848.

de Jesus, A., Antunes, P., Santos, R., & Mendonça, S. (2018). Eco-Innovation in the Transition to a Circular Economy: An Analytical Literature Review. *Journal of Cleaner Production*, 172, 2999–3018.

Dietz, T., Börner, J., Förster, J., & von Braun, J. (2018). Governance of the Bioeconomy: A Global Comparative Study of National Bioeconomy Strategies. *Sustainability*, 10(9), 3190.

Droste, N., D'Amato, D., & Goddard, J. J. (2018). Where Communities Intermingle, Diversity Grows – The Evolution of Topics in Ecosystem Service Research. *PLOS ONE*, 13(9), e0204749.

El-Chichakli, B., von Braun, J., Lang, C., Barben, D., & Philp, J. (2016). Policy: Five Cornerstones of a Global Bioeconomy. *Nature*, 535(7611), 221–223.

European Commission. (2013). Communication from the Commission to the European Parliament, the Council, the European Economic and Social Committee and the Committee of the Regions Green Infrastructure (GI) – Enhancing Europe's Natural Capital – COM(2013). Retrieved from https://eur-lex.europa.eu/legal-content/ES/TXT/PDF/?uri=CELEX:52013DC0249&from=EN

Eurostat. (2021a). Environmental Economy – Statistics on Employment and Growth. Retrieved from https://ec.europa.eu/eurostat/statistics-explained/index.php?title=Environmental_economy_%E2%80%93_statistics_on_employment_and_growth

Eurostat. (2021b). Private Investments, Jobs and Gross Value Added Related to Circular Economy Sectors. Retrieved from https://ec.europa.eu/eurostat/databrowser/view/cei_cie010/default/table?lang=en

Felipe-Lucia, M. R., Martín-López, B., Lavorel, S., Berraquero-Díaz, L., Escalera-Reyes, J., & Comín, F. A. (2015). Ecosystem Services Flows: Why Stakeholders' Power Relationships Matter. *PLOS ONE*, 10(7), e0132232.

Ferguson, P. (2015). The Green Economy Agenda: Business as Usual or Transformational Discourse? *Environmental Politics*, 24(1), 17–37.

Frenken, K., & Schor, J. (2017). Putting the Sharing Economy into Perspective. *Environmental Innovation and Societal Transitions*, 23, 3–10.

Geissdoerfer, M., Savaget, P., Bocken, N. M. P., & Hultink, E. J. (2017). The Circular Economy – A New Sustainability Paradigm? *Journal of Cleaner Production*, 143, 757–768.

Ghisellini, P., & Ulgiati, S. (2020). Circular Economy Transition in Italy. Achievements, Perspectives and Constraints. *Journal of Cleaner Production*, 243, 118360.

Global Bioeconomy Summit (2018). Conference Report Innovation in the Global Bioeconomy for Sustainable and Inclusive Transformation and Wellbeing. Retrieved from https://gbs2020.net/wp-content/uploads/2021/10/GBS_2018_Report_web.pdf

Gollner, C. (2020). EUROPE TOWARDS POSITIVE ENERGY DISTRICTS – FIRST UPDATE February 2020, Austria: Joint Programming Initiative (JPI) Urban Europe. Retrieved from https://policycommons.net/artifacts/2033983/europe-towards-positive-energy-districts/

Guenster, N., Bauer, R., Derwall, J., & Koedijk, K. (2011). The Economic Value of Corporate Eco-Efficiency. *European Financial Management*, 17(4), 679–704.

Guerry, A. D., Polasky, S., Lubchenco, J., … Vira, B. (2015). Natural Capital and Ecosystem Services Informing Decisions: From Promise to Practice. *Proceedings of the National Academy of Sciences*, 112(24), 7348–7355.

Haines-Young, R., & Potschin, M. (2010). The Links between Biodiversity, Ecosystem Services and Human Well-Being. In *Ecosystem Ecology*, Cambridge University Press, pp. 110–139.

Hart, J., & Pomponi, F. (2021). A Circular Economy: Where Will It Take Us? *Circular Economy and Sustainability*, 1(1), 127–141.

Hetemäki, L., Hanewinkel, M., Muys, B., Ollikainen, M., Palahí, M., & Trasobares, A. (2017). Leading the Way to a European Circular Bioeconomy Strategy. From Science to Policy.

Hobson, K. (2016). Closing the Loop or Squaring the Circle? Locating Generative Spaces for the Circular Economy. *Progress in Human Geography*, 40(1), 88–104.

Hobson, K., & Lynch, N. (2016). Diversifying and De-Growing the Circular Economy: Radical Social Transformation in a Resource-Scarce World. *Futures*, 82, 15–25.

Holmgren, S., D'Amato, D., & Giurca, A. (2020). Bioeconomy Imaginaries: A Review of Forest-Related Social Science Literature. *Ambio*, 49(12), 1860–1877.

Howe, C., Suich, H., Vira, B., & Mace, G. M. (2014). Creating Win-Wins from Trade-Offs? Ecosystem Services for Human Well-Being: A Meta-Analysis of Ecosystem Service Trade-offs and Synergies in the Real World. *Global Environmental Change*, 28, 263–275.

Hrabanski, M. (2017). Private Sector Involvement in the Millennium Ecosystem Assessment: Using a UN Platform to Promote Market-Based Instruments for Ecosystem Services. *Environmental Policy and Governance*, 27(6), 605–618.

IPBES. (2018). Intergovernmental Science-Policy Platform on Biodiversity and Ecosystem Services (2018). Summary for policymakers of the regional assessment report on biodiversity and ecosystem services for Europe and Central Asia of the Intergovernmental Science-Policy Platform on Biodiversity and Ecosystem Services. Retrieved from doi:10.5281/zenodo.3237428

Issa, I., Delbrück, S., & Hamm, U. (2019). Bioeconomy from Experts' Perspectives – Results of a Global Expert Survey. *PLOS ONE*, 14(5), e0215917.

Kirchherr, J., Piscicelli, L., Bour, R., … Hekkert, M. (2018). Barriers to the Circular Economy: Evidence from the European Union (EU). *Ecological Economics*, 150, 264–272.

Kirchherr, J., Reike, D., & Hekkert, M. (2017). Conceptualizing the Circular Economy: An Analysis of 114 Definitions. *Resources, Conservation and Recycling*, 127, 221–232. https://doi.org/10.1016/j.resconrec.2017.09.005

Korhonen, J., Nuur, C., Feldmann, A., & Birkie, S. E. (2018). Circular Economy as an Essentially Contested Concept. *Journal of Cleaner Production*, 175, 544–552.

Kovacic, Z., Strand, R., Funtowicz, S., Benini, L., & Jesus, A. (2021). Growth without Economic Growth.

Kröger, M., & Raitio, K. (2017). Finnish Forest Policy in the era of Bioeconomy: A Pathway to Sustainability? *Forest Policy and Economics*, 77, 6–15.

Ladu, L., & Blind, K. (2017). Overview of Policies, Standards and Certifications Supporting the European Bio-Based Economy. *Current Opinion in Green and Sustainable Chemistry*, 8, 30–35.

Lewandowski, M. (2016). Designing the Business Models for Circular Economy – Towards the Conceptual Framework. *Sustainability*, 8(1), 43.

Loiseau, E., Saikku, L., Antikainen, R., … Thomsen, M. (2016). Green Economy and Related Concepts: An Overview. *Journal of Cleaner Production*, 139, 361–371.

Loorbach, D., Schoenmaker, D., & Schramade, W. (2020). *Finance in Transition: Principles for a Positive Finance Future*, Rotterdam: Rotterdam School of Management, Erasmus University. Retrieved from www.rsm.nl/fileadmin/Images_NEW/Positive_Change/2020_Finance_in_Transition.pdf

Lorek, S., & Spangenberg, J. H. (2014). Sustainable Consumption within a Sustainable Economy – Beyond Green Growth and Green Economies. *Journal of Cleaner Production*, 63, 33–44.

Luederitz, C., Abson, D. J., Audet, R., & Lang, D. J. (2017). Many Pathways Toward Sustainability: Not Conflict But Co-Learning Between Transition Narratives. *Sustainability Science*, 12(3), 393–407.

Mastini, R., Kallis, G., & Hickel, J. (2021). A Green New Deal without Growth? *Ecological Economics*, 179, 106832.

McAfee, K. (2012). The Contradictory Logic of Global Ecosystem Services Markets. *Development and Change*, 43(1), 105–131.

McDowall, W., Geng, Y., Huang, B., … Doménech, T. (2017). Circular Economy Policies in China and Europe. *Journal of Industrial Ecology*, 21(3), 651–661.

Merino-Saum, A., Clement, J., Wyss, R., & Baldi, M. G. (2020). Unpacking the Green Economy Concept: A Quantitative Analysis of 140 Definitions. *Journal of Cleaner Production*, 242, 118339.

Merli, R., Preziosi, M., & Acampora, A. (2018). How Do Scholars Approach the Circular Economy? A Systematic Literature Review. *Journal of Cleaner Production*, 178, 703–722.

Meyer, R. (2017). Bioeconomy Strategies: Contexts, Visions, Guiding Implementation Principles and Resulting Debates. *Sustainability*, 9(6), 1031.

Millar, N., McLaughlin, E., & Börger, T. (2019). The Circular Economy: Swings and Roundabouts? *Ecological Economics*, 158, 11–19.

Millennium Ecosystem Assessment. (2005). *Ecosystems and Human Well-being: Synthesis*, Washington, DC. Retrieved from www.millenniumassessment.org/documents/document.356.aspx.pdf

Murray, A., Skene, K., & Haynes, K. (2017). The Circular Economy: An Interdisciplinary Exploration of the Concept and Application in a Global Context. *Journal of Business Ethics*, 140(3), 369–380.

Mustalahti, I. (2018). The Responsive Bioeconomy: The Need for Inclusion of Citizens and Environmental Capability in the Forest Based Bioeconomy. *Journal of Cleaner Production*, 172, 3781–3790.

Neill, A. M., O'Donoghue, C., & Stout, J. C. (2020). A Natural Capital Lens for a Sustainable Bioeconomy: Determining the Unrealised and Unrecognised Services from Nature. *Sustainability*, 12(19), 8033.

Oliveira, M., Miguel, M., van Langen, S. K., … Genovese, A. (2021). Circular Economy and the Transition to a Sustainable Society: Integrated Assessment Methods for a New Paradigm. *Circular Economy and Sustainability*, 1(1), 99–113.

O'Neill, K., & Gibbs, D. (2016). Rethinking Green Entrepreneurship – Fluid Narratives of the Green Economy. *Environment and Planning A: Economy and Space*, 48(9), 1727–1749.

Palahi, M., Pantsar, M., Costanza, R., … Fioramonti, L. (2020). Investing in Nature to Transform the Post COVID-19 Economy: A 10-point Action Plan to Create a Circular Bioeconomy Devoted to Sustainable Wellbeing. *Solutions*, 2(11).

Pearce, D., Markandya, A., & Barbier, E. (2013). *Blueprint 1: For a Green Economy*, Routledge.

Pedersen, S., Gangås, K. E., Chetri, M., & Andreassen, H. P. (2020). Economic Gain vs. Ecological Pain – Environmental Sustainability in Economies Based on Renewable Biological Resources. *Sustainability*, 12(9), 3557.

Pfau, S., Hagens, J., Dankbaar, B., & Smits, A. (2014). Visions of Sustainability in Bioeconomy Research. *Sustainability*, 6(3), 1222–1249.

Priefer, C., Jörissen, J., & Frör, O. (2017). Pathways to Shape the Bioeconomy. *Resources*, 6(1), 10.

Ramcilovic-Suominen, S., & Pülzl, H. (2018). Sustainable Development – A 'Selling Point' of the Emerging EU Bioeconomy Policy Framework? *Journal of Cleaner Production*, 172, 4170–4180.

Reike, D., Vermeulen, W. J. V., & Witjes, S. (2018). The Circular Economy: New or Refurbished as CE 3.0? – Exploring Controversies in the Conceptualization of the Circular Economy through a Focus on History and Resource Value Retention Options. *Resources, Conservation and Recycling*, 135, 246–264.

Robinson, D. J. (2015). Building a Green Economy. In *The Energy Economy*, New York: Palgrave Macmillan US, pp. 173–191.

Ronzon, T., Piotrowski, S., M'barek, R., Carus, M., & Tamošiūnas, S. (2018). Jobs and Wealth in the EU Bioeconomy (JRC-Bioeconomics). European Commission, Joint Research Centre(JRC).

Ronzon, T., Piotrowski, S., Tamosiunas, S., Dammer, L., Carus, M., & M'barek, R. (2020). Developments of Economic Growth and Employment in Bioeconomy Sectors across the EU. *Sustainability*, 12(11), 4507.

Rugani, B., Maia de Souza, D., Weidema, B. P., … Verones, F. (2019). Towards Integrating the Ecosystem Services Cascade Framework Within the Life Cycle Assessment (LCA) Cause-Effect Methodology. *Science of The Total Environment*, 690, 1284–1298.

Russell, M., Gianoli, A., & Grafakos, S. (2020). Getting the Ball Rolling: An Exploration of the Drivers and Barriers Towards the Implementation of Bottom-Up Circular Economy Initiatives in Amsterdam and Rotterdam. *Journal of Environmental Planning and Management*, 63(11), 1903–1926.

Sabato, S., & Fronteddu, B. (2020). A Socially Just Transition Through the European Green Deal? *SSRN Electronic Journal*. doi:10.2139/ssrn.3699367

Sanz-Hernández, A., Esteban, E., & Garrido, P. (2019). Transition to a Bioeconomy: Perspectives from Social Sciences. *Journal of Cleaner Production*, 224, 107–119.

Sauvé, S., Bernard, S., & Sloan, P. (2016). Environmental Sciences, Sustainable Development and Circular Economy: Alternative Concepts for Trans-Disciplinary Research. *Environmental Development*, 17, 48–56.

Schäpke, N., & Rauschmayer, F. (2014). Going Beyond Efficiency: Including Altruistic Motives in Behavioral Models for Sustainability Transitions to Address Sufficiency. *Sustainability: Science, Practice and Policy*, 10(1), 29–44.

Schoenmakere, M. de, Hoogeveen, Y., Gillabel, J., & Manshoven, S. (2018). The Circular Economy and the Bioeconomy: Partners in Sustainability. EEA Report, (8/2018). Retrieved from www.eea.europa.eu/publications/circular-economy-and-bioeconomy

Schröder, P., Anantharaman, M., Anggraeni, K., & Foxon, T. J. (2019). *The Circular Economy and the Global South* (P. Schröder, M. Anantharaman, K. Anggraeni, & T. J. Foxon, Eds.), Routledge. doi:10.4324/9780429434006

Sikdar, S. (2019). Circular Economy: Is There Anything New in this Concept? *Clean Technologies and Environmental Policy*, 21(6), 1173–1175.

Smith, A. C., Harrison, P. A., Pérez Soba, M., … Wyllie de Echeverria, V. (2017). How Natural Capital Delivers Ecosystem Services: A Typology Derived from a Systematic Review. *Ecosystem Services*, 26, 111–126.

Stegmann, P., Londo, M., & Junginger, M. (2020). The Circular Bioeconomy: Its Elements and Role in European Bioeconomy Clusters. *Resources, Conservation & Recycling: X*, 6, 100029.

ten Brink, P., Mazza, L., Badura, T., Kettunen, M., & Withana, S. (2012). Nature and Its Role in the Transition to a Green Economy. A TEEB Report. Forthcoming Www. Teebweb. Org and Www. Ieep. Eu.

The Ellen MacArthur Foundation. (2015). Towards a Circular Economy: Business Rationale for an Accelerated Transition. Retrieved from https://ellenmacarthurfoundation.org/towards-a-circular-economy-business-rationale-for-an-accelerated-transition

Tomaselli, M. F., Hajjar, R., Ramón-Hidalgo, A. E., & Vásquez-Fernández, A. M. (2017). The Problematic Old Roots of the New Green Economy Narrative: How Far Can it Take Us in Re-Imagining Sustainability in Forestry? *International Forestry Review*, 19(1), 139–151.

Toppinen, A., D'Amato, D., & Stern, T. (2020). Forest-Based Circular Bioeconomy: Matching Sustainability Challenges and Novel Business Opportunities? *Forest Policy and Economics*, 110, 102041.

UNEP. (2011). Towards a Green Economy: Pathways to Sustainable Development and Poverty Eradication. Retrieved September 16, 2022, from https://sustainabledevelopment.un.org/index.php?page=view&type=400&nr=126&menu=35

Urban Nature Atlas. (2021). A Collection of More than 1000 Inspiring Nature-based Solutions from European Cities and beyond. Retrieved September 16, 2022, from https://una.city/

Vivien, F.-D., Nieddu, M., Befort, N., Debref, R., & Giampietro, M. (2019). The Hijacking of the Bioeconomy. *Ecological Economics*, 159, 189–197.

Winans, K., Kendall, A., & Deng, H. (2017). The History and Current Applications of the Circular Economy Concept. *Renewable and Sustainable Energy Reviews*, 68, 825–833.

World Economic Forum, & AlphaBeta. (2020). New Nature Economy Report II: The Future of Nature and Business, Switzerland, Cologny/Geneva. Retrieved from www3.weforum.org/docs/WEF_The_Future_Of_Nature_And_Business_2020.pdf

Wunder, S., Brouwer, R., Engel, S., … Pinto, R. (2018). From Principles to Practice in Paying for Nature's Services. *Nature Sustainability*, 1(3), 145–150.

Zeug, W., Bezama, A., & Thrän, D. (2020). *Towards a Holistic and Integrated Life Cycle Sustainability Assessment of the Bioeconomy: Background on Concepts, Visions and Measurements*, Leipzig: Helmholtz-Zentrum für Umweltforschung (UFZ).

Part II

4 Environmental Economics and the Bioeconomy

> ## Learning Objectives
>
> To understand and be able to have a critical discussion:
>
> - about the origin of the debate on environmental economics.
> - about the concepts of efficiency and optimality in allocation.
> - about welfare economics and market failures.
> - about the concepts of sustainability (both strong and weak).
> - about capital sustainability.

4.1 Definition and History of Environmental Economics

When approaching environmental economics, a natural question arises: what does 'environmental' stand for? Generally speaking, environmental economics is the application of the principles of economics to the study of how environmental resources are managed.

Economics can be divided into *microeconomics* – which studies the behaviour of individuals and small groups – and *macroeconomics*, the study of the economic performance of economies as a whole. *Environmental economics* is founded on both, with an inclination towards microeconomics, as it focuses primarily on how individuals and groups make decisions about transforming and managing scarce resources to increase human wealth, in its broadest sense. Environmental economics is an analytical subject: it not only describes the state of the environment and its change, but it is concerned also with the causes of its condition and with solutions to improve the economic institutions to adequately consider environmental impacts.

Another distinction is therefore necessary between *positive* and *normative economics*. The first studies how an economic system works by observing it and how people make decisions based on given circumstances. It attempts to establish any cause-and-effect relationships or behavioural associations which can help ascertain and test the development of economics theories. Normative economics, instead, is the study of 'what ought to be'. It focuses on opinion-oriented prescriptive and value judgements aimed towards economic development. Both approaches are deployed in environmental economics and will be analysed in this chapter.

While environmental economics as a distinct subject is relatively new, concerns with resource and environmental issues are not. In the eighteenth and nineteenth centuries, '*classical*' *economists* considered these issues at a time when the industrial revolution was rapidly growing. One of their main focuses was the study of what determined standards of living and economic growth; in this respect, natural resources, especially land, were seen as a key element. It followed that, being land finite and assuming diminishing returns, classical economists saw as inevitable a stationary state and therefore considered economic development as temporary.

In addition to this, Malthus (1766–1834) theorised the famous model in which he assumed fixed land quantity, growing population, and diminishing returns in agriculture. Therefore, a decline in output per capita and living standards was deemed inevitable. These assumptions were reformulated by Ricardo (1772–1823), who considered land to be available in parcels of different quality and agricultural output as expandable (both by extending cultivable land and by improving land productivity). Still, returns to the land input were considered to be diminishing. Mill (1806–1873) further elaborated on these approaches, recognising the importance of technical progress and knowledge in agriculture and the economy as a whole and relaxing the physical constraints set by his colleagues. He also introduced new considerations on natural resources, viewed not exclusively under extractive lenses but also intrinsically valuable for humans (such as the beauty of the countryside). In 1857, he wrote that

if the earth must lose that great portion of its pleasantness which it owes to things that the unlimited increase of wealth and population would extirpate from it, for the mere purpose of enabling it to support a larger, but not a happier or better population, I sincerely hope, for the sake of posterity, that they will be content to be stationary long before necessity compels them to it.

By the end of the nineteenth century, a new field of study in economics emerged: '*neoclassical*' *economics*. While classical economists interpreted value as arising from the labour power embodied in output, neoclassicals saw value as determined in exchange, thereby reflecting preferences and costs of production; price and value started to be seen as coincident. A shift from the analysis of the aggregate level of the economy towards the firm-level structure of economic activity and its allocative efficiency also occurred. With rapid economic expansion ongoing during the past three decades of the nineteenth century, neoclassical economists were also less concerned with the finiteness of resources and the consequent decline of economic growth. However, the concept of diminishing returns was not abandoned but rather was formalised within the marginalist framework.

Neoclassical economists revolutionised the methodological approach to the economy: Jevons (1835–1882) and Menger (1840–1921) formalised the theory of consumer preferences in terms of utility and demand theory. Walras (1834–1910) developed the General Equilibrium Theory, founded on the concepts of efficiency and optimality. Marshall (1842–1924) elaborated a partial equilibrium supply-and-demand-based analysis of price determination widely adopted in the study of economics. These are the foundations of modern environmental economics too.

In the first decades of the twentieth century, the abrupt interruption of economic growth (which started with the Wall Street Crash of 1929) led to new approaches, such as *Keynes*' (1883–1946) theory of income and output determination. The main aim was to provide an explanation for the persistently high unemployment and enduring recession, with a focus on aggregate supply and demand – a macroeconomics approach. Though Keynes did not tackle environmental issues, his work indirectly stimulated new developments in neoclassical theories, especially dealing with economic growth. While previous models did not take into account physical constraints to economic growth, more recent ones (from the 1970s onward) started to consider natural resources and to elaborate on their efficient and optimal depletion.

Another relevant development concerns 'welfare economics', the aim of which is to theorise the desirability of a given allocation of resources over other possible allocations. Inevitably, ethical considerations came into play. Traditionally, classical and neoclassical economists based their views on the utilitarian philosophy stemming from the theories of Hume, Bentham, and Mill. According to this view, social welfare is seen as an average of the total utility levels enjoyed by single individuals in society. To help understand the best allocation of resources, the main reference is usually Pareto (1897), who developed a principle of allocative efficiency – also known as Pareto optimality, that is a state of affairs in which there is no alternative state that would make some people better off without making anyone worse off. Conversely, a state of affairs *x* would be Pareto-inefficient (or suboptimal) if and only if there is some state of affairs *y* such that no one strictly prefers *x* to *y* and at least one person strictly prefers *y* to *x*. Under perfect market competition, it is always possible to reach Pareto optimality (the first theorem of welfare economics states conditions under which the allocation associated with any competitive market equilibrium is Pareto-optimal).

Whenever this condition cannot be attained, 'market failures' arise. These are exemplified by 'externalities', that is, situations occurring when producing or consuming a good affects third parties not directly related to the transaction. Externalities can be either positive or negative. Pollution, as we will see, is a classic example of a negative externality.

The first comprehensive studies on externalities can be traced back to Marshall (1890), while the first work concentrating on pollution as an externality belongs to Pigou (1920). Only by the 1970s did modern approaches to pollution gain increasing attention in economics. In parallel, other branches of environmental economics focused on the recreational value of the natural environment with a cost-benefit analysis.

In short, *natural resource economics* and *environmental economics* have distinct roots in the core of modern mainstream economics. The former emerged mainly out of neoclassical growth economics, the latter out of welfare economics and the study of market failure. Both can be said to date from the early 1970s, though of course, earlier contributions can be identified. We will further explore both fields in this chapter.

In addition, another relevant distinction deserves our attention. It is the long-standing divide between *environmental economics* and *ecological economics*. The latter dates back to the 1980s, when ecologists and economists teamed together and prompted the development of a new interdisciplinary field of study. Economics and ecology share the common root 'eco', derived from Greek 'oikos', which stands for 'household'. Though, it could be said that the former studies human interactions, while the latter focuses on interactions between organisms and the environment. Clearly, humans and nature are strictly related, if not indivisible. That is why ecological economists are concerned with the way humans organise their activity and its effects on nature and ecosystems.

Under this approach, the economic system is no longer seen as separated from the environment but rather as part of the planet and its functioning. Among the first economists to adopt this view was Boulding (1966), who exposed the need to consider the laws of nature and their effects on the material basis for economic activity. A fundamental principle of ecological economics is that human economic activity must be limited by the environment's carrying capacity. Carrying capacity is defined as the population level and consumption activities that the available natural resource base can sustain without depletion.

Therefore, the fundamental difference with environmental economics is that ecological economics is concerned with putting economics in the larger context of the earth sciences and their laws – combining several methodologies – while environmental economics applies economic concepts and theories to the environment and its resources – with a neoclassical approach.

These two economic fields can be seen both as alternative and as complementary. While this chapter, as the title goes, is mainly concerned with environmental economics, ecological economics will be presented in detail in Chapter 5. In any case, only by combining these two fields can one fully grasp the meaning of 'sustainable bioeconomy'.

Figure 4.1 (adapted from Folke & Kåberger 1991) proposes a schematic conceptual model to illustrate how environmental economics and ecological economics recombine in a space which goes from social to natural science and spanning from single to multiple evaluation criteria for analysing the interactions between ecological and economic systems. There are several perspectives within each box as well

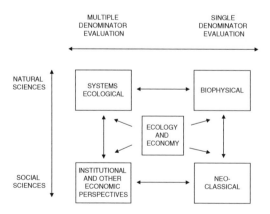

Figure 4.1 A schematic conceptual model of ecological and economic perspectives and approaches to environmental issues.
Source: Folke and Kaberger (1991)

as intermediate forms – at the vertical, horizontal, and cross-sectional levels – represented by the arrows in the model. Especially during the 1980s, the boundaries between the different boxes have become more indefinite, which implies that there is an ongoing melding and integration of various approaches, concepts, and methods but also an increased diversification of interfaces and contexts aimed at linking the natural environment and the economy.

4.2   Efficiency, Optimality, Market Failures, and the Environment

As already anticipated, two fundamental concepts in environmental economics are those of 'efficiency' and 'optimality'. We will briefly explore both concepts and present the core principles of welfare economics. Then we will turn our attention to 'market failures' and look at environmental issues through the lenses of 'public goods' and 'externalities'.

At any given time, an economy will have access to particular quantities of productive resources. Individuals have preferences about the various goods that can feasibly be produced using the available resources. An 'allocation of resources' describes what goods are produced and in what quantities they are produced, which combinations of inputs are used, and how the outputs of those goods are distributed among people (consumers).

As mentioned, an allocation of resources can be defined as 'efficient' if it is not possible to improve the condition of one or more individuals without worsening the condition of anyone else (i.e. the *Pareto optimality*). The opposite holds true when there is an inefficient allocation – that is, if it is possible to improve someone's position without worsening the position of anyone else (i.e. *suboptimality*).

4.2.1   The General Economic Equilibrium Theory and the Two Fundamental Theorems of Welfare Economics

This is the centrepiece of a popular theory in neoclassical economics: the *General Equilibrium Theory* (GET). This model describes the mechanisms for achieving the simultaneous equilibrium of all markets in an economic system. The GET demonstrates that the equilibrium achieved in perfect competition markets corresponds to a Pareto-optimal use of resources needed to produce the goods on those markets.

For an economic system to be in a Pareto-optimal situation, it needs to be efficient at three distinct levels:

A. That of the allocation of final goods among different consumers (*consumption optimum*)
B. That of the allocation of the various production inputs (*production optimum*)
C. That of the choice of the final goods to produce (*general optimum*)

Let us take consumption optimum into consideration. Imagine a barter economy with two consumers – free to choose if and how to exchange – and two goods produced

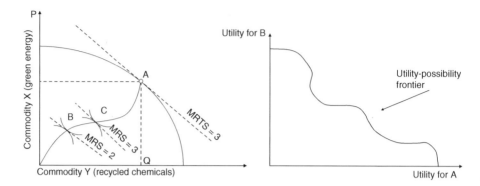

Figure 4.2 The Pareto optimum in consumption and the utility-possibility frontier.

in a given quantity. Under these conditions, to determine which exchanges will take place, we will use a graphical representation, called Edgeworth box.

Points A, B, and C in Figure 4.2 (left panel) represent some of the possible efficient allocations which satisfy both individuals' utility at their best. The union of all these points represents the 'contracts curve'. The same reasoning applies to a more advanced economic system in which competition and goods' prices are taken into consideration. The contracts curve can be transformed into a 'utility-possibility frontier', where each combination of utility for both A and B is interpreted in terms of their preferences (Figure 4.2 right panel). We therefore obtained a graphical representation of the consumption optimum.

The same approach can be repeated on the production side, allowing to obtain the production optimum (b). For the economic system to be in equilibrium (c), the two conditions of efficiency analysed (consumption and production) are necessary but not sufficient: the goods to be produced need also to be chosen in a way that is compatible with consumers' willingness to pay. Combining the production and consumption optimum, one can find the general optimum, which is usually expressed as: MRS = MRT, where MRS is the marginal rate of substitution (expressing consumers' preferences) and MRT is the marginal rate of Transformation (expressing producers' preferences).

As an example, we could apply the GET to the circular bioeconomy context: let us assume that commodity x corresponds to green energy produced using residual biomasses and specifically municipal solid waste (MSW) in a *waste-to-energy* circular economy framework. Turning waste into energy can be one key to a circular economy, enabling the value of products, materials, and resources to be maintained on the market for as long as possible, minimising waste and resource use. However, MSW could also be effectively used to produce other goods. For instance, the *waste-to-chemical* approach allows the use of such waste as feedstock for the synthesis of new products. Available technologies allow for the transformation of waste into valuable syngas, through a high-temperature conversion carried out under a pure oxygen environment. This could be used as a building block for the synthesis of a wide range of carbon-recycled chemicals. Let us assume that such recycled chemicals correspond to commodity *y* in our framework. On the one hand, the consumption optimum will allow the various combinations of green energy/recycled chemicals which correspond to consumers utility maximisations to be identified. On the other hand, the production optimum will guarantee the efficient allocations of the MSW to the many alternative combinations of the two commodities. Finally, the choice of the final quantities of energy/recycled chemicals to produce will be identified through the satisfaction of the general optimum condition.

Therefore, this model states that under the assumption of markets operating in perfect competition, every single agent's maximising behaviour (for its own satisfaction) leads to an efficient situation. The only information needed concerns market prices and each individual's own preferences. Starting from these premises, welfare economics infers two Fundamental Theorems:

- The *First Fundamental Theorem* of welfare economics states that, in a complete and free market, a competitive equilibrium – when and if is reached – is a Pareto optimum.
- The *Second Fundamental Theorem* of welfare economics states that any Pareto optimum can be supported as a competitive equilibrium for some initial set of endowments. This implies that any desired Pareto-optimal outcome can be supported, with any redistribution of initial wealth.

4.2.2   Market Failures: Markets Are Not Perfectly Competitive

According to the Second Theorem, market allocation is efficient but to obtain a specific Pareto optimum, a redistribution is needed. That is where state intervention comes into play. This might be even more necessary whenever the assumptions underlining the First Theorem do not hold true in the real world. Specifically, the following conditions need to be met:

A. Markets exist for all goods and services produced and consumed.
B. All markets are perfectly competitive.
C. All transactors have perfect information.
D. Private property rights are fully assigned in all resources and commodities.
E. No externalities exist.
F. All goods and services are private goods, so that no public goods exist.

In a real-world scenario, several of these assumptions are often impaired, leading to 'market failures'. One simple example is the absence of perfect competition. For a market to be in this situation, several conditions need to be simultaneously met:

B1. Infinite number of operators.
B2. No economies of scale.
B3. Freedom of entry and exit.
B4. Perfect information and absence of transaction costs.
B5. No agreements, understandings, and cartels.
B6. Homogeneity of products.

There are many examples of failures in terms of perfect competition. One case in point is that in real market conditions, monopolies and oligopolies often arise. There are many reasons why a monopoly exists, such as the ownership of a given natural resource or a legal institutional setting (e.g. public utilities providing energy, water). A monopolistic market is characterised by a unique producer, barriers to entry into the market, economies of scale (the bigger the company, the less the costs) and higher prices for consumers with lower production. Most importantly, it does not result in an efficient allocation of resources.

The same can be said for oligopolies. In this (more frequent) situation, there are few, large producers. Each of them sets a price taking into consideration other competitor's behaviour, often leading to a non-Pareto-efficient equilibrium. Whenever the competitors collude and reach an agreement on the price, a cartel is established. To prevent this from happening, public authorities usually enact anti-monopolistic regulations.

In most cases, companies incur considerable costs to enter into a market, and therefore are also likely to stay longer than efficiency would suggest. So-called hit-and-run strategies may not be easily feasible, also considering that leaving could lead to certain losses (sunk costs), both in terms of capital invested to enter and of experience and know-how acquired. This problem is particularly stringent in the circular bioeconomy meta-sector, in which new bio-based products face tough competition from conventional products which can rely on lower production costs, a favourable regulatory framework, and a dominant position in the market (see Box 4.1).

Another example of real world situations is that perfect information and product homogeneity are hardly met in real markets. Consumers are usually not capable of gathering all the information regarding product prices, especially now when 'pricing to market' strategies purposely adapt to prices based on specific market conditions. For instance, the very same good (e.g. a car) could be cheaper in another country, and yet almost no consumer would be eager to incur extra costs and time to buy it there. Finally, products are increasingly differentiated, as a basic marketing rule. Advertising is mainly aimed at making one product stand out in its own niche over its competitors.

As seen above, the lack of perfect competition is just one among many other examples of market failures. For our purposes, two other interesting failures are the existence of externalities and of public goods.

4.2.3   Market Failure: Externalities and Public Goods

As briefly mentioned above, an *externality* occurs when a production or consumption activity of one subject influences the welfare of another subject, negatively or positively, without the latter being compensated (in the case of a negative impact) or paying a price (in the case of a positive impact) equal to the cost or benefit incurred/received. Externalities thus indicate the effect of an activity on people who had no decision-making role in the activity, leading to divergences between private and social costs.

Externalities could also concern *public goods*, which are characterised by two main attributes: non-rivalry and non-excludability. Pure public goods are both

Box 4.1 Perfect Information and the Circular Bioeconomy – The Role of Labels, Certifications, and Standards

The lack of perfect information is particularly relevant when considering the emerging circular bioeconomy. As mentioned, one of the conditions to be met for the two fundamental welfare economic theorems to hold is that all trans-actors have perfect information. This condition is rarely met in the real world, and it is even more so when considering the circular bioeconomy meta-sector. Indeed, information concerning the environmental (and social) impact of specific goods is asymmetrically distributed between producers and consumers. As an example, let's consider the production of a bioplastic bottle. The producer will have the full set of information on the bio-based content of the bottle, the production process employed, the feedstock utilised, etc. This information is fundamental in assessing the overall impact the good has on the environment. However, consumers often have only scant information about all these aspects. Therefore, their purchasing decisions might be distorted, and this will reflect on prices. To reduce these information asymmetries, there is growing attention to sustainability assessments, leading to the definition of standards, certification schemes, and eco-labels. These are valuable instruments through which companies can demonstrate their commitment to lowering the environmental impact of their products and processes, reducing at the same the information asymmetry between producer and consumer.

However, existing standards often favour conventional materials. As a result, excellent bio-based alternatives to fossil-based products are not accepted because they do not have the same properties as fossil material. To be able to make the transition to a circular and bio-based economy, fully fledged bio-based alternatives to fossil materials and products must be introduced on a large scale. However, existing legislation and regulations hinder the introduction of new bio-based products, whereas sustainability standards, certifications, and eco-labels should favour the development of a level playing field between conventional and bio-based products.

non-rivalrous and non-excludable. Typical examples are lighthouses or nature conservation: users cannot be prevented from enjoying the benefits of such public goods for failing to pay for them. Also, use by one person neither prevents access to other people nor does it reduce availability to others. Other categories present mixed attributes: *club goods* (such as private parks, zoos, cinemas) are excludable (i.e. access can be restricted) but non-rivalrous (at least up to a certain congestion point). Instead, *common goods* are rivalrous but not excludable (e.g. foraging wild herbs, where permitted by the law, is an activity available to all, but foragers will compete for the resource). *Private goods* are both rivalrous and excludable (e.g. food, timber). Biodiversity, water and air quality, and overall environmental quality are essentially public goods. If the air is cleaned up for one person in an urban area, it is automatically cleaned up for everybody else in that community. In other words, the benefits accrue to everyone in the community, and it is almost impossible to restrict access to such benefits. However, with the growth of the world economy, some public goods are becoming increasingly rivalrous. To explain this point, let us refer to commons as natural resources that anyone can use freely; if these were improperly managed, they could be excessively used to the point of exhaustion. For instance, take an open pasture that serves as grazing land for cattle. In contrast to grasslands that are managed by exclusive owners who have it in their best interest to limit their livestock numbers to prevent overgrazing, grasslands open to unrestricted public use may be overgrazed by one party even if another party decides to restrict consumption by their cattle. Since those who choose to refrain from excessive use would ultimately miss out on profit-making opportunities, most would end up allowing their cattle to graze as much as possible. This therefore represents a scenario in which actors, motivated only by personal gain, would allow their cattle stock and consumption to reach levels that would completely deplete the grassland. This type of phenomenon was first depicted by Hardin (1968) in 'The Tragedy of the Commons'.

Private markets are likely to undersupply public goods, relative to efficient levels. To understand why, think of a lake, the shores of which are inhabited. The people use the lake for recreational purposes, but unfortunately, the water quality of the lake has been contaminated by an industrial plant that has since closed. It is possible to clean the water by using a fairly expensive treatment process. Each of the surrounding homeowners is willing to pay a certain amount to have the water quality improved. Once the efficient level of water quality has been identified, one could imagine relying on a competitive market system to get the contaminants in the lake reduced. Suppose a private firm attempts to sell its services to three homeowners. The firm goes to person A and tries to collect an amount equal to that person's true willingness to pay. But that person will presumably realise that once the lake is cleaned up, it is cleaned up for everybody, independently of each homeowner's contribution. So, A may have the incentive to underpay, relative to her/his true willingness to pay, hoping that the other homeowners will contribute enough to cover the costs of the clean-up. Clearly, everyone else may react in the same way.

As it seems, when a public good is involved, each person may have an incentive to have a free ride at the expense of others. A *free rider* is a person who pays for a good less than his/her true marginal willingness to pay, that is, a person who underpays when considering the benefits he/she receives.

4.2.4   State Intervention

In the examples provided in Section 4.2.3, market failures originate from a lack of due consideration of pollution or overconsumption damage costs (externality costs). Externalities can be addressed through various instruments, ranging from direct government-driven regulations to arrangements between private parties. Such instruments can be grouped into the following three intervention schemes (see Figure 4.3 and Box 4.2):

A. *Regulatory based:* direct environmental regulation (state-driven regulations and quality standards/levels)

B. *Information based:* direct negotiations and voluntary approaches (voluntary transactions between polluters and victims, voluntary approaches – including e.g. certification, corporate disclosure)

C. *Economic based:* environmental taxes and subsidies and emissions trading systems (ETSs) (fines or incentives aimed at improving environmental quality, tradable permits for emissions or other forms of environmental disruption)

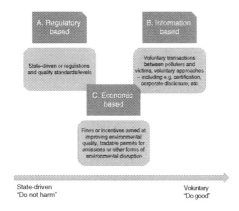

State-driven
"Do not harm"   Voluntary
                                                     "Do good"

Figure 4.3 Alternative interventions schemes.

Box 4.2 Governance of Plastic Pollution towards a Circular Bioeconomy

A range of policy instruments is being used by governing authorities, at local, regional, and national levels, to reduce plastics pollution. As discussed above, these can be divided into three categories: regulatory-based, economic-based, and information-based instruments. Examples are illustrated below:

Regulatory Based

policy statements – for example, National Plastics Waste Management Strategy, zero-waste policy

bans – for example, ban on single-use plastics, plastic waste landfill ban, ban on production and use of microbeads in products

trade policies – for example, ban on imported waste, support for trade initiatives that boost alternatives to single-use plastics products, targets on reducing trade in certain plastics

mandated labelling and information disclosure – for example, mandatory consumer information on recyclable material on plastic products

extended producer responsibility (EPR) schemes – for example, introduction of an EPR across the life cycle of the product, eco-design and material content

limit/restrict use – for example, restrict use of non-recyclable plastics

responsible handling – for example, recycling targets for plastic waste, introduction of separate collection streams for plastic products

eco-design standards – for example, targets to reduce add-ons like single-use plastic carry bags/holders for beverage cups, mandated percentage of recyclable material in products

procurement – for example, government procurement policy to avoid use of high-impact single-use plastic products

Economic Based

tax – for example, plastics beverage packaging tax, landfill and incineration taxes, pollution tax

levy – for example, levy on single-use plastic product producers/sellers

subsidy – for example, subsidies supporting innovation/production/research efforts on new materials

pay as you throw scheme – for example, charge for plastic waste disposal

payments – for example, deposit refund schemes

Information Based

research – for example, commission studies, reports, best practice development, undertake LCA (life cycle assessment)

voluntary labelling and information disclosure – for example, encourage voluntary disclosure schemes, certification, labelling of recyclable content

data collection/reporting – for example, collect data, show trends to support new behaviour

voluntary best practice guidance – for example, develop and disseminate best practice guidance

education/awareness raising – for example, education campaign on recycling

industry voluntary agreements – for example, promote voluntary actions by industry, voluntary industry targets

(*Source:* United Nations Environment Programme, 2021. *Addressing Single-use Plastic Products Pollution Using a Life Cycle Approach. Nairobi*)

Effective policies often require a mix of interventions to be used and should consider the broader context and needs of the society that will be affected by the policy.

4.2.4.1   Regulatory Based

These measures are direct legal regulations aimed at introducing or improving specific limitations to economic activities to prevent and reduce pollution. They are also referred to as '*command and control*' (CAC) measures where 'command' stands for the setting of environmental standards and 'control' for the sanctions imposed in case of violation.

Every country has a different legal system, which could be different in both procedural and substantive terms. Though, one could distinguish between two main categories of direct regulation: *emission criteria regulations* and *total emission amount regulations*.

The first are systems that categorically restrict contamination percentages among production emissions. More specifically, they set input coefficient restrictions of environmental resources (indicators of environmental resource utilisation that could also be called the pollution emission coefficient) per unit of production. The second regulations fix a cap on permissible pollution emission levels. To deliver their objectives, direct environmental regulations must ensure the highest level of compliance possible, as non-compliance would undermine their effectiveness. This can be achieved through appropriate policy implementation and enforcement. In the 'control' phase too, countries differ in terms of sanctions and their execution.

In terms of efficiency, environmental regulations should reach an optimal balance between extra costs for polluting companies and an effective reduction of pollution, with positive social externalities. How should socially optimal emission levels be determined in a specific and justifiable manner? First, the government must collectively decide the extent to which pollution should be curbed. Then, the entities that will be obliged to curb emissions, and to what extent, must be determined. All this depends on specific and contingent environmental policies (see Box 4.3).

Box 4.3 Regulatory Measures in the Circular Bioeconomy – The Single-Use Plastic Case

Single-use plastic products (SUPPs) are used once, or for a brief period of time, before being thrown away. The impacts of this plastic waste on the environment and our health are global and can be drastic. Single-use plastic products are more likely to end up in our seas than reusable options. The EU aims to become a forerunner in the global fight against marine litter and plastic pollution. To this end, in June 2019, the European Parliament approved the European Union (EU) Directive on the reduction of the impact of certain plastic products on the environment, commonly referred to as the Single-Use Plastics (SUP) Directive, which aims to reduce the volume and impact of certain plastic products on the environment. Through the SUP Directive, different measures are being applied to different products. These measures are tailored to get the most effective results, and to consider if more sustainable alternatives are available. When sustainable alternatives are easily available and affordable, single-use plastic products cannot be placed on the markets of EU Member States. This applies to cotton bud sticks, cutlery, plates, straws, stirrers, and sticks for balloons. It will also apply to cups, food and beverage containers made of expanded polystyrene, and to all products made of oxo-degradable plastic.

For other single-use plastic products, the EU is focusing on limiting their use through reducing consumption through awareness-raising measures introducing design requirements, such as a requirement to connect caps to bottles introducing labelling requirements, to inform consumers about the plastic content of products, disposal options that are to be avoided, and harm done to nature if the products are littered in the environment introducing waste management and clean-up obligations for producers, including EPR schemes. Specific targets include a 77 per cent separate collection target for plastic bottles by 2025 – increasing to 90 per cent by 2029; incorporating 25 per cent of recycled plastic in PET beverage bottles from 2025, and 30 per cent in all plastic beverage bottles from 2030.

4.2.4.2   Information Based

Direct Negotiations

Market mechanisms can lead to transactions and negotiations between the parties involved. The founding model of this idea is laid down in *Coase's Theorem* (1960), which has since become universally known in the field of environmental economics.

Coase's theorem states that bargaining between two economic agents can be considered a preferable solution to state intervention, but only if property rights are already defined and the negotiation and transaction costs between agents are close to zero. In essence, the theorem states that the market is able to solve independently the problem of externalities and social costs, but to do so it is necessary for property rights to be assigned upstream to economic agents.

To understand how Coase's theorem works, let us consider the following simple example. Consider an economy in which there are two firms (A and B) and that the production of firm A produces a negative externality (due to pollution) to firm B equal to the marginal damage (MD) curve depicted in Figure 4.4. Given that the marginal benefit (MB) of firm A equalled zero in Q_1, this will be the initial level of production of firm A, if property rights are assigned to firm A (i.e. firm A has the right to produce and pollute). However, firm A will agree to reduce the output of one unit if it receives in exchange an amount of money at least equal to the profit loss incurred by not producing that unit. On the other hand, company B would be willing to pay a certain amount so that that unit is not produced as long as it is less than the MD generated by the pollution associated with the production of that unit.

The agreement is possible if the profit lost by firm A is less than the amount that firm B is willing to pay. Looking at Figure 4.4, it must be verified that MD = MB. This condition is verified up to the production level of Q*. Therefore, firm B pays firm A to reduce the output until it reaches the level Q*, that is the volume of efficient production (also known as the optimal level of pollution).

Not possessing further information, it is not possible to establish the sum that will be paid. It will depend on the bargaining power of the two parties. However, the volume of production achieved will always be equal to Q*. It is important to note that

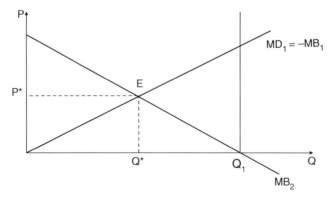

Figure 4.4 The Coase theorem and the optimal level of pollution.

compensation is not determined by the state or any other external party. It is the economic agents involved who determine the amount of compensation through a process of private bargaining.

Suppose now that the roles are reversed, and the property rights are instead assigned to the damaged firm B. In this case, firm A must pay compensation for polluting. Firm B is willing to accept a certain amount of pollution on the condition that it receives monetary compensation that is greater than the MD it must bear. Firm A finds it convenient to pay a certain amount to compensate for its pollution, provided that this amount is less than the benefit of producing an additional polluting unit of output. In this case, the initial level of production will be equal to zero, however through negotiation firm A will expand its production up to the optimal level of pollution Q*. The major difference from the previous case now is that it will be the polluting firm A compensating firm B (see also Chapter 3 for an example of compensation schemes).

As mentioned above, a direct negotiations model will only work if property rights are already defined and the negotiation and transaction costs between agents are close to zero. Indeed, these are conditions not usually achieved in the real world. Hence, there are some limitations to Coase's theorem that can be summarised as follows.

First, the Coase theorem is sensitive to its assumption of low transaction costs. In a negotiation, *transaction costs* are rarely close to zero, which is required in the Coase theorem. Based on the transaction costs, negotiation may or may not occur. For example, in many cases, it is difficult to bring many parties together or create capacity-building and resources to address the problem. So, a key criticism is that the theorem is almost always inapplicable in economic reality because real-world transaction costs are rarely low enough to allow for efficient bargaining.

Likewise, we saw that private property cannot be applied in every situation. Some goods are not subject to *pure private property rights* and are subject to representational issues and free riding.

Incomplete and asymmetric distribution of information can also represent a limitation to Coase theorem's applicability: it is often difficult to technically identify who produces the pollution and who suffers from it. This information implies an additional cost that adds up to the cost of the transaction. For instance, those affected by pollution may be forced to invest substantial financial resources to find the polluter, without having the certainty of finding them. When the cost of information is very high and/or the risks of failure in the search are high, the rightful owner of the property right (the polluter) abandons the negotiation a priori. Even if the search were entrusted to the state, in a cost/benefit analysis the cost of the search may not be compensated by the social revenue that can be obtained.

Finally, *inter-generational negotiation* might as well represent a cause of inapplicability of the Coase theorem. Oftentimes, the consequences of pollution do not affect current generations but rather the unborn. For example, the greenhouse effect or the hole in the ozone layer destabilises the ecosystem over time, producing effects only in the long term. Future generations cannot participate in any negotiation or bargaining with current generations, hence nullifying the Coasean bargaining effectiveness.

Along with these limitations and criticisms, there are other elements raising doubts on the effectiveness of the Coasean bargaining process in the presence of largely unbalanced power relationships. The Vittel case, presented in Box 4.4, provides an example of such a problem.

Box 4.4 Coasean Bargaining, Power Relationships, and the Case of Vittel

The Vittel valley, in north-eastern France, is famous for the low-lying Vosges mountains. Although agriculture has always been a centrepiece of the fertile territory's business, artesian springs have long claimed an increasingly relevant place in the local economy. Since the eighteenth century, the state introduced regulations for mineral springs as sources of natural remedies (Brei 2018). Then, in the nineteenth century, with the spread of mass production and developments in the property rights frameworks, the bottled market water expanded, paving the way for the widespread commercial exploitation of mineral waters.

The Vittel brand was established in the 1880s and in 1903, it sold a million bottles (Brei 2018; Everard 2011). In 1969, Nestlé acquired a significant amount of stocks in its parent company – reportedly attracted by its innovative decision to transition from glass bottles to plastic – when it was already a leading brand globally (Depres et al. 2008; Everard 2011; Lichfield 2004; Perrot-Maître 2006).

In parallel, in the late 1970s, boosted in part by Common Agricultural Policy (CAP) subsidies, an agricultural transition was in progress: farmers in the watershed implemented intensive maize-based systems, helping to make the area one of the most productive in France (Depres et al. 2008). With suboptimal manure management and overstocking, the massive use of fertilisers and pesticides started to seep contaminants into the groundwater, leading to an increase in aquifer nitrate concentrations (Barbier & Benoit 1996; Perrot-Maître 2014). This represented a direct existential threat to the Vittel brand, as French mineral water labelling regulations featured strict pollutant thresholds and restrictions on water treatment and origin labelling.

Vittel decided to engage in a private contract-based strategy to get farmers to implement aquifer-friendly management, but it lacked the scientific and agronomic expertise to spot the necessary changes or estimate their costs (Börner et al. 2017; Wunder et al. 2020). To tackle this challenge, Vittel partnered with INRA (the national agency for agronomic research) to launch a research program (AGREV) with socio-economic and agronomic components in 1989 (Barbier & Benoit 1996; Hernandez & Benoît 2011; Perrot-Maître 2014).

Three years later, Nestlé concluded the takeover of the Vittel brand and established an independent company, Agrivair, following smooth negotiations with the farmers. The resulting arrangements focused on granting usufructuary rights over company-owned lands, quashing farmers' debts, providing free technical assistance, and subsidising farmers' costs of switching to groundwater-friendly practices (which were developed through the AGREV studies). As of 2004, all remaining farmers had embraced the program and 92 per cent of the sensitive area was protected. At this point, Perrot-Maître (2006) considered the program to be successful, as it had achieved its core objective of mitigating the threat of nitrate pollution by modifying farming practices. The high renewal rate of these contracts, namely by the next generation of farmers, is often cited as the demonstration of a win–win outcome.

This case is an example for an evidence-based environmental management and the use of incentives to persuade problematic actors to change their behaviour for the benefit of all. Voluntary negotiation accomplished its goals efficiently and without diverting taxpayer funds directly to polluters.

In Vittel, the fundamental question was the basis for determining compensation. Should it be a function of the costs borne by farmers transitioning to more extensive production, or of the resulting benefits to the corporation? Unsurprisingly, Nestlé/Vittel and the farmers offered entirely opposing answers (Abildtrup et al. 2012; Grolleau 2013; Lawton 2015). So, who had the power to uphold their view?

As discussed in this chapter, the Coase theorem is generally taken to hold that the same Pareto-efficient outcome should be achieved regardless of the initial property rights assignment, as long as those rights are well-defined and transferable in the absence of significant transaction costs, asymmetric information, or government intervention (Zhang 2016; see e.g. Lewis & Polasky 2018). Simply put, farmers' costs for transitioning to and maintaining an aquifer-friendly relationship with management represent one bargaining curve, while the gains Nestlé/Vittel derive from cleaner water correspond to the other. The farmers' compensation had to cover their opportunity costs for the enforcement of new systems as a lower boundary, but it also could not exceed Nestlé/Vittel's net benefits (Capodaglio & Callegari 2018). In the 'distributionally blind' world of the Coase theorem, the bargaining process should lead to the same optimal outcome whether the farmers are fully liable for pollution or not liable at all (Ishiguro 2003; Meramveliotakis & Milonakis 2018, p. 50)

In Vittel, the relevant rights were unequivocal: farmers had a clear right to take action that would generate water quality measurements that were intolerable to Nestlé/Vittel. The clarity of the property rights allocation is presumably what made Vittel a candidate for a Coasean solution at the outset. If aquifer nitrate concentrations continued to rise (or if the company attempted to purify the water before bottling), the brand would lose its right to use the mineral water label – and it had good reason to believe that would be calamitous for brand value (Depres et al. 2008). Notably, although the farmers enjoyed an effective monopoly on the right to determine aquifer nitrate concentrations, they received a minor share of the benefits derived from maintaining them underneath the labelling threshold.

This result raises questions on possible flaws of the Coasean bargaining process related to unevenly distributed power relationships. Anyhow, Vittel shows that one's bargaining position matters a lot less than one might expect when there is a large power differential between parties. The company's ability to reconfigure information asymmetries, force successive individual bargaining, and – at least in principle – shape the local economy and will further jeopardises the applicability of the Coase theorem in its traditional 'distributionally blind' form.

Additional reading: Bingham (2021), https://doi.org/10.1016/j.ecoser.2021.101247

Voluntary Approaches

Voluntary limitations are another category through which the business world assumes obligations without direct oversight from the government. In these cases, pollution reduction environmental policies are defined, implemented, and enforced by the emitters themselves. Since they are voluntary and industry-created, they generally reflect overall feasibility and indirectly invite government participation. Sometimes, they could be even more efficient (or stringent) than public regulations, depending on the government's policy and its implementation schemes. They could also engage companies in beneficial competition, as customers may reward greener products and therefore more sales. However, it is important to ascertain that green marketing policies are not just 'greenwashing' measures but rather an effective step towards a more environmentally friendly business (see Box 4.5).

4.2.4.3   Economic Based

Environmental Taxes and Subsidies

This solution foresees state intervention that will impose an economic burden on polluting activities via direct taxation, based on tentatively optimal calculations. This tax is also referred to as 'Pigouvian tax', as it was first theorised by Pigou (1920).

Actually, the solution proposed by the English economist calls for the state to intervene through the introduction of both taxes and subsidies, to induce the economic agents who cause the externality, and to internalise the external costs or benefits: in this way, they will find it privately convenient to push their activity up to the social level.

The tax to be paid on each unit of output, therefore, must be equal to the marginal external cost (or marginal damage MD) at the social optimum point (see Figure 4.5):

Box 4.5 Voluntary Limitation: The New Plastics Economy Global Commitment

A case of voluntary limitation is the New Plastics Economy Global Commitment, which pools over 500 businesses, governments, and other organisations from around the world in the fight against plastic waste and pollution. Led by the Ellen MacArthur Foundation and the UN Environment Programme, the Global Commitment has already rallied to obtain over 450 signatories resolute to start building a circular economy for plastic. These comprise companies representing 20 per cent of all plastic packaging produced worldwide. All business and government signatories have signed up to a clear set of 2025 targets backed by common definitions and will report annually on progress to ensure transparency and continuity.

The Global Commitment and its vision for a circular economy for plastic are endorsed by the World Wide Fund for Nature (WWF), the World Economic Forum, the Consumer Goods Forum (a CEO-led organisation representing some 400 retailers and manufacturers from seventy countries), and forty universities, institutions, and academics. Also, more than fifteen financial institutions (with an excess of $2.5 trillion in assets under management) have supported the Global Commitment, and more than $200 million has been committed by venture capital funds to turn the plastic economy from a linear to a circular model.

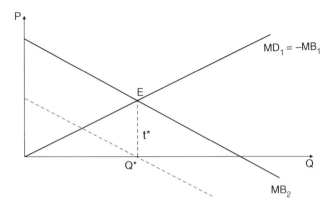

Figure 4.5 The Coase theorem and the environmental taxes.

$$t* = (Q*) = \mathrm{MB}(Q*)$$

Alternatively, the government could provide subsidies in return for emissions reductions: the cost-benefit analysis for the enterprise is the same, while for states it implies higher expenses – and no revenue, if not in terms of social benefits. This could mark a decisive point for taxes, as the revenues could be invested, redistributed, or simply deducted from other taxation schemes.

Pigouvian taxes and subsidies seem to be effective solutions to the problem of externalities, but their implementation is difficult. The main problem is represented by the need to measure the quantity and value of externalities to be able to determine the right tax or subsidy that corrects the inefficiency, without introducing other distortions in the systems (see Box 4.6). In the case of a tax, for example, the state needs to know the external costs caused by the activity of the firm, but it is often difficult to establish precisely and quantify in monetary terms the damages of pollution.

A further complication is the existence of information asymmetries between the polluting firm and the state. Moreover, the firm has no incentive to disclose this information and, knowing that it will be used to levy a tax, can distort it to incur lower taxation.

Emissions Trading Systems

A similar measure is the institution of an emission trading system (ETS). In this case, businesses are granted *emission certificates for a standardised quota of pollution output*. In many cases, the government has introduced emission permits that give companies the right to pollute up to a certain level. A market is then created to trade these allowances between companies and the organisations that own them.

Polluters need emission certificates available on the trading market, and if they pollute more than the permissible amounts pursuant to the certificates, they can buy additional emission rights from other polluters. If they pollute less than the amount

---

Box 4.6 When the Subsidy Goes in the Wrong Direction – The Controversial Case of Environmentally Harmful Subsidies

At present, there is no shared definition of an environmentally harmful subsidy (EHS). Stemming from the OECD's 1998 and 2005 definition of 'subsidy', one might define an EHS thus: 'A result of a government action that confers an advantage on consumers or producers, in order to supplement their income or lower their costs, but in doing so, discriminates against sound environmental practices.'

One of the greatest obstacles is determining the environmental noxiousness of subsidies, as all production and consumption activities have an environmental footprint. Broadly speaking, a subsidy is harmful to the environment if it leads to a higher level of production and consumption than would be the case without the measure. Against this background, another definition of EHS is the following: 'All other things being equal, the [environmentally harmful] subsidy increases the levels of output/use of a natural resource and therefore increases the level of waste, pollution and natural exploitation to those connected.'

The European Environmental Agency (EEA) valuation is that 75 per cent of total EU energy subsidies in 2001 are accounted for by fossil fuels, with coal as the largest recipient. A recent estimate of the Global Subsidy Initiative estimates producer and consumer subsidies to be no less than US$ 500 billion a year globally (GSI 2009): that is 1 per cent of the world gross domestic product, the amount that the Stern Review judged necessary to restrict the world temperature rise to 2°C (Stern 2006).

Reforming environmentally harmful subsidies is a key policy challenge for many countries. The European Parliament in July 2021 voted to make it legally binding for all Member States to phase out fossil fuel subsidies by 2025 and all other environmentally harmful subsidies as of 2027.

---

permitted by their certificates, they might sell their excess certificates. This is accomplished not through negotiations between factories and businesses but through the trading of emissions certificates allocated by the government. If other economic methods are conjunctively utilised to construe monetary value to environmental assets for them to be taken in by the market, externalities can actually be internalised.

Usually, the total permissible amounts of emissions are determined beforehand by the government, and this is a crucial factor to the success of the scheme. Aggregate emission levels are overseen by the government, and they are suppressed according to how many emissions certificates are issued.

Emission trading systems are a realistic measure as those who can easily decrease emissions can do so, and those who cannot easily do so can acquire the right to emit the amounts that they need. This way, an equal burden (marginal cost) is imposed on all businesses for decreasing emissions, and since businesses engage in optimising behaviour, the social costs of implementing reduction targets decreed by the government are minimised. However, in accordance with the Coase theorem, optimal emissions amounts are not dependent on how they are allocated at the start.

In the past few decades, ETSs have been experimented with by policymakers, such as the EU, which operates on the principle of cap-and-trade. A cap is set on the total amount of certain greenhouse gases that can be emitted by installations covered by the system. The cap is reduced over time so that total emissions decrease. Within this cap, installations buy or receive emission allowances that they can trade if necessary. Limiting the total number ensures that the available allowances have value.

At the end of each year, installations must surrender enough allowances to cover their emissions fully if they wish to avoid heavy fines. If a facility reduces its emissions, it can keep the unused allowances to cover future needs or sell them to another facility that is short of them. Trading creates flexibility and ensures that emission reductions happen when they are the most cost-effective. A robust CO_2 price also encourages investment in innovative, low-carbon technologies.

Trading schemes have also been implemented to secure biodiversity and habitats. Inter alia, habitat banking, and tradable development rights (TDR) expanded as a means for achieving 'no net loss' of biodiversity and of reconciling nature conservation with economic development goals. Both habitat banking and TDR have the capacity to contribute to biodiversity conservation targets and attain viable solutions with positive social impacts on local communities and landowners. They can also incentivise public–private co-operation in biodiversity conservation. Concurrently, these policy instruments are confronted with many theoretical and implementation challenges – such as the additionality and equivalence of offsets, endurance of land-use planning provisions, monitoring of offset performance, or delays between restoration and the resulting conservation benefits.

A definite and binding regulatory approach is a condition for the success of habitat banking and TDR. In exchange, these schemes offer robust incentives for compliance with provisions and secure a more equitable allotment of the benefits and costs of land-use controls and preservation (Santos et al. 2015).

4.2.5   The Role of the State beyond Environmental Externality

As anticipated, these four lines of action can be combined by policymakers depending on contingent circumstances and policy orientations. We should also bear in mind that these solutions are specifically aimed at resolving environmental externalities. Many other actions are required to solve wholly pollution and environmental depletion, implying, among others, a shift from a linear fossil-based economy towards a circular bioeconomy.

For these purposes, an active role of governments in the economy can help in leaping towards a new system, with so-called *industrial policies*, that is, the set of measures undertaken by the government to promote or prevent structural change in the economy.

A clear example can be found in the EU 'Green Deal' presented at the end of 2019. This plan aims to foster major changes in Europe's economic structure, including transitions from fossil fuels to renewables, and from diesel to electric cars. This will be a broad and radical change for the economy, as well as a major socio-economic transformation. With the Green Deal, the EU recognised that energy and climate policies alone are not sufficient to pursue climate neutrality. For instance, a strategy based only on increasing the price of coal would remain sterile, especially if it were accompanied by a popular uprising. Only a broader policy, encompassing economic, industrial, fiscal, labour, innovation, and social policy aspects, can address such an important challenge.

The justification for such a comprehensive industrial policy is provided by the same market failures we have presented. More specifically, knowledge spillovers, co-ordination failures, informational asymmetries, economies of scale, and market concentration (monopolistic and/or oligopolistic positions) can hamper green innovations and the desired transition.

One of the main arguments in favour of industrial policy relates to research and development (R&D) and technology policy concerns knowledge spillovers. Since markets do not provide sufficient incentives for private investment in research – because of the non-excludable and non-rivalrous nature of knowledge – private investments could be much lower than the socially desired level. Governments can intervene by granting strong intellectual property (IP) rights with patents and by funding research in universities and enterprises. A co-ordinated state-led approach can also improve failures in optimal co-ordination across production chains, where single companies could pursue different goals with different means.

The lack of information about future profitability can be another obstacle to innovation. If any entrepreneurial activity inherently carries its own risks, green innovation could magnify uncertainties on whether projects will be impactful enough, not conflicting with each other, and not subject to political cycles. In addition, smaller companies usually suffer disadvantages in terms of information and R&D capacity compared to larger ones.

Last but not least, production costs can be too high to invest in the first place. Even if future economies can pay off, sometimes entry barriers can deter innovation, at the advantage of the already existing, often more polluting companies. This could be exacerbated by the presence of monopolies and/or oligopolies which raise the price to enter the market and to survive enough to reap the benefits of green innovation. Often, capital markets can provide the financial resources to overcome these challenges, but since they are subject to market failures too, public intervention could be providential.

4.3   The Sustainability Debate: The Pursuit of Optimality and Role of Posterity

Economic theory incorporates the concept of *sustainability* into the study of growth and development. We are now assuming a dynamic perspective, which considers the current and the potential future effects of economic activities on the capital stock, which includes all natural resources available in the economy. As mentioned in Chapter 3, *natural capital* is defined as the stock of natural ecosystems, which produces a flow of goods or services in the future. Natural capital can also provide services such as waste recycling or erosion control (Costanza 2008).

One of the traditional classifications of natural capital and its functions is the one offered by Pearce and Turner (1990), which is known as 'source-sink-service'. The main function (the source) of natural capital is its ability to provide raw materials (e.g. oil and minerals) that are essential in economic production. The sink component of natural capital refers to the capacity of natural systems to absorb and transform the waste products generated by human activities. Finally, the service function – also referred to as the life support function – consists of the provision of services that keep ecosystems and the biosphere intact.

The concept and definition of natural capital is fundamental as it determines what is 'sustainable development'. The production of goods takes place over time; that is, it has a process nature. The natural resources that are exploited in this process are flows. The task is to understand how the overall output of the system is not reduced if the flow of natural resources is reduced in time because of human activity.

First, it should be noted that economic sustainability is more feasible when the amount of capital needed to replace the loss of services provided by natural capital is smaller. The issue of *capital substitutability* is central to working out a solution to the economic sustainability issue. According to the factor substitutability hypothesis, an increase in structures, knowledge, and skills must be able to compensate for the decrease in natural capital to ensure the maintenance, over time, of production capacities and the satisfaction of the well-being of the population. In essence, this is the Hartwick–Solow criterion, based on which natural capital erosion can be replaced with *artificial capital.*

Turner et al. (1996) place the emphasis on the sum of quantities of these two capitals which must remain *constant* over time; it is substantially implied that with the progress of human civilisation and the consequent utilisation of natural resources, a loss of weight percentage of natural capital over time in favour of artificial capital is acceptable. According to this view, an economy which goes by the name of *weak sustainability* is sustainable if it saves enough to be able to offset the depreciation of natural and artificial capital; this means that even when natural resources are fully exploited and the environment is contaminated, if the economic system provides the financial means to invest in the restoration of ecosystems and for the production of new capital, then it is possible to compensate for losses incurred.

To summarise, weak sustainability posits that natural capital erosion is not a problem if:

- the revenues generated by the extraction of non-renewable resources are saved and reinvested in artificial capital (plants, infrastructure, human capital);
- artificial and natural capital are perfect substitutes; and
- non-renewable resources are extracted according to an efficient plan.

This kind of sustainability is opposed by the idea of *strong sustainability*, which argues for the inflexibility of natural resources because they are mostly irreplaceable.

There would not be any remedy to their degradation and therefore they are not replaceable even with the increase of other values, such as social or economic ones.

Here, natural capital is not simply a reservoir to be drawn on. It is a complex set of systems that, through a delicate network of balances, performs a multiplicity of functions – first life support. As Daly (1996) and Barbier (1987) state, the natural environment and artificial capital are complementary rather than substitutes. Hence, the rate of utilisation of renewable resources must not exceed their rate of regeneration. The release of pollutants and waste into the environment must not exceed its load-bearing capacity, and the stock of non-renewable resources must remain constant over time. Essentially, according to this view, the current generation should leave to future generations at least the same stock of natural capital that it currently enjoys.

Strong sustainability also considers the knowledge developed by biological disciplines and adds two important elements: the presence of *radical uncertainty* and *critical thresholds*. The complexity of the mechanisms governing the biosphere on the one hand makes the effects of many of our actions unpredictable, while making us aware of the existence of irreversible thresholds beyond which equilibria lose their stability. The use of the *precautionary principle*, which could correspond to what traditional economists call a moderate aversion to risk, is therefore what is called for by proponents of the strong sustainability principle.

Ultimately, strong sustainability is defined on *ecological grounds*. To ecologists, sustainability means maintaining the resilience of ecosystems. While traditional economists stem from human interests, defined mainly in terms of consumption, ecologists start from the properties of the system of which humans are a part. This does not mean that the ecological approach ignores human interests, rather it includes them within the continued functioning of the biosphere (Common et al. 1995).

The difference between weak and strong sustainability lies not only in the very definition of natural capital, but also in a different assessment of the *role that growth and the market can play in environmental protection*. On the one hand, weak sustainability considers economic growth to be unquestionable and focuses on resource efficiency and the implementation of internalisation mechanisms through market instruments that consider the environment. On the other hand, strong sustainability argues for the conservation of natural resources, according to which the economic system must minimise the use of resources by reducing production and even population levels.

No definition of sustainability is free of flows: there is no form of development which can be said to be perfectly in line with the definition of strong sustainability, as some alteration of natural capital is inherent in every process of growth, even the most eco-friendly. But also the adoption of the weak sustainability principle poses significant risks, given the irreversibility that characterizes most environmental decisions. In conclusion, to pursue sustainable development, it is desirable for economic theory to be increasingly open to ecology and other natural sciences, as well as social sciences and ethics. A balanced and precautionary approach, based on the complementarity of artificial and natural capital, may help too (Costanza 1989).

Take-Home Message

Sustainable bioeconomy is based on a combination of environmental economics, which offers a description of the state of the environment, its changes, causes, and solutions to improve economic institutions, and ecological economics, which is concerned with putting economics in the larger context of earth sciences.

Two fundamental concepts in environmental economics are those of 'efficiency' and 'optimality', derived from the GET. Starting from GET, welfare economics infers its two fundamental theorems, whose assumptions are often not met in the real world, leading to market failures, which are exemplified by externalities.

Externalities, resulting from insufficient consideration of pollution or overconsumption damage costs, can be addressed through regulatory (direct environmental regulation such as state-driven regulations and quality standards), information (direct negotiations and voluntary approaches), and economic-based instruments (environmental taxes and subsidies and ETSs).

An active role of governments in the economy can help to leap towards a new system, with so-called industrial policies, that is, the set of measures undertaken by the government to promote or prevent structural change in the economy, as exemplified by the Green Deal.

The concept and definition of natural capital, that is, the stock of natural ecosystems, is fundamental as it determines what is 'sustainable development'.

The issue of capital substitutability is central in working out a solution to the economic sustainability issue as it states that economic sustainability is more feasible when the amount of capital needed to replace the loss of services provided by natural capital is smaller.

A distinction can be made between weak and strong sustainability; the difference lies in the definition of natural capital but is also based on a different assessments of the role that growth and the market can play in environmental protection.

Learning Exercises

1. What does the concept of externality mean? How is it related to the principle of allocative efficiency?
2. What are the fundamental theorems of welfare economics? Which conditions are necessary to satisfy them?
3. What are the main characteristics of monopolistic and oligopolistic markets?
4. Which main intervention schemes can be used to address market failures deriving from the costs of (especially environmental) externalities?
5. What does the Coase theorem state? What are its main limitations?

Online Resources

Lecture 'Ecosystem services: governance & policy instruments'. Available at: www2.helsinki
.fi/fi/unitube/video/9eea51f9-fb2b-4384-a47d-028e3a6d7219

References

Abildtrup, J., Jensen, F., & Dubgaard, A. (2012). Does the Coase Theorem Hold in Real Markets? An Application to the Negotiations Between Waterworks and Farmers in Denmark. *Journal of Environmental Management*, 93(1), 169–176.

Barbier, E. B. (1987). The Concept of Sustainable Economic Development. *Environmental Conservation*, 14(2), 101–110.

Barbier, M., & Benoit, M. (1996). Programme AGREV. Synthèse des investigations menées de 1992 à 1995, sous la responsabilite scientifique de l'Institut National de la Recherche Agronomique.

Bingham, L. R. (2021). Vittel as a Model Case in PES Discourse: Review and Critical Perspective. *Ecosystem Services*, 48, 101247.

Börner, J., Baylis, K., Corbera, E., … Wunder, S. (2017). The Effectiveness of Payments for Environmental Services. *World Development*, 96, 359–374.

Boulding, K. E. (1966). The Economics of the Coming Spaceship Earth. In H. Jarrett, ed., *Environmental Quality in a Growing Economy, Resources for the Future*, Baltimore: Johns Hopkins University Press, pp. 3–14.

Brei, V. A. (2018). How is a Bottled Water Market Created? *WIREs Water*, 5(1). doi:10.1002/wat2.1220

Capodaglio, A., & Callegari, A. (2018). Can Payment for Ecosystem Services Schemes Be an Alternative Solution to Achieve Sustainable Environmental Development? A Critical Comparison of Implementation between Europe and China. *Resources*, 7(3), 40.

Coase, R. (1960). The Problem of Social Cost. *The Journal of Law and Economics*, 3, 1–44.

Common, M. (1995). *Sustainability and Policy: Limits to Economics*, Cambridge: Cambridge University Press.

Costanza, R. (1989). What is Ecological Economics? *In Ecological Economics*, 1, 1–7.

Costanza, R., & Cleveland, C. (2008). Natural Capital. *The Encyclopedia of Earth*, 31. Retrieved from http://editors.eol.org/eoearth/wiki/Natural_capital

Daly, H. E. (1996). *Beyond Growth*, Boston: Beacon Press.

Depres, C., Grolleau, G., & Mzoughi, N. (2008). Contracting for Environmental Property Rights: The Case of Vittel. *Economica*, 75(299), 412–434.

Everard, M. (2011). *Common Ground: The Sharing of Land and Landscapes for Sustainability*, New York: Bloomsbury Publishing.

Folke, C., & Kåberger, T. (1991). Recent Trends in Linking the Natural Environment and the Economy. In *Linking the Natural Environment and the Economy: Essays from the Eco-Eco Group*, Dordrecht: Springer Netherlands, pp. 273–300.

Grolleau, G. (2013). Chapter 9: Collective Action Case Study – France. In *Providing Agri-environmental Public Goods through Collective Action*, Paris: OECD Publishing, pp. 183–193.

GSI. (2009). *Achieving the G-20 Call to Phase out Subsidies to Fossil Fuels: Policy Brief*, Geneva: IISD.

Hardin, G. (1968). The Tragedy of the Commons. *Science*, 162(3859), 1243–1248.

Hernandez, S., & Benoît, M. (2011). Gestion durable de la ressource en eau : l'utilisation du paiement pour service environnemental au service de la protection des captages. *Annales Des Mines – Responsabilité et Environnement*, N° 63(3), 87–95.

Ishiguro, S. (2003). Comparing Allocations Under Asymmetric Information: Coase Theorem revisited. *Economics Letters*, 80(1), 67–71.

Lawton, J. (2015). Payments for Ecosystem Services: A best practice guide.

Lewis, D. J., & Polasky, S. (2018). An Auction Mechanism for the Optimal Provision of Ecosystem Services Under Climate Change. *Journal of Environmental Economics and Management*, 92, 20–34.

Lichfield, J. (2004, September 16). Eau dear, what can the matter be? Retrieved from 16/09/2022 www.independent.co.uk/news/world/europe/eau-dear-what-can-the-matter-be-32590.html

Marshall, A. (1890). *Principles of Economics*. London (8th Ed. Published in 1920): Macmillan.

Meramveliotakis, G., & Milonakis, D. (2018). Coasean Theory of Property Rights and Law Revisited: A Critical Inquiry. *Science & Society*, 82(1), 38–66.

Pareto, V. (1897). The New Theories of Economics. *Journal of Political Economy*, 5(4), 485–502.

Pearce, D. W., & Turner, R. K. (1990). *Economics of Natural Resources and the Environment*, Baltimore: Johns Hopkins University Press.

Perrot-Maître, D. (2006). *The Vittel Payments for Ecosystem Services: A Perfect PES Case?* London, UK: International Institute for Environment and Development.

Perrot-Maître D. (2014). The Vittel Case: A Public-Private Partnership in the Mineral Water Industry. Case studies on Remuneration of Positive Externalities (RPE)/ Payments for Environmental Services (PES), Rome. Retrieved from www.fao.org/3/a-bl927e.pdf

Pigou, A. C. (1920). *The Economics of Welfare*, First Edition, London: Macmillan.

Santos, R., Schröter-Schlaack, C., Antunes, P., Ring, I., & Clemente, P. (2015). Reviewing the Role of Habitat Banking and Tradable Development Rights in the Conservation Policy Mix. *Environmental Conservation*, 42(4), 294–305.

Stern, N. (2006). Stern Review: The Economics of Climate Change.

Turner, R. K., Subak, S., & Adger, W. N. (1996). Pressures, Trends, and Impacts in Coastal Zones: Interactions between Socioeconomic and Natural Systems. *Environmental Management*, 20(2), 159–173.

United Nations Environment Programme. (2021). Addressing Single-Use Plastic Products Pollution using a Life Cycle Approach. Retrieved from www.unep.org/resources/publication/addressing-single-use-plastic-products-pollution-using-life-cycle-approach

Wunder, S., Börner, J., Ezzine-de-Blas, D., Feder, S., & Pagiola, S. (2020). Payments for Environmental Services: Past Performance and Pending Potentials. *Annual Review of Resource Economics*, 12(1), 209–234.

Zhang, D. (2016). Payments for Forest-based Environmental Services: A Close Look. *Forest Policy and Economics*, 72, 78–84.

5 Sustainability Transition and the Bioeconomy

Learning Objectives

To understand and be able to discuss critically:

- the main transition frameworks.
- the main transition pathways.
- the specificities of a transition from a linear and fossil-based economy to a circular bioeconomy.
- the role of policy measures.

5.1   Setting the Theoretical Framework

In the environmental sciences, most theories of systemic change show how transformation within complex and interdependent systems composed of multiple actors and multiple interests – in our case the transition to a sustainable development model – is linked to multi-level change, requiring several strategies and innovations aimed at greater efficiency. Indeed, a trajectory of genuine sustainable development cannot be based on technological and productive innovation alone.

Usually, policymakers tend to adopt a *top-down approach* to sustainable development, making sustainability a policy planning issue and implementing policy interventions with the aim of helping individuals and communities to adopt more environmentally sustainable lifestyles and of greening mainstream businesses. However, policymakers are also increasingly opening the field to citizens and local communities to contribute more actively to the sustainability transition, within a *bottom-up approach*.

We conceive sustainable transition as the set of processes aimed at making our development model more environmentally friendly. Sustainable transition is therefore both an objective and at the same time a set of processes. There is a large body of literature which, using a *multi-level perspective (MLP)*, analyses and attempts to frame social changes that can develop from the ecologisation of production systems towards sustainable development (Bosman & Rotmans 2016; Geels 2010; Schot &

Geels 2008). This can be at macro, meso, or micro systemic level. In this framework, transition is understood as a non-linear interaction process of three socio-technical levels:

- The 'niches': limited and protected spaces where radical innovations are created and developed;
- The 'regimes': the areas of social practices and the rules and institutions that constrain actions in existing systems;
- The 'landscape': the general background against which the macro-processes are situated.

According to this scheme, innovations develop in niches but have a chance to spread in regimes – which tend to be self-preserving – when changes in the landscape are such as to destabilise them from the outside. In this sense, the alignment between niches, regimes, and landscapes enables radical innovations to produce technological leaps that can promote important social changes by modifying socio-technical regimes.

5.2   Approaches to Transition and Innovation

Before assessing MLPs, we should first consider other related theoretical approaches to transition and innovation:

- *Strategic niche management* (SNM)
- *Transition management* (TM)
- *Technological innovation systems* (TIS)

5.2.1   Strategic Niche Management

This theory focuses on detecting the circumstances under which a niche can be successfully developed. It is a technique developed to facilitate the introduction and dissemination of new technologies through social experiments (Caniëls & Romijn 2008; Schot & Geels 2008). It concentrates on innovations that target socially desirable long-term goals – such as sustainability – which faces a mismatch with the existing system of infrastructure and regulations.

Much of the SNM theory is linked to the intensive *networking activities* that all the actors involved in the process of 'incubation' of the niche are required to carry out. Briefly, we could say that according to scholars, the real factor that triggers this evolutionary process is the widest possible involvement of actors such as enterprises, public institutions, and researchers.

However, there are other relevant factors, such as the *quality and nature* of these interactions between entities, which the SNM does not analyse systematically. In fact, it is difficult to use this theory to draw a general model from empirical studies conducted on technological niches structurally different from each other.

Generally speaking, the SNM considers a series of *conditional factors* which can promote or hinder niche processes. These factors can be classified within a range of influences over the process, from weaker to stronger conditions. Among those which are believed to be the most influential, researchers identify the existence of sheltered spaces for incubation, where the technology can be experimented without external pressures from a technical and economic point of view. Another strong condition is the opportunity for continuous evaluation and incremental improvement, by means of interacting with stakeholders. Also, the technology should exhibit temporal increasing returns or learning economies, be open to development in further directions, and be attractive for certain applications (i.e. the advantages of the new technology must overcome the disadvantages).

Turning our attention to weaker conditions, a first example is the instability of the established regime. When issues cannot be solved within the existing technologies and parameters, alternative solutions might be incentivised. Another condition often cited by scholars is the institutional and public support base, which is not always given at the first stage of innovative processes, also depending on how radical they are.

Last, but not least, policy intervention can be crucially impactful, as it can guide the learning and development processes. Policy interventions can improve networking and exchanges within the society and directly incentivise emerging technologies with taxes and/or subsidies (more on this will be developed in the final paragraph of this chapter).

As a final remark, it is worth noting here that the SNM includes a series of steps that are believed to define the formation process of a technological niche:

- *Choice of the technology*. The decision should be based on multiple criteria, such as the potential and inspirational influence on stakeholders and feasibility, in connection with user needs and values. Within this process, great importance is attached to innovative entrepreneurs who can lead and act as pioneers.
- *Selection of an experiment*. The innovation process should first focus on simple experiments and proceed with a trial-and-error approach. Therefore, a balance must be found between ambition and realism: the experiment should aim high but not too high as to impair the process by wasting too much time and effort. When it comes to sustainability, the choice between environmental goals and market feasibility can be imposed already at this stage.
- *Experiment implementation*. This phase is crucial as it requires co-ordination between innovators and other stakeholders, such as partners, competitors, consumers, and policy makers. The main goal is to induce learning in networks, find potential problems, identify end users, adjust the technology to the existing socio-technical regime, and set up communication strategies. Policy makers should assume the role of enabler and catalyst, rather than regulator or technology sponsor (Kemp et al. 1998). Financial support may help too, but is not always the most effective instrument.
- *Scaling up*. This is the final step, where the technological niche starts to spread in the market. It is a gradual process that implies dismantling protection and opening up the technology to the already established network, and beyond. Protection should be lifted when the experiment led to positive results, but also when negative outcomes demonstrate the wastefulness of further incubation.

5.2.2   Transition Management

Transition management (TM) is an approach which concentrates on accelerating and facilitating technological transitions within a multi-actor scenario. Through a long-term perspective made of multiple and constant interventions, TM aims at defining a transition path towards a new structure, whether characterised by the objective of greater sustainability or by other issues deemed as central in a given period (Foxon et al. 2010; Kemp et al. 2007; Rotmans et al. 2001).

The main principles which underline TM are:

- *long-term thinking* aimed to define the framework for short-term policies;
- *multi-domain, multi-actor, and multi-level thinking*;
- *learning-by-doing* approach;
- keeping *innovation* alongside with *improvement*;
- *wide playing field* aimed to leave multiple options open on the table.

In its more mature form, TM allows the development of these principles through four types of interventions: addressing current development objectives and challenges, defining a shared agenda to create a single sense of power and responsibility, activating joint projects, reflecting, and weighting up. Therefore, it is an open-ended process involving the so-called development rounds, where what has been achieved in terms of content, process dynamics, and knowledge is periodically evaluated. The stakeholders engaged in the transition process evaluate in each interim round the set interim transition objectives, the transition process itself, and the transition experiments.

This is especially important for complex transitions such as health and environmental ones, which cannot be constrained to a pure quantitative and risk-based analysis. Such transitions also require qualitative studies assessing the socio-political issues at stake.

There are a number of key obstacles affecting a transition's governance:

- *Dissent on the best strategy and the desired end goals.* The sustainability transition is an example of how difficult it is to reach consensus on the required actions. For these reasons, it is all the more important to constantly review and discuss the strategy, and to define common parameters.
- *Fragmentation of power.* In democratic systems, the transition cannot be managed by a unique authority; instead, it requires co-ordination between institutions and stakeholders. When contrasting views exist, it is essential to reach a consensus at least on the main long-term goals.
- *Defining short-term steps.* The transition consists of a step-by-step development guided by the end goal. Yet, policy makers might struggle with finding the right short-term approach. They should adopt a forward-looking strategy, without excluding a backward reasoning, especially when the transition has already started.
- *Lock-in.* By choosing the best available option at the beginning of a transition while others are still in development stage, future development will be likely dominated by that specific option leading to a lock-in effect. For these reasons, maintaining a wide playing field is fundamental.

• *Political myopia.* Political cycles are shorter than the transition process, which could involve different generations. This means that short-term policies could hamper the longer-term goals of the transition, as they are not politically rewarding. As a solution, some scholars suggest establishing a transition arena, where policy making is detached from contingent political issues and vested rights (Loorbach & Rotmans 2006).

For these reasons, TM should involve a multi-level governance model structured on three tiers: the strategic level, where a long-term vision is defined; the tactical level, where coalition building and agenda setting are performed; and the operational level, where the experimentation is carried out.

In short, TM is aimed at influencing, organising, and co-ordinating processes at different levels so that these processes are aligned and synergetic. It is concerned with the co-evolution of technology and society through analysing interactions and feedback between various 'subsystems' and by elaborating these insights to increase the likelihood that these subsystems (and thus the whole system) move into a more long-term (and in our case, sustainable) direction.

5.2.3   Technological Innovation Systems

A technological innovation system (TIS) can be defined as a set of networks of actors and institutions jointly interacting in a specific technological field and contributing to the generation, diffusion, and utilisation of variants of a new technology and/or a new product (Hekkert et al. 2007; Markard & Truffer 2008).

A TIS is defined as follows:

• It includes different actors, which share a common view of the innovation field, but who are pursuing different innovation strategies or controlling different resources.
• It is characterised by a certain division of tasks among the involved actors, which together form an 'innovation value chain'.
• It comprehends various institutions, both external and internal to the innovation system.
• It is distinguished by an already existing, yet immature market with competing suppliers.

The purpose of analysing a TIS is to assess the development of a specific technological field in terms of both the structures and processes that support or hinder it. To do this, a TIS focuses not only on knowledge diffusion but also on the actual exploitation of business solutions by adopting a dynamic approach where innovation is gradually developed in multiple blocks.

In order to reach these goals and be able to compare different TISs, each TIS usually includes the following components:

1. *Entrepreneurial activities.* Entrepreneurs turn knowledge into innovation following business opportunities. They usually undertake market research and organise projects and experiments to determine the potential of the emerging technology.

2. *Knowledge development.* It concerns different types of learning activities, the most important categories being learning-by-searching (research and development processes) and learning-by-doing (field and/or lab experiments).

3. *Knowledge diffusion through networks.* Networks are essential to incentivise the exchange of knowledge among all actors. Diffusion activities include partnerships between actors, workshops, and conferences. The TIS approach also stresses the importance of the interaction between actors of different backgrounds and to recur to learning-by-using, where user-producer interactions provide for additional information.

4. *Guidance of the search.* Activities shaping the needs, requirements, and expectations of actors to ensure their support of the emerging technology. They might be individual or collective (as institutional policies) and positive or negative. The former facilitates the process, while the latter slows it down or even hinders it. Also, the guidance might be narrowly focused or more open to variety: a balance should be found.

5. *Market formation.* To stimulate innovation, it is usually necessary to create temporary niche markets, with financial support and/or ad-hoc taxation policies.

6. *Resource mobilisation.* It consists of the allocation of financial, material, and human capital and usually includes investments and subsidies. Also the mobilisation of natural resources – as biomass, oil or natural gas – might be relevant.

7. *Creation of legitimacy and counteract resistance to change.* Since an emerging technology often leads to resistance from dominant actors with vested interests, other actors must counteract them. Advocacy coalitions include political lobbies and advice activities on behalf of such interest groups; though they do not have the power to change formal institutions directly, they can influence them and therefore their legislation.

5.3   The Multi-Level Perspective

The MLP is related to all the previous theories, as it focuses on the obstacles to change and tries to systematise the network of relations of all the actors involved in the transition process. Hence, it could be said it is the most holistic and comprehensive one.

As already mentioned, it distinguishes between three main socio-economic structures (Bosman & Rotmans 2016; Geels 2010; Geels & Schot 2007). The first (higher) level is called the *socio-technological landscape*. It consists of a series of structural trends that can assume the most varied nature – political, environmental, technological, etc. However, they are not easily detectable as they are essentially unpredictable. The term 'landscape' is used because it is the only one of the three levels that does not have a direct empirical underpinning. Landscape acts in the background but is situated at the apex of the model as it is the one able to effectively modify the other two levels.

On the other hand, the *socio-technological regime* is placed in between the other two levels. It represents the existing economic and social reality within a sector and consists of everything that regulates and substantiates an existing economic sector (incubation). It comprises actors and technological trajectories which include, among others, consumers, suppliers, financial networks, research networks, authorities, policy systems, and their trajectories. They create the forms and the rules of economic activity of the socio technological regime. Although this is a heterogeneous group of elements, it allows technologies to develop through the connection that the social groups imposes on them.

A socio-technological transition basically consists of a regime change. The breadth and strength of the links within the regime mostly make it a real barrier that is difficult to surmount for technological innovations that develop in niches. This is why socio-technological transitions occur only under specific circumstances.

Finally, there are *technological niches*. These are 'sheltered spaces', such as R&D laboratories, in which consumers have special demands and offer to support emerging innovations. Niches are fundamental as they are the natural level for innovations to develop, applying pressure on the regime to incorporate the needs and expectations arising from the bottom (citizens, grassroots movements, researchers' communities, etc.). As with the other two levels, they are constituted by an almost unpredictable number of actors who gain more power and visibility when the links within them are more structured.

It should be noted that a transition does not always mean an upward movement to allow a changeover to a new socio-technological regime, but rather the opposite can happen too. The thrust can originate from the landscape, as macroeconomic events can put even more pressure on the regime than the niches do. However, for socio-technological changes to take place, the timing in which the pressure for modification occurs is fundamental. It may occur when an innovation niche is fully developed and, therefore, capable of replacing the dominant socio-technological regime, or when niches have not completed their strive to maturity and, therefore, are unable to align with macroeconomic trends and pressure.

This process is represented in Figure 5.1, in which pressure coming from the landscape level aligns with pressure coming from sufficiently mature niche innovations. Such a scenario could allow the transition from a linear fossil-based model to a circular bio-based one. In this case, the pressure coming from the landscape can open a window of opportunity for one (or more) mature niches to replace the incumbent regime and establish a new stable and more sustainable configuration. This pressure could be associated with growing concern on global climate change and associated extreme weather conditions (including exceptional drought conditions, extreme heat).

Hence, the MLP shares a great deal with the SNM with its focus on niche formation and the process that brings it to maturity. One could say that SNM can fit in the MLP framework as a thorough explanation of its lower level and therefore better understand its interactions with the regime and landscape.

As Lopolito et al. (2011) mention, SNM can help understand why some technologies succeed while others fail to prevail. In particular, in addition to what we mentioned previously, niche formation processes might be classified into three sub-processes (Figure 5.2):

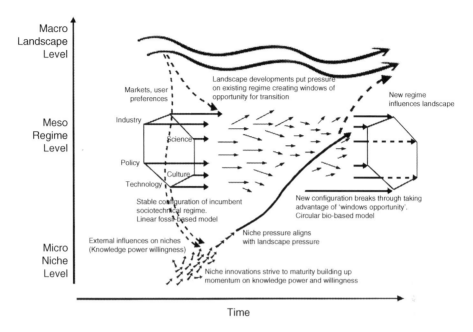

Figure 5.1 Socio-technological transitions processes.
Source: Geels (2002)

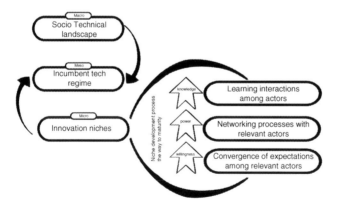

Figure 5.2 Multi-level approach and the niche formation mechanisms.
Source: Lopolito et al. (2011)

- *Willingness*. It is the convergence of expectations of the actors towards a common project. This represents the starting point for the development of a technological niche. As observed by Geels & Smit (2000), when a new technology emerges a political lobbying process takes place to convince the policy maker, companies, and other institutional actors to invest in it, building up momentum and expectations.

The process of expectation formation gains momentum when an increasing number of participants share the same positive expectations, which are accompanied by tangible results obtained through experimentation. The process becomes simpler when the technological potential becomes credible, that is, when it is supported by solid empirical data and when it addresses issues not solved by the dominant technology. This encourages actors to invest time and money in a technology that does not have market value yet.

- *Power.* The process of niche development is strongly influenced by the presence and the distribution of power within the network of local actors. Such a network of actors is necessary to influence policy choices and to bring in other relevant actors, such as potential investors. A powerful actor is any stakeholder who is able to bring added value to the network. However, even very influential actors often do not have all the necessary prerequisites for the final development of the niche.

The presence of powerful subjects is important both from an individual perspective and from a network point of view. At the individual level, an adequate level of power is instrumental in promoting and improving the technology; at the collective level, when a group of actors achieves enough power, it can define the niche formation. It could be said that they operate as a positive externality for the whole group, thanks to which the niche enjoys a sufficient level of influence compared to the others.

- *Knowledge.* It is necessary to focus on the acquisition of an adequate level of knowledge, which can be a positive externality as well. This requirement depends very much on the complexity of the technological transition. It is essential to integrate the technical expertise of the various companies experimenting with new technologies, paving the way for technological spillovers to occur. Hence, research and development activities within the niche are very important.

This knowledge gaining process occurs for individual enterprises through learning by doing and for network activities through the exchange of useful information between companies. It is therefore a learning process based on intensive interactions among stakeholders.

5.4   Transition Pathways

In the previous paragraph, we laid down the theoretical foundations of technological transitions from a static perspective. Now we can move forward and explore how the MLP defines transition processes within a dynamic outlook. The aim is to describe how the niches, the regime and the landscape mutually interact and what combinations can arise. Geels et al. (2007, 2010) classified the *transition pathways* into four main categories, in addition to a 'zero' category named Reproduction Process.

In this specific case, the trajectories are predictable and therefore do not cause a regime shift because the regime itself takes up the trajectories and adapts to their subsequent positioning. In the *Reproduction Process* niches and landscapes are not influential; radical niche innovations may arise but have few chances to break through as the regime stays dynamically stable. This does not exclude intrinsic innovations within the established regime (i.e. firms' competition, investments, R&D, mergers, and acquisitions), but disarranging the set of existing rules is excluded.

If there is moderate pressure from the landscape, there can be a regime change if the trajectories of the other two levels converge with the macroeconomic orientation (fully developed niches and influenced regime). In this pathway category, commonly defined as *Transformation*, the landscape is influenced by the action of regime actors, as well as outsiders. Societal pressure can be a driving force to change regulations: scientists and engineers may develop technical arguments to support the transformation; outsiders may introduce alternative technologies, etc. The whole process however might also involve conflicts and contestations, which are gradually solved with the reorientation of the development trajectories. Therefore, via cumulative adjustments, new regimes arise, yet without forcefully disrupting the basic architecture of the regime. This scenario could be better defined as an update or an addition, rather than real destruction. Hence, regime actors usually survive notwithstanding the changes they have to undergo.

The transformation pathway, for instance, powered the transition in Holland from cesspools to sewerage systems. Outsiders were represented by doctors, who warned about the correlation between poor hygienic conditions and infectious diseases. However, despite this new information, regime actors (mainly the government) initially underestimated the issue and introduced only limited innovations. When, at the end of the nineteenth century, urbanisation arose because of industrialisation, the pressure on the regime started to increase. Engineers and doctors teamed up and stimulated the introduction of alternative solutions, such as central collection and reuse of excrements, also thanks to steam pumps.

This driving force pushed for a shift in the civic and cultural perception of low hygiene and a rise in democratisation which in turn increased pressure on regime actors to develop alternative solutions, such as sewerage systems. If the trajectories of the regime are no longer co-ordinated with those of the other levels, a 'vacuum' is created. This gap can be filled by the work of the niches, which can realign their trajectories with those of the regime either when a very structured niche develops or when all niches converge their efforts to fill the vacuum. This dynamic process represents the second category of transformation pathway and is called *Dealignment and Realignment*.

In this scenario, the regime is under a significant landscape pressure. As a consequence, incumbents gradually lose faith in the regime and reduce investments. The vacuum arises when the distrust widens enough to kickstart the transition to alternatives. However, in this case there is no ready solution to fill the void; rather, usually multiple niches start developing. Hence, a period marked by intense competition leads to experimentation and development, until one niche becomes dominant. This is when the dealignment and realignment is accomplished.

An example of this scenario is the transition from horse-drawn carriages to automobiles. When the US was exploding as an economic power in the late nineteenth century, the horse-based regime was placed under pressure. There were hygiene concerns as well as urbanisation issues which started to favour a transition to electric-powered solutions. The enthusiasm for electricity from the business world caused the transition from horse-drawn trams to electric trams. Then, in the 1890s, automobiles started to gain attention too, especially petrol-powered ones – initially mainly used for racing and touring purposes. In this context, the introduction of the Model T Ford gradually became a dominant niche, and rapidly scaled up as mass production systems lowered costs. The political, cultural, and economic interests favoured the expansion of gasoline cars, up to becoming a symbol of the American lifestyle.

The third category of transformation pathway is the *Technological Substitution*, which occurs when there is a specific shock at the macro level, or any other unpredictable and extraordinary event in the landscape. In such cases, The regime ceases to exist, as it is unable to react to the shock. Socio-technological trajectories have conflicting and unpredictable trends. The absence of a technological regime leads to an increasing demand for services or goods by the population. Niches, if fully developed, form a new regime that could replace the previous one. Therefore, this is a more disruptive pathway compared to the previous one. An example can be found in the transition from sailing ships to steamships. Sailing ships were dominant in the mid nineteenth century, while steamships were still confined to niche level. The British Empire started to subsidise this niche market to speed up the postal system across its domains. In 1848, political revolutions and the Irish famine constituted a shock that drove migration from Europe to America. Steamships were more apt for the massive movement of passengers for trans-Atlantic routes. In addition, in 1869 the Suez Canal was opened, favouring steamships, as sailing ships could not cross it and had to go around Africa. By 1890, steamships replaced sailing ships as the dominant regime, winning an economic competition.

Finally, it could happen that niches act to solve local problems and in doing so create a network of trajectories capable of influencing the regime. In other words, niches are developed, but integrate the needs of the regime, without leading to a transformation. In such a case one speaks of *Reconfiguration*. In this pathway, the new regime grows out of the old one and experiences substantial changes in its basic architecture, contrary to what happens in the transformation pathway. This happens especially in distributed socio-technical regimes (such as agriculture), where transitions are not powered by a single innovation but rather by a sequence of different and complementary innovations.

An example is the transition from traditional factories to mass production in America, which was pushed by a multi-cluster innovation. One field where huge changes occurred was the labour organisation, as in the mid nineteenth century the mechanisation of many tasks reduced and consequently changed human labour. Other innovations like materials and batteries shaped new product design and repair. These and other technological advancements sustained the shift to mass factory production, helped by the spread of electricity and the pressure from industrial engineers and economic competition. Eventually, the transition to mass production was completed as a result of multiple component innovations interacting with the existing regime. There was no single breakthrough technology, rather a series of new solutions, pushed by a favourable landscape.

The timing and nature of the pressures of the socio-technical landscape are not the only factors that can influence transition trajectories. To explore the influence of other factors – primarily agency and institutions – and transitioning from one trajectory to another, Geels et al. (2016) analysed the above four pathway categories from an 'endogenous enaction' perspective, emphasising the ways in which innovations are interpreted and acted upon by key actors and coalitions and innovations are institutionalised.

For the technological substitution pathway, they propose a bifurcation of the actors and institutions involved in the process. As for actors, they could either be new firms struggling against the established regime or a differentiated set of outsiders (such as activists, social movements, and companies with other core businesses). As for institutions, they propose two patterns: the first includes a limited institutional change, where niches have to compete within the existing set of rules ('fit-and-conform'); the second allows adjustments of the rules and institutions to allow the niche innovation, with potential power-struggles ('stretch-and-transform').

The four transition pathways are schematically represented in Figure 5.3.

Concerning the transformation pathway, Geels et al. (2016) consider that incumbent actors are likely not to remain stuck in the established regime, therefore reorienting themselves towards new technologies with organisational adjustments. They also posit that technological change might not only include incremental change, as it could incorporate innovations ('competence adding') and partially or fully reorient. These alternatives would also entail a deeper transformation of the institutional regime.

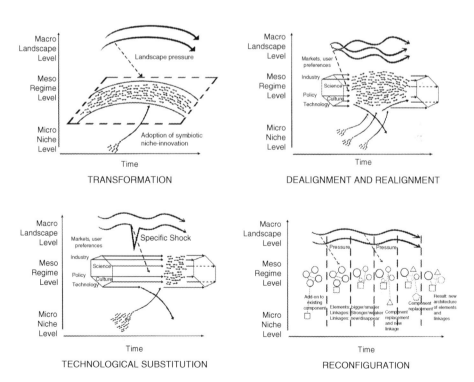

Figure 5.3 Typologies of socio-technical transition pathways.
Source: Geels and Schot (2007)

The reconfiguration pathway on the other hand could allow alliances between incumbent actors and new entrants. It could also encompass additions to the existing regime, only subsequently leading to 'innovation cascades' which would reconfigure the system architecture. Institutional support in this case is seen as a gradual process eventually leading to a new drift.

Finally, the dealignment and realignment pathway maintains the regime's main features. Geels et al. (2016) underline that in such a scenario it is important to have the landscape pressure to open space for new actors and technologies, while institutions are believed to suffer prolonged uncertainty, until a final replacement occurs.

5.5   The Circular Bioeconomy Transition

Changing a linear system into a circular one requires critical systemic transitions. Such transition-oriented developments generally do not arise spontaneously, although in certain cases external changes might stimulate systemic change (such as the introduction of new regulations or intensive societal debate). Often, these systemic changes must be engendered by intended decisions and actions from powerful regime actors. System transitions are thereby dependent on the impact of purposeful change processes organised by the stakeholders involved.

The transition towards a bioeconomy is complex, involving several sub-transitions: untwining the agricultural sector from the fossil sector, unwinding the chemical sector from the fossil sector, converting the chemical sector into a food-health sector, and shifting the focus in the forestry sector from bulk to high-end speciality products (Bosman & Rotmans 2016). It can also intensify pressure on bioresources and hence on biomass production itself, aside from existing demands and expected additional requirements for carbon sequestration for climate protection.

The full implementation of a comprehensive circular bioeconomy strategy may cause additional demand and competition, therefore requiring appropriate supply – and demand-side measures (see next paragraph).

Unless coupled with such measures and further technological innovations, bioeconomy transitions are likely to increase the demand for land, water, and other natural resources, and consequently the risk of resource degradation in forests and other ecosystems and their biodiversity, functions, and services. Depending on the context and transition pathway, some of the negative impacts could even risk being higher per unit of bio-based products compared to fossil-based products (Sillanpää & Ncibi 2017)

Therefore, a circular bioeconomy transition must involve a *holistic approach* to the production, sourcing, use, and consumption of bioresources, including the scale, intensity, and length of this use, as well as recycling, reuse, and disposal, also avoiding rebound effects where feasible. However, current strategies focusing on the promotion of bioresources have not yet comprehensively addressed these challenges and have primarily assessed the potential of the bioeconomy to deliver added value and economic growth of individual sectors. In this respect, the integration of circularity concepts into bioeconomy transition pathways is essential (Figure 5.4).

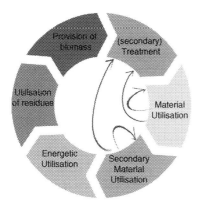

Figure 5.4 Integrating circularity in the bioeconomy.
Source: Fritsche and Rösch (2020)

In this sense, the bio-based sector is key for using renewable biological resources and processes to substitute fossil-based products. Bio-based products go far beyond mere biomass processing. They capitalise on the unprecedented advances in life sciences and biotechnology (including microbiology, microbiomes, and enzyme technologies) that, coupled with the digital revolution, allow the use of nature's biological assets, its biochemicals and biomaterials, and its biomimetic assets (its functions and processes) to generate new sources of economic value and future revenue (Hetemäki et al. 2017).

Indeed, the interest in the transition from fossil to bio-based products has revitalised traditional sectors by bringing forward opportunities to diversify their products. Innovation capitalises on the skills of making use of biomass for bio-based production, in traditional sectors such as pulp, woodworking, textiles, and wood-based construction.

For instance, the pulp, paper, and board industry developed new cellulose-based applications that can replace fossil-based textiles and plastics. The regeneration of pulp, paper, and board has also yielded solutions for the better exploitation of side streams for biofuel production and is also now seen progressively in markets, including fine and commodity chemicals, healthcare, automotive, consumer goods, and construction. Some low-tech products, such as composites and packaging materials, have lower added value but also lower cost and risk, and are therefore interesting for their large potential for replication in a diversity of regions and contexts (European Commission 2018).

Advances in bio-based innovation enhance the circularity of the bio-based sector and the whole bioeconomy by enabling the processing of current side streams, residues, and wastes into products. New technologies also enable biowaste and residues from farms and the forest-based sector, from cities or from the food sector to be transformed into bio-based products such as chemicals, organic fertilisers, biofuels, and also heat and power, if a more circular use is not possible. For instance, food-processing industries are exploring the potential of converting residues into bio-based products, such as chemicals and biofuels (Pagotto & Halog 2016; Stegmann et al. 2020).

Several *niches* are already developing in the sub-sectors of the circular bioeconomy, and the landscape seems to be increasingly pressing on the established regime. Morone et al. (2016) presented an assessment of this pressure with respect to the transition to sustainable waste management in southern Italy. It was concluded that from 2007 to 2014, a certain degree of landscape pressure was exerted on local municipalities. Both public institutions (mainly via economic channels) and civil society stakeholders (via political channels) were found to be influencers, in addition to indirect pressure mechanisms which also generated competition-imitation behaviours between municipalities.

In Morone et al. (2015), instead, the niche maturity level of the *bioplastics technology* was assessed, by means of the SNM theory and the already mentioned classification (willingness, power, knowledge). The result was that the niche was not fully exploiting its potential, as information circulated inefficiently within the social network. The most knowledgeable actors were confined in peripheral positions, while sceptical subjects benefitted from a more central position. The results can help improve co-operation and policy making, to drive further expectations convergence (and therefore the transition).

As for a more general outlook, Bosman and Rotmans (2016) and Antikainen and Valkokari (2016) offer an interesting analysis of the *sustainability transition in Finland*, one of the pioneering countries in the field. Building on a multi-phase and MLP, Bosman and Rotmans (2016) assessed the stage of development of the Finnish bioeconomy strategy. The country is naturally well placed since 60 per cent of the territory is covered by forests and four out of its ten top export products are related to forestry and related industries. The bioeconomy is already estimated to account for 16 per cent of GDP and is growing, thanks to a highly educated population, intersectoral co-operation and innovative capacity.

In Finland, there is consensus on the inevitability of the transition, but the sense of urgency varies among stakeholders. Some are more satisfied with the current stage of development and argue for an incremental approach; others are more focused on the obstacles and flaws and advocate for a more radical innovation approach. However, the authors report that there is no centralised control of the transition: the Ministry of Economic Affairs and Employment is the most pivotal public actor but lacks full acknowledgement from business and civil society sectors. The silos-fragmentation of the economy is seen as a major obstacle, considering that the bioeconomy cuts through all economic sectors. Moreover, in the particular Finnish case, the forestry industry is dominated by three large companies which hold the key to much of the bioeconomy transition.

Bosman and Rotmans (2016) estimate that Finland is on the brink of a take-off phase, but that it still lacks fundamental driving factors (urgency, common understanding, and ownership). Most of the transition pressure is confined to the micro-level, while the major barriers lie in the landscape and the established regime.

The government laid down a bioeconomy transition strategy in 2014, which confirms both the potential behind such a transition and its challenges. Interestingly enough, the main obstacles might be that the bioeconomy is already a solid sector and therefore it is approached with a business-as-usual way of thinking. The risk of the traditional players' dominance is that new actors and innovations are prevented from stepping in. Therefore, there is a need for better interaction between the various actors, especially at the regime level, thereby ensuring an active engagement and entitlement of the transition from both private and public stakeholders.

Antikainen and Valkokari (2016) reached a similar conclusion from a circular economy transition perspective. While Finnish businesses are familiar with sustainability, there seems to be a lack of frameworks for supporting the business model innovation. The authors stressed on the importance of systemic rather than single-business innovation and conceded that re-design is often more burdensome for established companies within an existing business ecosystem – such as the forestry industry – rather than for newcomers.

D'Amato et al. (2020) detected comparable constraints regarding Finnish small and medium enterprises (SMEs). Co-operation and dialogue along value chains have been confirmed to be a priority. Networking and joining forces are all the more important, given the potential lack of financial resources for smaller companies, thus hampering innovation. The authors highlight the need for either a regulatory pressure or a shift in customer demand to create future opportunities.

Although every case is different, these evaluations could be extended to other countries, considering that the circular bioeconomy transition is slowly taking place, and pressure at the niche level can already be seen. The landscape and the regime already adapted and opened to sustainable innovation, but much wider and systemic changes lie ahead and require game-changing policy making.

5.6   Policy Measures to Prompt a Just Transition

As explained earlier in this chapter, the sustainability transition is a complex, multi-level, and multi-faceted process. The need for co-ordination and alignment among the actors involved might require direct government intervention, although not purely from a 'command-and-control' position. The rising political capital of a circular bioeconomy is however coupled with a risk that potential benefits will be overstated to favour technological goals in spite of socio-ethical and ecological implications. In particular, issues such as establishing which goals are served by a circular bioeconomy and how social and environmental value will be created should not be decided by a restricted group of actors from developed countries, considering that a circular bioeconomy has global impacts. Policy making and implementation should engage a wide variety of stakeholders who can provide insights and support on the problems circular bioeconomy is dealing with (Kershaw 2021).

We propose to distinguish between measures of four kinds that governments could implement on a national and international scale to support a just transition:

- *Regulation.* Regulatory policy is the first and natural field of intervention for policymakers. From a general perspective, introducing limitations to the most harmful activities for the environment can be important, yet not sufficient. Regulatory frameworks should be deeply reformed to suit a circular bioeconomy better; the current legal systems were conceived and adapted to a kind of economy which is going to fade away. Product design and consumption will be hugely impacted, and the very concept of 'property' is already opening up to new paradigms. A rethinking of what a public good is and how it can benefit the needs of both the market and society would be helpful. Aside from this, regulation could shape a better landscape by ensuring the implementation of common standards. For instance, wood construction suffers from a lack of standards, which limits its deployment in highrise buildings (Hetemäki et al. 2017). The same could be said about waste and secondary raw materials, as safety concerns hinder trade and reuse. As the OECD (2018) has pointed out, even the development of common definitions (e.g. what the bioeconomy, a biowaste, and a biorefinery are) would be beneficial for reducing uncertainty and therefore supporting investment. By intervening, regulators could build an enabling architecture through which both newcomers and incumbents can co-exist and thrive whilst moving towards a sustainable business model. Also, the establishment of recognised labels would help the bio-based economy as consumers would be able to distinguish between products and gather the necessary information for more conscious and (possibly) environmental-friendly choices.

- *Prompting a change in stakeholder behaviour.* Another desirable intervention from the government implies a less direct approach, that is nudging consumers and producers towards more sustainable behaviours. This intervention is based on 'nudging', a concept developed by Thaler and Sunstein (2009), which is among the pillars of behavioural economics. Moving from the assumption of individual's bounded rationality, the authors suggest that policymakers 'gently push' citizens towards socially beneficial choices with subtle hints, cues, and other suggestions.

  Green nudging solutions include the aforementioned ecolabels, which signalling a 'green premium' in products can appeal to customers even when prices are higher than the competition. In addition, setting more sustainable solutions as the default option could help to accelerate the transition, as consumers usually show a 'status quo bias' and 'inertia'. This has already been tested in the case of electricity supply plans and of cash withdrawal, where the 'Print' option for receipts was placed on the left, while the average right-handed person is more willing to select the right option (in this case, not printing the receipt). Other examples include nudging in culinary choices and social influencing exploiting imitation behaviours.

- *Subsidies and incentives.* These interventions concentrate on the economic and financial side. Economic policy strategies can be disruptive when they successfully guide market forces towards desired objectives, such as the sustainability transition. Measures could include higher taxation for the use of materials and the selling of products conflicting with the circular bioeconomy transition, as well as subsidies and financial support for innovative technologies and products in line with the desired goal. The OECD stresses also the importance of subsiding research and development in the field, at both upstream (laboratory-based research) and downstream levels (industry).

  Green finance investments can have a pivotal role in creating the necessary ecosystem for a shift in the economic development model. These policies include two aspects: the reform and innovation of existing financial tools, an exploration of the type of fiscal policy and the feasible way to raise money for green finance development; and the reform of existing fiscal revenue management and distribution policy, namely the efficiency and direction in the use of fiscal funds (Owen et al. 2018; Wang & Zhi 2016).

- *Policy mixes between stabilisation and destabilisation of regimes.* Last, but not least, policymakers are required to find the equilibrium point between destabilisation and stabilisation of the established regime, as no easy and quick transition will be possible. We have seen that the transition dynamics can be very different and are highly influenced not only by technological innovation but also by social and cultural forces. Kivimaa and Kern (2016) argue that policy interventions could boost a 'creative destruction', a process first described by Schumpeter according to which entrepreneurs and their innovation destabilise the existing regime and throw out of the market obsolete technologies.

According to Turnheim and Geels (2012), the climate crisis can accelerate destabilisation, yet it is not the only factor at play. They argue that social concerns are equally important but not pressing enough to destabilise the regime without concurring economic factors (such as improving service and quality, user freedom, and energy independence). They also point out that public support depends not only on the urgency of issues but also on the existence of attractive alternative visions. Here, a shared cultural and social drive towards destabilisation is key.

However, Turnheim and Geels (2012) also sustain that existing industry regimes are likely to persist and resist technical change for a long time, until the social, political, and economic pressure increases. It is necessarily a gradual and mid-to-long-term process, in which policymakers will have the difficult task of balancing between the declining regime and the rising one. The alignment of social and economic pressure should not be taken for granted, as shifting towards a bio-based economy might entail disruption in supply chains and in commodity markets, with potential inflationary pressures, and therefore higher costs for consumers. This task could be even more difficult with low fossil fuel prices and global economic stagnation while the recovery from the pandemic crisis could both accelerate the pressure for transition and pose additional challenges.

Take-Home Message

Sustainable transition can be considered a set of processes aimed at making our development model more environmentally friendly.

Strategic niche management (SNM), transition management (TM), technological innovation systems (TIS), and the multi-level perspective (MLP) are the main theoretical approaches to describe sustainable transitions and innovation.

According to the MLP, transition is a non-linear interaction process of three socio-technical levels: the niches, that is, 'sheltered spaces' where innovation happens; the regimes, that is, the existing economic and social reality within a sector; and the landscape, comprehending structural trends of various nature.

Transition processes have been described from a dynamic outlook as transition pathways, divided into four categories: transformation, dealignment and realignment, technological substitution, and reconfiguration.

Circular economy transition, which is a complex, multi-level, and multi-faceted process, must involve a holistic approach to production, consumption, reuse, recycling, and disposal.

The bio-based sector is central for the use of renewable biological resources and processes to substitute fossil-based products.

There are already a number of niches developing in different sub-sectors of the circular bioeconomy, and the landscape seems to be increasingly pressing on the established regime.

The need for co-ordination and alignment among the actors involved in the transition might require a direct government intervention, which can take several forms (regulations, prompting a change in stakeholders' behaviour, subsidies and incentives, policy mixes between stabilisation and destabilisation of regimes).

Learning Exercises

1. What are the socio-technical levels that characterise the multi-level perspective (MLP)?
2. What are the main transition pathways of a socio-technological regime in the MLP theory?
3. What do strategic niche management, transition management, and technological innovation systems theories state?
4. What are the key obstacles affecting the governance of a transition?
5. What are the measures that governments could implement to support the sustainability transition?

References

Antikainen, M., & Valkokari, K. (2016). A framework for sustainable circular business model innovation. *Technology Innovation Management Review*, 6(7), 5–12.

Bosman, R., & Rotmans, J. (2016). Transition governance towards a bioeconomy: A comparison of Finland and the Netherlands. *Sustainability*, 8(10), 1017.

Caniëls, M. C. J., & Romijn, H. A. (2008). Strategic niche management: Towards a policy tool for sustainable development. *Technology Analysis & Strategic Management*, 20(2), 245–266.

D'Amato, D., Veijonaho, S., & Toppinen, A. (2020). Towards sustainability? Forest-based circular bioeconomy business models in Finnish SMEs. *Forest Policy and Economics*, 110, 101848.

European Commission. (2018). A sustainable bioeconomy for Europe: Strengthening the connection between economy, society and the environment. European Commission.–2018.–URL: https://Ec.Europa.Eu/Research/Bioeconomy/Pdf/Ec_bioeconomy_Strategy_2018.Pdf(Дата Обращения 25.02. 2020).

Foxon, T. J., Hammond, G. P., & Pearson, P. J. G. (2010). Developing transition pathways for a low carbon electricity system in the UK. *Technological Forecasting and Social Change*, 77(8), 1203–1213.

Fritsche, U., & Rösch, C. (2020). The Conditions of a Sustainable Bioeconomy. In *Bioeconomy for Beginners*, Berlin, Heidelberg: Springer Berlin Heidelberg, pp. 177–202.

Geels, F. W. (2002). Technological transitions as evolutionary reconfiguration processes: A multi-level perspective and a case-study. *Research Policy*, 31(8–9), 1257–1274.

Geels, F. W. (2010). Ontologies, socio-technical transitions (to sustainability), and the multi-level perspective. *Research Policy*, 39(4), 495–510.

Geels, F. W., Kern, F., Fuchs, G., … Wassermann, S. (2016). The enactment of socio-technical transition pathways: A reformulated typology and a comparative multi-level analysis of the German and UK low-carbon electricity transitions (1990–2014). *Research Policy*, 45(4), 896–913.

Geels, F. W., & Schot, J. (2007). Typology of sociotechnical transition pathways. *Research Policy*, 36(3), 399–417.

Geels, F. W., & Smit, W. A. (2000). Failed technology futures: Pitfalls and lessons from a historical survey. *Futures*, 32(9–10), 867–885.

Hekkert, M. P., Suurs, R. A. A., Negro, S. O., Kuhlmann, S., & Smits, R. E. H. M. (2007). Functions of innovation systems: A new approach for analysing technological change. *Technological Forecasting and Social Change*, 74(4), 413–432.

Hetemäki, L., Hanewinkel, M., Muys, B., … Potočnik, J. (2017). *Leading the Way to a European Circular Bioeconomy Strategy*, Vol. 5, European Forest Institute Joensuu, Finland.

Kemp, R., Loorbach, D., & Rotmans, J. (2007). Transition management as a model for managing processes of co-evolution towards sustainable development. *International Journal of Sustainable Development & World Ecology*, 14(1), 78–91.

Kemp, R., Schot, J., & Hoogma, R. (1998). Regime shifts to sustainability through processes of niche formation: The approach of strategic niche management. *Technology Analysis & Strategic Management*, 10(2), 175–198.

Kershaw, E. H., Hartley, S., McLeod, C., & Polson, P. (2021). The sustainable path to a circular bioeconomy. *Trends in Biotechnology*, 39(6), 542–545.

Kivimaa, P., & Kern, F. (2016). Creative destruction or mere niche support? Innovation policy mixes for sustainability transitions. *Research Policy*, 45(1), 205–217.

Loorbach, D., & Rotmans, J. (2006). *Managing Transitions for Sustainable Development. In Understanding Industrial Transformation*, Dordrecht: Kluwer Academic Publishers, pp. 187–206.

Lopolito, A., Morone, P., & Sisto, R. (2011). Innovation niches and socio-technical transition: A case study of bio-refinery production. *Futures*, 43(1), 27–38.

Markard, J., & Truffer, B. (2008). Technological innovation systems and the multi-level perspective: Towards an integrated framework. *Research Policy*, 37(4), 596–615.

Morone, P., Lopolito, A., Anguilano, D., Sica, E., & Tartiu, V. E. (2016). Unpacking landscape pressures on socio-technical regimes: Insights on the urban waste management system. *Environmental Innovation and Societal Transitions*, 20, 62–74.

Morone, P., Tartiu, V. E., & Falcone, P. (2015). Assessing the potential of biowaste for bioplastics production through social network analysis. *Journal of Cleaner Production*, 90, 43–54.

OECD. (2018). *Meeting Policy Challenges for a Sustainable Bioeconomy*, OECD. doi:10.1787/9789264292345-en

Owen, R., Brennan, G., & Lyon, F. (2018). Enabling investment for the transition to a low carbon economy: government policy to finance early stage green innovation. *Current Opinion in Environmental Sustainability*, 31, 137–145.

Pagotto, M., & Halog, A. (2016). Towards a circular economy in Australian agri-food industry: An application of input-output oriented approaches for analyzing resource efficiency and competitiveness potential. *Journal of Industrial Ecology*, 20(5), 1176–1186.

Rotmans, J., Kemp, R., & Asselt, M. (2001). Transition management: A promising policy perspective. In *Interdisciplinarity in Technology Assessment*, Berlin, Heidelberg: Springer Berlin Heidelberg, pp. 165–197.

Schot, J., & Geels, F. W. (2008). Strategic niche management and sustainable innovation journeys: Theory, findings, research agenda, and policy. *Technology Analysis & Strategic Management*, 20(5), 537–554.

Sillanpää, M., & Ncibi, C. (2017). *A Sustainable Bioeconomy*, Cham: Springer International Publishing. doi:10.1007/978-3-319-55637-6

Stegmann, P., Londo, M., & Junginger, M. (2020). The circular bioeconomy: Its elements and role in European bioeconomy clusters. *Resources, Conservation & Recycling: X*, 6, 100029.

Thaler, R. H., & Sunstein, C. R. (2009). *Nudge: Improving Decisions About Health, Wealth, and Happiness*, Penguin.

Turnheim, B., & Geels, F. W. (2012). Regime destabilisation as the flipside of energy transitions: Lessons from the history of the British coal industry (1913–1997). *Energy Policy*, 50, 35–49.

Wang, Y., & Zhi, Q. (2016). The role of green finance in environmental protection: Two aspects of market mechanism and policies. *Energy Procedia*, 104, 311–316.

6 The Role of Bioeconomy towards Safe and Just Sustainability Transformations

> **Learning Objectives**
>
> To understand and be able to discuss critically:
>
> - the basic principles of ecological economics.
> - the concepts of planetary boundaries and doughnut economics.
> - the potential of the bioeconomy to shape safe and just sustainability transformations.

6.1 Ecological Economics, Weak and Strong Sustainability

The foundational ideas for ecological economics emerged in the 1970s and 1980s in an international climate of concern over population growth, finite resources, and pollution. The need for a new and hybrid field stemmed from the observation that traditional economic paradigms did not accurately represent and address the relationship between the economy and the environment, and that ecology did not address the issue of human dependency on ecological processes (Costanza & Daly 1987). In 1988, the International Society of Ecological Economics was established, followed a year later by the peer-reviewed academic journal *Ecological Economics*:

> The initiators [of the field] shared the basic view that the human economy and the ecological systems are much more intertwined than is usually recognised. [...] Instead of describing the relationship between the economy and nature in terms of interfaces between two basically different systems (nature provides resources, sink capacity and direct utility for the economy), these economists emphasised that the human economy is embedded in nature, and that the economic processes can also be conceptualised as natural processes in the sense that they can be seen as biological, physical and chemical processes. [...] In other words, the society could be seen as an "organism" with a "social metabolism" (Røpke 2005, p. 266).

Ecological economics thus advocates that economic and social systems are embedded in and indissoluble from the biosphere (Figure 6.1). Well-functioning ecological systems are recognised as life-supporting for human viability and prosperity, and thus fundamental to both. This implies acknowledging the flows of materials, energy, and services from the biosphere to human society and the economy (see the

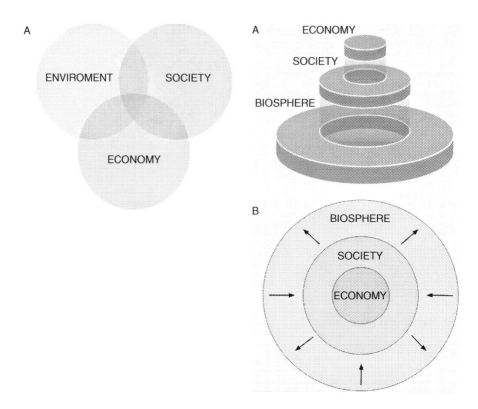

Figure 6.1 Two alternative representations of sustainability. On the left, the environment, society, and the economy are equal and interlinked. On the right, society and the economy are embedded in and indissoluble from the environment (biosphere).
Source: Folke et al. (2016)

concept of ecosystem services in Chapter 3) and the flows (e.g. pollutants, emissions, heat) and feedback (e.g. ecosystem management, restoration, and conservation) from society and the economy to the biosphere (Braat & de Groot 2012; Giampi-etro 2019). Ecological economics is a fundamentally interdisciplinary field, mainly linking ecology and economics, but including theories, notions, and methods from a vast array of other disciplines, such as, for example, political sciences, psychology, philosophy, and theology. It is thus characterised by a high degree of pluralism of opinions and views (Dube 2021), and it is also strongly transdisciplinary, meaning that non-academic stakeholders are often included at various stages of the research co-creation process. System thinking is an important approach to understanding intertwined ecological and economic systems in terms of flows of energy and matter (Røpke 2004). Cornerstone notions in the field are the limits to the material growth of the economy, the need for equity and resource redistribution across space and time (also beyond the human species), and the recognition of multiple and intrinsic values of nature (linking to the idea of the irreplaceability and incommensurability of natural capital) (Costanza & Daly 1987; Røpke 2005).

In the first volume of *Ecological Economics*, Costanza (1989, p. 2) clarified the position of ecological economics with regard to the limits to growth and prosperity: '[c]urrent economic paradigms (capitalist, socialist, and the various mixtures) are all based on the underlying assumption of continuing and unlimited economic growth. This assumption allows problems of inter-generational, intra-generational, and inter-species equity and sustainability to be ignored (or at least postponed), since they are seen to be most easily solved by additional growth'. Against this notion, technological optimists believe that technology and innovation will be able to expand these biophysical limits indefinitely and allow for continued growth. Technological pessimists instead argue that technology will not be able to fully 'circumvent fundamental energy and resource constraints and that eventually economic growth will stop' (ibid.).

An assumption of technological optimism tolerates the idea of high substitution potential between natural capital with human-made capital (e.g. built and financial capital, such as equipment, building, infrastructure; money, and economic assets). However, in reality, basic life-supporting functions performed by nature are difficult, expensive, or impossible to substitute artificially. Examples are the provision of food, clean water, and air; regulation of global and local climate, pests, and diseases, and maintenance of individual psychological and physical health and community peace and well-being. Ecological economics thus suggests that natural capital is poorly or only moderately substitutable with other forms of human-made capital. This stance, along with technological circumspection and acknowledgement of the limits to growth, locates ecological economists closer to a strong (in opposition to a weak) sustainability perspective (Table 6.1 and Box 6.1).

While full substitutability of natural with man-made capital is impossible, a certain measure of substitution between types of capital is realistically necessary (Goodland & Daly 1996). How much substitution is acceptable, and for what purposes?

Table 6.1 Comparison between weak and strong sustainability

Weak sustainability	Strong sustainability
Environment as a provider of resources, sink capacity, and amenity values for society and the economy	Environment as a super-system containing society and the economy
Natural capital and man-made capital perfectly substitutable	Natural capital and man-made capital not perfectly substitutable (multi-functionality of natural capital)
Sustainability requires maintaining a total amount of capital, composed of natural capital and/or man-made capital	Sustainability requires maintaining a minimum amount of natural capital and a minimum amount of man-made capital
Technological positivism and economic growth	Technological circumspection and limits to growth
Commensurability and comparability of values	Incommensurability and incomparability of values
Monetary valuation or other unidimensional measures	Multiple and complementary measures for valuation

Source: Gardner 2004; Munda 1997

> **Box 6.1** Capital Substitutability and the Commensurability and Comparability of Values
>
> *Natural capital* (includes non-renewable capital such as fossil resources and minerals, and renewable capital such as ecosystems and their functions, see Chapter 3). *Human-made capital* includes financial capital (assets in terms of money value), built capital (artificial material resources, e.g. machines, infrastructures), human capital (individual skills, talent, education), and social capital (social fabric, relations, trust, shared values). There are a number of issues that affect the degree of substitutability, called elasticity, between natural and human-made capitals. For example, ecosystems are multi-functional, meaning that a forest can simultaneously provide several benefits, such as timber, food and genetic resources, climate, water and soil regulation, recreation and tourism, scientific, and educational and spiritual values. Human-made capital can usually perform only one or a handful of such functions. Moreover, 'adequate substitutes exist for some components of natural capital (e.g. water filtration facilities for water purification provided by intact ecosystems), whereas there may be no cost-competitive substitute for other components (e.g. soil microbes to maintain soil fertility and nutrient recycling)' (Cohen et al. 2019, p. 428). Ultimately, substitutability should be determined empirically, and may depend strongly on the geographical and temporal scale of the analysis. However, there is evidence to suggest low to moderate levels of substitutability between natural capital and human-made capital (ibid.).
>
> The amount of natural capital that is acceptable and necessary for conversion into human-made capital should thus be decided by evidence-backed policymaking. However, such estimations require methodologies to *measure and compare* different values, and this taps into another important divide between weak and strong sustainability. Under a weak sustainability perspective, multiple values can be measured by using a unidimensional measure (i.e. a single currency type, e.g. money), which conveniently also allows for a comparative assessment (e.g. in cost-benefit analysis). In strong sustainability, values may be deemed to be incommensurable, which does not mean that a value is infinite, but that it is not possible to quantify it, especially in monetary terms. This also leads to difficulties in comparing different kinds of values. Strong sustainability thus proposes that optimal solutions to social and environmental problems should be assessed through multi-criteria approaches (O'Neill 2020).

A few decades since the initial establishment of ecological economics as a field, the emerging concept of the bioeconomy has not been able to answer fully this and other unresolved fundamental questions (Giampietro 2019). A good overview of the bioeconomy against weak and strong sustainability issues is provided by Bennich and Belyazid (2017). Based on key notions from ecological economics and sustainability science, this chapter discusses the potential and limitations of the bioeconomy to shape pathways towards sustainability transformations. Section 6.2 defines sustainability transformations and presents the recent concepts of planetary boundaries and doughnut economics, which stress the dependency of human well-being on planetary ecological health, and highlight the need to pursue solutions that are both safe in terms of planetary health and just in terms of inter- and intra-generational equity. Section 6.3 examines the bioeconomy, considering key issues in ecological economics and sustainability science, namely the growth paradigm, justice, and equity.

6.2   Planetary Boundaries and Doughnut Economics

Several scholars have argued that, as humanity, we are now operating in the Anthropocene, an unofficial term that has been proposed to indicate a new geological epoch – following the Holocene – characterised by the uncertainty and non-linearity of global impacts from human intervention (Bai et al. 2016). Great socio-economic accelerations (e.g. sharp increases in population growth, gross domestic product, energy and water use, and other similar trends) can be observed as having taken place since the second half of the past century, along with worrisome trends in the Earth system, such as ocean acidification, atmospheric carbon dioxide, and degradation of the terrestrial biosphere (Steffen et al. 2015a).

Given these disturbing trends, the concept of planetary boundaries was proposed in 2009 by a group of international scientists to define a 'safe operating space for humanity' (Rockström et al. 2009; Steffen et al. 2015b). The framework (Figure 6.2) includes nine interlinked sub-systems of the biosphere and identifies quantitative risk areas for each of them. The sub-systems include (1) stratospheric ozone depletion, (2) atmospheric aerosol loading, (3) ocean acidification, (4) disruptions of biogeochemical flows, (5) freshwater use and changes in the hydrological cycle, (6) land conversion, (7) biodiversity loss and extinctions, (8) climate change, and (9) introduction of novel entities (e.g. synthetic organic pollutants, radioactive materials, micro-plastics, and genetically modified organisms). The authors of that article suggest that crossing certain biophysical thresholds may result in large-scale, non-linear, and/or irreversible changes, with dangerous or disastrous consequences for humanity. The concept of planetary boundaries has had important traction among sustainability scientists, policymakers, and practitioners (Barbier & Burgess 2017; Haffar & Searcy 2018).

The planetary boundaries framework has recently been further combined with the complementary idea of social needs (Raworth 2012, 2017). The result is a framework shaped like a doughnut (Figure 6.2). Doughnut economics represents an economy in which society's needs are met without compromising the nine sub-systems of the planet. Societal needs are identified as food, health, education, income and work, political voices, social equity, gender equality, housing, networks, energy, and water. Doughnut economics reiterates the dependence of human well-being on planetary health. It also calls for deep social inequalities to be addressed globally, with minimum standards of living not being met by millions of people, and with four planetary boundaries already having been assessed as being in the risk zone (climate change, biodiversity loss, nitrogen and phosphorus loading, and land conversion).

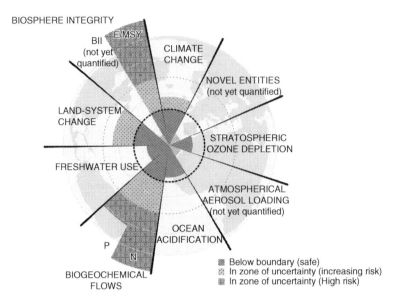

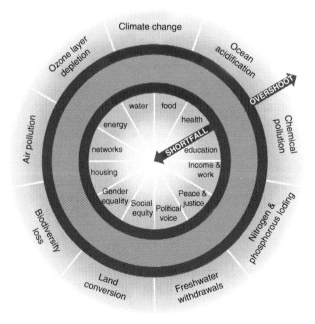

Figure 6.2 The planetary boundaries framework (left) and the doughnut economy framework of social and planetary boundaries (right). Sources: modified from Lokrantz J./ Azote (2022), already based on Steffen et al. (2015b); Kate Raworth and Christian Guthier, Doughnut Economics Action Lab (2020), based on Raworth (2017).

Within this framework, social and environmental stresses are no longer portrayed as economic "externalities": Instead, the planetary and social boundaries are the starting point for assessing how economic activity should take place. The economy's over-arching aim is no longer economic growth in and of itself, but rather to bring humanity into the safe and just space – inside the doughnut – and to promote increasing human well-being there. (Raworth 2012, p. 8).

The doughnut economics framework

aims to specify the social and planetary boundaries between which humanity can thrive but does not suggest specific pathways for getting into that safe and just space, or for thriving there. […] There are likely to be many possible pathways in that space, which will be aligned with different cultures, visions and values, and with different costs, risks, and distributions of power and benefits between social groups. So, there will be a range of outcomes for social justice. This makes the process of adjudicating between them a deeply political one (Leach et al. 2013, p. 86).

In other words, the doughnut framework does not offer a one-size-fits-all solution but rather provides a canvas against which complementary and competing pathways of change may be hypothesised (Leach et al. 2015; Stirling 2015) (Figure 6.3 and Box 6.2).

At the time of writing this book, little literature has thoroughly examined the bioeconomy alongside the concepts of planetary boundaries or doughnut economics. However, the EU updated its Bioeconomy Strategy in 2018, in which it acknowledges the term 'planetary boundaries', stating that

[t]o ensure that the bioeconomy operates within the planetary boundaries, first and foremost a robust assessment of the amounts, types, qualities and impacts of the sustainable production and use of biomass from all sources is needed. Impacts include the implications of land use (and its changes) on biodiversity and other essential parameter of ecosystems on land and sea, as well as on the local, regional and sometimes global socio-economic systems (European Commission 2018, p. 91).

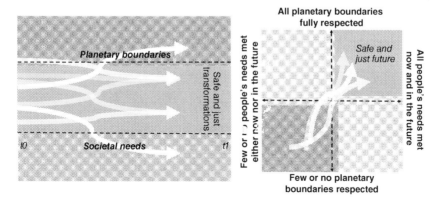

Figure 6.3 Potential pathways of change within the planetary and social boundaries. Inspired to: Leach et al. (2013)

> **Box 6.2** Transitions and Transformation Pathways towards Sustainability
>
> Socio-technical transitions, social-ecological transformations, and sustainability pathways are concepts used in sustainability science to frame 'thinking about ex-ante processes of change' (Patterson et al. 2017, p. 11).
>
> Sustainability pathways is a term that is also used to describe open-ended, dynamic, and value-laden potential alternatives for the future. This means that efforts to shape such pathways involve dealing with a plurality of values and worldviews, and with multiple narratives prescribing how change should happen (Leach et al. 2013b).
>
> The term 'sustainability transitions' (see Chapter 5) is used in reference to the well-known multi-level perspective framework, which captures the reconfiguration of regimes and actors in socio-technical systems, such as, for example, energy, food, or waste systems (Geels 2019). Several potential transition pathways can be envisioned but may however become stalled or locked-in along the way, depending on the reconfiguration dynamics of the system.
>
> The term 'sustainability transformations' is used to understand possible or desirable 'pathways [or trajectories] of sustainable environmental and societal change within the looming Anthropocene', including the dynamics between actors bearing the costs or enjoying the benefits of such changes. It is used to assess changes in socio-ecological or socio-technical-ecological systems (Patterson et al. 2017, p. 2). As for sustainability transitions, change in this context emerges from the interplay of top-down and bottom-up dynamics.

6.3   Prosperity and Justice in the Bioeconomy

6.3.1   The Growth Paradigm

The politically dominant interpretation of the bioeconomy is growth-oriented, with a positive attitude about the potential of science, innovation, and technology in mitigating trade-offs between economic, social, and ecological goals (Vivien et al. 2019). The key contribution to sustainability from this perspective is represented by a global shift in the premises for producing feed/food, commodities, and energy: from the exploitation of fossils to the (circular) utilisation of biomass-based resources (see Chapter 3).

Assuming that full substitution of fossil-based products is possible in practice, net sustainability requirements would imply that (1) bio-based resources should be considered as a substitute for fossils exclusively when the first outperforms the latter from a sustainability viewpoint, and the best-performing substitute should be preferred, and (2) fossil resources spared from this substitution should not be redirected to and used in other sectors or purposes (Harmon 2019; Jander & Grundmann 2019; Lewandowski et al. 2018). Gathering the evidence base to implement the first principle may already prove difficult. Environmental and social impacts of bio-based products depend on a number of factors, such as the type and source origin of the biomass, processes, and logistics associated with manufacturing, retailing, and product/service use and end-of-life treatment options. For example, even when considering only the issue of greenhouse gases, calculations about emission savings due to substitution of fossil-based products with bio-based ones rely on a number of assumptions that greatly affect the accuracy of the estimates (Asada et al. 2020). Moreover, available methodologies are unable to fully capture multiple sustainability aspects in a comprehensive and holistic manner, especially for the purpose of informing long-term predictions (Otto et al. 2021).

Some academics have recently reclaimed the bioeconomy[1] as compatible with degrowth or postgrowth ideas (Ghisellini et al. 2016; Giampietro 2019). Degrowth and postgrowth advocates argue that 'the biosphere cannot conceivably sustain ever-increasing consumption' and that if the current economic system remains on a growth path, '[a]verage material living standards will decrease' along with setbacks in 'many of the major advancements of the industrial era associated with high economic output per capita, including improved education and health' (Crownshaw et al. 2019, p. 122). This argument is supported by the observation there is currently no evidence that absolute decoupling of economic growth from environmental burden is possible, despite technological improvements (Giampietro & Funtowicz 2020; Mastini et al. 2021; Parrique et al. 2019; Vadén et al. 2020; Ward et al. 2016).

Whilst a number of countries in the global North have recently managed to reduce greenhouse-gas emissions while still growing their economies, it is highly unlikely that such decoupling will occur more widely in the near future, rapidly enough at global scale and for other environmental impacts. This is because renewable energy, electrification, carbon-capturing technologies and even services all have resource requirements, mostly in the form of metals, concrete and land.

In addition, relative environmental gains from technological improvement may be lost to unchecked rebound or leakage effects, meaning additional environmental impacts in space or time (Korhonen et al. 2018).

In the face of a potential destructive scenario that unchecked growth may bring about, several scholars have suggested that a planned, voluntary paradigm shift aimed at prosperity, rather than growth, would be preferable (Jackson 2009; Mastini et al. 2021). The basic principle of a planned paradigm change (whether degrowth or postgrowth) is that there is a need to redefine human well-being beyond economic growth, thus, for instance, adopting indicators alternative to gross domestic product in decision-making (Box 6.3). Degrowth would also entail reducing overproduction and overconsumption by satisfying the needs (rather than wants) of all people (Heik-kurinen & Bonnedahl 2018; Wiedmann et al. 2020).

---

[1] Chapters 1–3 of this book show that the bioeconomy is a boundary concept. This means that while definitions have been coined in the policy, industry, and scientific communities, such definitions are loose enough so that multiple societal actors are able to operate under the bioeconomy 'banner' despite their diverging perspectives, agendas, and goals.

> **Box 6.3** Measures of Prosperity
>
> *Gross domestic product* (GDP) – which represents the monetary market value of final goods and services within a country – is currently widely used as an indicator of economic performance and, to a certain extent, of prosperity and well-being. However, among its several limitations, GDP fails to account for trade-offs between economic development and environmental or human health.
>
> *Alternative indicators* have been proposed by governments and non-governmental organisations as a way to measure the quality of life, with examples such as the Genuine Progress Indicator, the Happy Planet Index, the Human Development Index, and the Inclusive Wealth Index. These indicators are based on a range of aspects, including human health, education, subjective life satisfaction, and/or environmental health. The 2018 Inclusive Wealth Index report (Managi & Kumar 2018) shows that globally, the contribution of natural capital to the Inclusive Wealth Index has declined since 1990, while the proportion of produced and human capital has increased, along with GDP. Per capita growth in inclusive wealth was observed in eighty-nine countries out of 140. The report also found that the Inclusive Wealth Index is more conservative in measuring the growth of a nation compared to the Human Development Index and to GDP.

6.3.2   Inclusiveness and Justice

An important principle in ecological economics and in sustainability science is the equitable value redistribution across societal actors in space and time. Scheidel et al. (2018) suggest that 'changes in socio-metabolic configurations [such as those that would take place under a bioeconomy] redefine the distribution of environmental benefits and burdens across different actors'. One of the key social goals of the bioeconomy is the creation of 'modern jobs in rural areas, thus counteracting both the limited geographical distribution of accessible fossil resources and the current concentration of job and income opportunities in urban areas. The bioeconomy will enable areas poor in fossil but rich in bio-based resources to improve income and development opportunities' (Lewandowski et al. 2018).

The bioeconomy is thus expected to cater to the needs of developed and emerging/developing economy countries. In developing countries, the bioeconomy is expected to replace the 'natural economy', 'where heavy reliance on subsistence farming and traditional biomass degrade the resource base with low economic returns' (Johnson 2017, p. 289). 'Emerging industrial economies such as China and India see biotechnology as a nascent field of innovation in which they can quickly compete. Brazil, South Africa and Malaysia are investing to add value to their vast biological resources' (El-Chichakli et al. 2016, p. 221). In places like Europe, Japan, and the United States, expanding the bioeconomy is seen as a means of industrial renewal and wealth creation through science, technology, and innovation (ibid.).

Some aspects critical to equity and justice, such as rural-urban dynamics and global North-South dynamics, are only partly acknowledged in the bioeconomy. Despite expectations, natural resource-rich rural areas and the Global South may be 'stuck' in the role of producers and manufacturers. For example, 'biotechnology infrastructure and skilled employees are found mostly in high-income countries, whereas local biological know-how and reuse culture are strong in developing countries. Supply chains should create local jobs, with manufacturing close to the raw-material base' (El-Chichakli et al. 2016, p. 222). Important issues also include the access and use of genetic resources and traditional knowledge (in particular the appropriation and monopoly by a few actors with no benefit redistribution to local communities), knowledge and technology transfer versus intellectual property rights on biotechnologies or other innovations, and biosafety and bioethics risks (e.g. with regard to genetically modified organisms) (Hamilton 2008; Sheppard et al. 2011).

Resource, energy, food security, and self-sufficiency at the national or regional level remain important ambitions in the bioeconomy against predictions of population growth, although this raises concerns over competition with increasing demands for other biomass uses. In particular, the role of biofuels and bioenergy has been an object of controversy during the past decade due to potential competition with food production, even though some scholars maintain that sustainable biofuels can still play a role in energy security (Johnson 2017). Lewandowski et al. (2018, p. 14) suggest that '[i] n a sustainable bioeconomy, the use of bio-based resources should be optimized with regard to two main criteria. First, the demand for high-quality food for the world's population should be satisfied. Second, the remaining bio-based resources should ideally be allocated with regard to the maximal ecological, social and economic benefit. This holistic approach in resource allocation is a major pillar of a sustainable bioeconomy and can serve as a blueprint for sustainable and general resource allocation strategies'.

Remaining concerns about the bioeconomy are the potential replication of existing power structures (related to e.g. gender, class, ethnicity), or the creation of new forms of inequality, as well as the persistence of models related to extractivism and the commodification of nature (Ramcilovic-Suominen & Pülzl 2018). In addition, while biotechnology promises to release some environmental and ethical pressures that come with animal farming (e.g. via novel, synthetic foods), the bioeconomy is largely based on an anthropocentric and utilitarian worldview (Neill et al. 2020). The perceived role of forms of life other than humans is largely restricted to that of providers of raw materials or beneficial functions (e.g. nature-based solutions, biomimicry), with only marginal discussions about animal welfare and inter-species sustainability (Bergmann 2019).

6.4   To Be Continued…

As pointed out by Zeug et al. (2020, pp. 1–2),

[r]enewable or bio […] does not necessarily mean sustainable. Sustainability is not an intrinsic characteristic but rather a promising potential of BE [i.e., the bioeconomy] and only if sustainability is a central objective of the economy itself.' The authors continue, 'Means to monitor progress in reaching the targets set in BE policies and strategies is lacking in many countries. Not only due to a lack of appropriate methods, but also due to a lack of a clear

Table 6.2 Perspectives on ecological economics notions in the bioeconomy

Ecological economics principles	Perspectives under the bioeconomy
Substitutability of natural capital	Remains a context-dependent question to be addressed empirically.
Planetary boundaries	Briefly acknowledged in the 2018 Bioeconomy Strategy by the European Union but largely missing from the overall discussion and literature on the bioeconomy.
Multiple social needs	Rural development and employment is a key societal goal, while other social needs remain marginally addressed.
Limits to growth	The politically dominant interpretation of the bioeconomy is pro-growth and technology-positivist. Some degrowth and postgrowth advocates reclaim the bioeconomy.
Equity and justice	Global North–South dynamics and inter-generational justice are loosely recognised in the bioeconomy. Inter-species justice and ethics remain largely unaddressed.

definition of the BE concept and of concrete and measurable targets and objectives, e.g., different interpretations of sustainability and economy as well as missing clear connection to target systems like the SDGs [i.e., the Sustainable Development Goals].

Table 6.2 shows a summary of whether and how central questions that are perpetually debated in ecological economics and in sustainability science are addressed by the bioeconomy.

In Chapter 3, we suggested that the bioeconomy could be interpreted as one of the sets of solutions available to define pathways of change towards sustainability (Aguilar et al. 2018; D'Amato 2021). The bioeconomy should be complemented with other solution types, such as those proposed by the green and circular economy – as it increasingly is. However, even mixed solution packages may not be sufficient to maintain the economy within planetary safe ecological boundaries, if exclusively focusing on technology-driven, relative (rather than absolute) reductions of ecological footprint. Moreover, just sustainability transformations also imply the need for a more equitable per capita distribution of resources and prosperity in space and time that also considers non-humans (Scheidel et al. 2018; Wiedmann et al. 2020).

Take-Home Message

- Ecological economics is an inter- and trans-disciplinary field of science advocating that well-functioning ecological systems are fundamentally linked to human viability and prosperity.
- Ecological economists generally embrace a strong sustainability perspective, characterised by circumspection towards the potential of technology to solve all

sustainability challenges, low tolerance to substitutability of natural capital with human-made capital, and acceptance of biophysical limits to economic growth.

• The concepts of planetary boundaries and doughnut economics suggest that we need to pursue ecologically safe and societally just transformations for humanity to survive and prosper.

• Because of its conceptual plasticity, the bioeconomy is, in principle, compatible with both weak and strong sustainability perspectives.

• A weak sustainability perspective limits the potential for the bioeconomy to contribute to shaping just and safe transformations.

Learning Exercises

1. What are the key principles of ecological economics in comparison to environmental economics?
2. What are the nine sub-systems of the planetary boundaries framework, and which ones have already been overshot?
3. What are the social boundaries in the doughnut economics framework, and what does a safe and just space for humanity mean?
4. What are the potential contribution and limitations of the bioeconomy to shaping sustainability pathways for humanity to thrive within a safe and just space?

Online Resources

National Doughnuts Data Explorer, Version 1.0. Available at: https://doughnuteconomics.org/tools-and-stories/22.

Online course: Pathways to sustainability. STEPS Centre. Available at: https://steps-centre.org/online-course-pathways-to-sustainability/.

Seminar 'Evidence gathering and integration in sustainability science: Methodological challenge and advancements', University of Helsinki/Helsinki Institute of Sustainability Science (4.9.2019). Available at: www.helsinki.fi/fi/unitube/video/57f41759-c823-4bc1-9b9a-651dcf206d6e

Seminar 'Justice and power in the context of global bioeconomy', University of Helsinki/Helsinki Institute of Sustainability Science. Available at: www.helsinki.fi/fi/unitube/video/7ed9ccc3-0e8e-4d4d-80fb-ca1e4ee0384a

References

Aguilar, A., Wohlgemuth, R., & Twardowski, T. (2018). Perspectives on Bioeconomy. *New Biotechnology*, **40**, 181–184.

Asada, R., Cardellini, G., Mair-Bauernfeind, C., … Stern, T. (2020). Effective Bioeconomy? a MRIO-based Socioeconomic and Environmental Impact Assessment of Generic Sectoral Innovations. *Technological Forecasting and Social Change*, **153**, 119946.

Bai, X., van der Leeuw, S., O'Brien, K., ... Syvitski, J. (2016). Plausible and Desirable Futures in the Anthropocene: A New Research Agenda. *Global Environmental Change*, **39**, 351–362.

Barbier, E., & Burgess, J. (2017). Natural Resource Economics, Planetary Boundaries and Strong Sustainability. *Sustainability*, **9**(10), 1858.

Bennich, T., & Belyazid, S. (2017). The Route to Sustainability – Prospects and Challenges of the Bio-Based Economy. *Sustainability*, **9**(6), 887.

Bergmann. (2019). Interspecies Sustainability to Ensure Animal Protection: Lessons from the Thoroughbred Racing Industry. *Sustainability*, **11**(19), 5539.

Braat, L. C., & de Groot, R. (2012). The Ecosystem Services Agenda: Bridging the Worlds of Natural Science and Economics, Conservation and Development, and Public and Private Policy. *Ecosystem Services*, **1**(1), 4–15.

Cohen, F., Hepburn, C. J., & Teytelboym, A. (2019). Is Natural Capital Really Substitutable? *Annual Review of Environment and Resources*, **44**(1), 425–448.

Costanza, R. (1989). What is Ecological Economics? *Ecological Economics*, **1**(1), 1–7.

Costanza, R., & Daly, H. E. (1987). Toward an Ecological Economics. *Ecological Modelling*, **38**(1–2), 1–7.

Crownshaw, T., Morgan, C., Adams, A., ... Horen Greenford, D. (2019). Over the Horison: Exploring the Conditions of a Post-Growth World. *The Anthropocene Review*, **6**(1–2), 117–141.

D'Amato, D. (2021). Sustainability Narratives as Transformative Solution Pathways: Zooming in on the Circular Economy. *Circular Economy and Sustainability*, **1**(1), 231–242.

Dube, B. (2021). Why Cross and Mix Disciplines and Methodologies?: Multiple Meanings of Interdisciplinarity and Pluralism in Ecological Economics. *Ecological Economics*, **179**, 106827.

El-Chichakli, B., von Braun, J., Lang, C., Barben, D., & Philp, J. (2016). Policy: Five Cornerstones of a Global Bioeconomy. *Nature*, **535**(7611), 221–223.

European Commission. (2018). A Sustainable Bioeconomy for Europe: Strengthening the Connection between Economy, Society and the Environment: Updated Bioeconomy Strategy SWD/2018/431. Retrieved from https://op.europa.eu/en/publication-detail/-/publication/edace3e3-e189-11e8-b690-01aa75ed71a1/

Folke, C., Biggs, R., Norström, A. V., Reyers, B., & Rockström, J. (2016). Social-ecological Resilience and Biosphere-based Sustainability Science. *Ecology and Society*, **21**(3), 41. http://dx.doi.org/10.5751/ES-08748-210341

Gardner, T. (2004). Limits to Growth? – A Perspective on the Perpetual Debate. *Environmental Sciences*, **1**(2), 121–138.

Geels, F.W. (2019). Socio-technical Transitions to Sustainability: A Review of Criticisms and Elaborations of the Multi-level Perspective. *Current Opinion in Environmental Sustainability*, 39, 187–201. https://doi.org/10.1016/j.cosust.2019.06.009

Ghisellini, P., Cialani, C., & Ulgiati, S. (2016). A Review on Circular Economy: The Expected Transition to a Balanced Interplay of Environmental and Economic Systems. *Journal of Cleaner Production*, **114**, 11–32.

Giampietro, M. (2019). On the Circular Bioeconomy and Decoupling: Implications for Sustainable Growth. *Ecological Economics*, **162**, 143–156.

Giampietro, M., & Funtowics, S. O. (2020). From Elite Folk Science to the Policy Legend of the Circular Economy. *Environmental Science & Policy*, **109**, 64–72.

Goodland, R., & Daly, H. (1996). Environmental Sustainability: Universal and Non-Negotiable. *Ecological Applications*, **6**(4), 1002–1017.

Haffar, M., & Searcy, C. (2018). Target-Setting for Ecological Resilience: Are Companies Setting Environmental Sustainability Targets in Line with Planetary Thresholds? *Business Strategy and the Environment*, **27**(7), 1079–1092.

Hamilton, C. (2008). Intellectual Property Rights, the Bioeconomy and the Challenge of Biopiracy. *Genomics, Society and Policy*, **4**(3), 26.

Harmon, M. E. (2019). Have Product Substitution Carbon Benefits Been Overestimated? A Sensitivity Analysis of Key Assumptions. *Environmental Research Letters*. doi:10.1088/1748-9326/ab1e95

Heikkurinen, P., & Bonnedahl, K. J. (2018). Dead ends and liveable futures: A framework for sustainable change. In K. J. Bonnedahl & P. Heikkurinen, eds., *Strongly Sustainable Societies: Organising Human Activities on a Hot and Full Earth* , Abingdon, Oxon; New York: Routledge, 2019. | Series: Routledge studies in sustainability: Routledge. doi:10.4324/9781351173643

Jackson, T. (2009). *Prosperity Without Growth: Economics for a Finite Planet*, Routledge.

Jander, W., & Grundmann, P. (2019). Monitoring the Transition Towards a Bioeconomy: A General Framework and a Specific Indicator. *Journal of Cleaner Production*, 236 (117564). doi:10.1016/j.jclepro.2019.07.039

Johnson, F. X. (2017). Biofuels, Bioenergy and the Bioeconomy in North and South. *Industrial Biotechnology*, **13**(6), 289–291.

Korhonen, J., Honkasalo, A., & Seppälä, J. (2018). Circular Economy: The Concept and Its Limitations. *Ecological Economics*, **143**, 37–46.

Leach, M., Newell, P., & Scoones, I. (2015). *The Politics of Green Transformations*, London: Routledge. doi:10.4324/9781315747378

Leach, M., Raworth, K., & Rockström, J. (2013). Between Social and Planetary Boundaries: Navigating Pathways in the Safe and Just Space for Humanity. In *World Social Science Report 2013*, Paris, France: OECD Publishing and UNESCO Publishing, pp. 84–89.

Lewandowski, I., Gaudet, N., Lask, J., Maier, J., Tchouga, B., & Vargas-Carpintero, R. (2018). Context. In *Bioeconomy: Shaping the Transition to a Sustainable, Biobased Economy*. Springer Open University of Hohenheim. doi:10.1007/978-3-319-68152-8_2

Managi, S., & Kumar, P. (2018). *Inclusive Wealth Report 2018*, London: Routledge. doi:10.4324/9781351002080

Mastini, R., Kallis, G., & Hickel, J. (2021). A Green New Deal without Growth? *Ecological Economics*, **179**, 106832.

Munda, G. (1997). Environmental Economics, Ecological Economics, and the Concept of Sustainable Development. *Environmental Values*, **6**(2), 213–233.

Neill, A. M., O'Donoghue, C., & Stout, J. C. (2020). A Natural Capital Lens for a Sustainable Bioeconomy: Determining the Unrealised and Unrecognised Services from Nature. *Sustainability*, **12**(19), 8033.

O'Neill, J. (2020). What Is Lost through No Net Loss. *Economics & Philosophy*, **36**(2), 287–306.

Otto, S., Hildebrandt, J., Will, M., Henn, L., & Beer, K. (2021). Tying Up Loose Ends. Integrating Consumers' Psychology into a Broad Interdisciplinary Perspective on a Circular Sustainable Bioeconomy. *Journal of Agricultural and Environmental Ethics*, **34**(2), 8.

Parrique, T., Barth, J., Briens, F., Kuokkanen, A., & Spangenberg, J. H. (2019). Evidence and Arguments against Green Growth as a Sole Strategy for Sustainability. *European Environmental Bureau.* https://eeb.org/wp-content/uploads/2019/07/Decoupling-Debunked.pdf

Patterson, J., Schuls, K., Vervoort, J., … Barau, A. (2017). Exploring the Governance and Politics of Transformations Towards Sustainability. *Environmental Innovation and Societal Transitions*, **24**, 1–16.

Ramcilovic-Suominen, S., & Pülsl, H. (2018). Sustainable Development – A 'Selling Point' of the Emerging EU Bioeconomy Policy Framework? *Journal of Cleaner Production*, **172**, 4170–4180.

Raworth, K. (2012). *A Safe and Just Space for Humanity: Can We Live Within the Doughnut?*, Oxfam. www-cdn.oxfam.org/s3fs-public/file_attachments/dp-a-safe-and-just-space-for-humanity-130212-en_5.pdf

Raworth, K. (2017). *Doughnut Economics: Seven Ways to Think Like a Twenty-First Century Economist*. London: Penguin Random House.

Rockström, J., Steffen, W., Noone, K., … Foley, J. A. (2009). A Safe Operating Space for Humanity. *Nature*, **461**(7263), 472–475.

Røpke, I. (2004). The Early History of Modern Ecological Economics. *Ecological Economics*. 50(3–4), 293–314. doi:10.1016/j.ecolecon.2004.02.012

Røpke, I. (2005). Trends in the Development of Ecological Economics from the Late 1980s to the Early 2000s. *Ecological Economics*, **55**(2), 262–290.

Scheidel, A., Temper, L., Demaria, F., & Martínes-Alier, J. (2018). Ecological Distribution Conflicts as Forces for Sustainability: An Overview and Conceptual Framework. *Sustainability Science*, **13**(3), 585–598.

Sheppard, A. W., Gillespie, I., Hirsch, M., & Begley, C. (2011). Biosecurity and Sustainability within the Growing Global Bioeconomy. *Current Opinion in Environmental Sustainability*, **3**(1–2), 4–10.

Steffen, W., Broadgate, W., Deutsch, L., Gaffney, O., & Ludwig, C. (2015a). The Trajectory of the Anthropocene: The Great Acceleration. *The Anthropocene Review*, **2**(1), 81–98.

Steffen, W., Richardson, K., Rockström, J., … Sörlin, S. (2015b). Planetary Boundaries: Guiding Human Development on a Changing Planet. *Science*, **347**(6223). http://dx.doi.org/10.1126/science.1259855

Stirling, A. (2015). Emancipating Transformations: From Controlling 'The Transition' to Culturing Plural Radical Progress. In *The Politics of Green Transformations*, Abingdon, Oxon, New York: Routledge, pp. 54–67.

Vadén, T., Lähde, V., Majava, A., … Eronen, J. T. (2020). Decoupling for Ecological Sustainability: A Categorisation and Review of Research Literature. *Environmental Science & Policy*, **112**, 236–244.

Vivien, F.-D., Nieddu, M., Befort, N., Debref, R., & Giampietro, M. (2019). The Hijacking of the Bioeconomy. *Ecological Economics*, **159**, 189–197.

Ward, J. D., Sutton, P. C., Werner, A. D., Costanza, R., Mohr, S. H., & Simmons, C. T. (2016). Is Decoupling GDP Growth from Environmental Impact Possible? *PLOS ONE*, **11**(10), e0164733.

Wiedmann, T., Lensen, M., Keyßer, L. T., & Steinberger, J. K. (2020). Scientists' Warning on Affluence. *Nature Communications*, **11**(1), 3107.

Zeug, W., Besama, A., & Thrän, D. (2020). Towards a Holistic and Integrated Life Cycle Sustainability Assessment of the Bioeconomy: Background on Concepts, Visions and Measurements, UFZ Discussion Paper.

Part III

7   LCA, LCC, and S-LCA Applied to the Bioeconomy

Learning Objectives

To understand and be able to discuss critically:

- the need for a life cycle thinking perspective in the assessment of the bioeconomy.
- the current status of the assessment methods for evaluating the sustainability of the bioeconomy.
- the holistic assessment of the bioeconomy towards safe and just sustainability transformations.

7.1   The Need for Life Cycle Thinking

Developing bio-based, recyclable, and biodegradable products as replacements for fossil-based materials has been included in the bioeconomy strategy of both EU Member States and non-EU countries during the past decade (EC 2018). However, the shift towards bio-based products and processes requires the effective use of biological sources and processing methods which can help countries ensure their supply security by reducing their dependency on fossil-based raw materials (Antar et al. 2021). Bio-based products can potentially make the economy more sustainable by lowering environmental impacts, especially in terms of CO_2 emissions by avoiding the use of fossil resources and the carbon storage potential in well-managed ecosystems (e.g. forests) and products (long-lived wood products) (Carus & Dammer 2018). They can even provide further advantages in economic and social terms, such as novel product characteristics with better biodegradability or lower toxicity (Sijtsema et al. 2016). Therefore, the bio-based products sector has been declared to be a priority area with high potential for future growth, reindustrialisation, and addressing societal challenges (de Besi & McCormick 2015).

Bio-based products are often acknowledged as sustainable by definition since they are derived from potentially renewable raw materials such as plants, crops, trees, and algae. However, considering solely the raw materials is not enough to assess the sustainability performance of any product. Let us consider the installation of bamboo flooring against concrete flooring in the United States or in a European country, as a well-known example. Bamboo is a green, renewable, eco-friendly, and durable material, which will cause less damage to the environment than concrete flooring (in terms of raw materials) (Yu et al. 2011). However, bamboo flooring is mostly produced in China and should be transported by ship or truck to end-users across the globe. As a result, the transportation of bamboo flooring creates more pollution in terms of net carbon emissions and therefore bamboo flooring cannot be considered sustainable. Building upon this example, there is an obvious need to go beyond the traditional focus on the production site and manufacturing processes and consider the entire stages of a product, which is called *life cycle thinking*. The life cycle stages of a product under evaluation start from the extraction of the raw materials; go through manufacture, distribution, use, possible reuse/recycling; and then end with final disposal. Consequently, representative overall scores should be calculated to produce a realistic idea about the actual impacts (Figure 7.1).

Moreover, it is important to extend the scope of current life cycle thinking to cover all three dimensions of sustainability to provide a full overview of the examined bio-based products. This is because better environmental performance might not necessarily mean better scores for indicators related to social and economic issues, and indeed improvements in one of the sustainability dimensions may occur at the expense of the other dimensions. This phenomenon is known as *sustainability trade-offs*. For example, growing dedicated energy crops with lower environmental impacts compared to

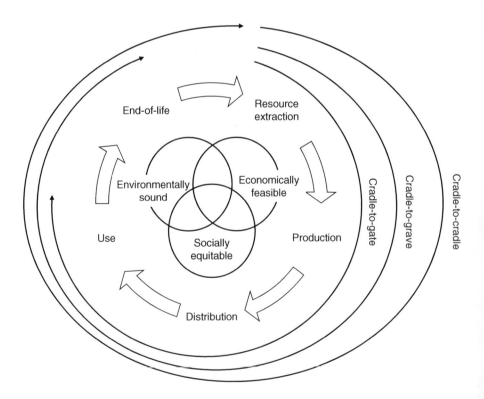

Figure 7.1 Life cycle thinking perspective.

the extraction of fossil fuel energy can cause competition with other land uses, such as agriculture or nature conservation, and could lead to adverse socio-economic impacts by, for example, increasing the risk of food security or contributing to biodiversity loss (Vera et al. 2022). As a result, a holistic sustainability assessment with scientifically sound tools and methods should be performed to depict the full impact on each dimension of sustainability and thus overcome the issues related to trade-offs.

From the theoretical framework of life cycle thinking, some tools have emerged to assess the impacts on different dimensions of sustainability such as life cycle assessment (LCA or sometimes referred as E-LCA), life cycle costing (LCC), and social life cycle assessment (S-LCA) for environmental, economic, and social dimensions, respectively. Moreover, more effort has been exerted on the combination of these tools to obtain an overarching representative score for the overall sustainability performance via using, for example, life cycle sustainability assessment (LCSA) and multi-criteria decision analysis (MCDA). In the following subsections, both individual assessment methods and combined assessment methods are covered in detail.

7.2 Life Cycle Assessment (LCA)

The environmental dimension of sustainability has been heavily addressed in the LCA community because of the global and urgent nature of challenges such as the overexploitation of natural resources, climate change, and waste generation against the exponential increase in the human population and corresponding rapid urbanisation. Many tools and methods have been proposed for evaluating the environmental performance of products, but a specific focus has been placed on LCA also known as *environmental life cycle assessment* (E-LCA). LCA is defined as 'the compilation and evaluation of the inputs, outputs and the potential environmental impacts of a product system throughout its life cycle' by ISO 14040 and 14044 standards (ISO 2006a, 2006b).

The framework of the LCA methodology is defined by the ISO 14040 and 14044 standards with four successive steps, namely, goal and scope definition, inventory analysis, impact assessment, and interpretation (Figure 7.2). Building on this framework, tools to cover economic aspects (e.g. LCC) and social aspects (S-LCA) have also been developed, although they are still in progress compared to the very well-developed LCA structure.

7.2.1 Goal and Scope Definition

The first step of LCA, *goal and scope definition*, is crucial since it includes several foundational considerations such as the aim, system boundary, target audience, functional unit, allocation, and cut-off criteria, which have considerable effects on the outcomes of the study. The aim of conducting an LCA study can differ according to the needs of the target audience. For example, the aim can be product development and improvement, strategic planning, decision-making, or marketing. The proceeding steps are mainly built

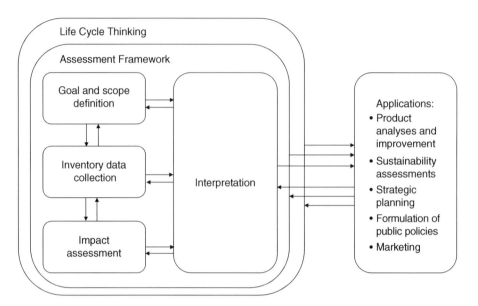

Figure 7.2 Life cycle assessment framework.
Source: ISO 14040, 14044

upon the aim of the study. The target audience of the LCA method is significantly diverse depending on the aim. It can be useful for future engineers and technologists who want to practice sustainability analysis. As an approach, LCA can assist product-oriented professionals in sustainable product development and improvement. From an environmental standpoint, LCA offers companies an opportunity to improve their performance in the context of corporate social responsibility. Finally, LCA can provide a scientific basis for academics who study sustainability and circular bioeconomy.

In principle, deciding which stages, processes, and elementary flows to include in an LCA study is known as *system boundary definition* through which mass, energy, and environmental relevance have been established as the cut-off criteria used to exclude any insignificant inputs, outputs, or unit processes from a study. Again, according to the aim of the study and the availability of inventory data, different system boundaries can be selected such as gate-to-gate, cradle-to-gate or cradle-to-grave. *Cradle* is the term used for the raw material phase while *grave* represents the end of life. Accordingly, cradle-to-grave means considering the life cycle impacts of a product starting from the raw material extraction and covering the end-of-life activities. *Gate* indicates any intermediate point between cradle and grave. Usually, the cradle-to-gate system boundary is used to calculate the impacts related to production activities. In some specific cases, it is also possible to use a gate-to-gate system boundary to identify the impacts related to one or two specific phases such as only the transportation of products. Recently, the system boundaries have been extended to cradle-to-cradle in such a way that, theoretically, no waste would be produced, and everything would be used as a source for something else. This is the foundational thinking in the circular economy model.

The functional unit is also defined during the first phase. By definition, the *functional unit* is 'the measure that permits performance quantification of the product system' and acts as the reference for all the input and output material/energy flows. In other words, it is the basis according to which the result from the LCA is expressed. For example, an LCA study comparing bio-based products with their fossil-based counterparts can be performed considering two mulch films (i.e. thin protective barriers for fertile soil) from different raw materials such as bioplastics and fossil-based plastics. In this example, the functional unit can be selected as one hectare of soil to be covered by these films, and the environmental impacts can be expressed per hectare of soil (Yilan et al. 2023).

7.2.2   Inventory Analysis

The life cycle *inventory analysis* phase includes the compilation and quantification of (i) energy carriers and raw materials used; (ii) emissions to the atmosphere, water, and soil; and (iii) different types of land use for a given product system throughout its life cycle. The purpose of developing a life cycle inventory is to calculate the quantities of inputs and outputs involved in delivering a specific functional unit of the product system under study, which typically produces a list of substances with identified quantity as the outcome.

During the inventory analysis, data collection is the most time- and energy-consuming step. According to the availability, two types of data can be used during this phase. The *primary data* or *foreground data* is process-specific, on-site data that can be collected via measurements, interviews, and annual reports. Otherwise, the *secondary* or *generic* or *background data* can be used if the collection of primary data is not possible. Secondary data can be gathered from LCA databases such as ecoinvent or previously published LCA studies. At the end of the inventory analysis phase, a comprehensive list of substances with their corresponding quantities and various units is compiled. Using this comprehensive dataset to deduce conclusions is almost impossible due to the amount of information involved. To overcome this issue, collected inventory data is converted into cumulative scores (i.e. impacts) during the impact assessment phase.

7.2.3   Impact Assessment

The third phase is *life cycle impact assessment*, which is aimed at understanding and evaluating the magnitude and significance of the potential environmental impacts of a product system. During this phase, inventory data are converted to indicator scores for impact categories that represent environmental issues. For example, the inventory data regarding fossil resource use represent the indicator scores for global warming potential.

The selection of the *impact assessment method* depends on the aim of the study as well as the requirements of the target audience. In general, impact assessment methods can be divided into two categories: *single-issue* and *multiple-issue methods*. Single-issue methods are generally preferred to obtain an overview of the production process without including all the related environmental impacts associated with the generation activity. Some widely studied single-score impact assessment methods are cumulative energy demand (CED), cumulative exergy demand (CExD), and global warming potential (GWP).

For a comprehensive analysis, multiple-issue methods are required. Multiple-issue methods are further divided into two categories as *midpoint* and *endpoint methods*. Midpoint indicators are usually named *impact categories*, while endpoint indicators are known as *damage categories*, which are used to express several impact category indicators into a specific area of protection. The *area of protection* is defined as a cluster of parameters that imply recognisable value to society, for example, human health, natural resources, natural environment, and man-made environment.[1] During the impact assessment phase, at first, inventory results are weighted, and midpoint indicators are obtained. Similarly, midpoint category indicators are weighted and summed to reach endpoint category scores such as human health, ecosystems, and resources. A final weighting is performed to aggregate the endpoint categories into a single score, and this score makes it easier to compare environmental burdens across different scenarios (Figure 7.3).

When aggregating data from inventory results into single scores, uncertainties tend to increase due to the assumptions made and the limitations resulting from the weighting method chosen. Impact categories include, for example, climate change, acidification, eutrophication, and land use change. On the other hand, three damage categories that can be included in the analysis are human health, ecosystems, and resources (Table 7.1).

To explain better the difference between these two, let us consider the waste disposal stage of mulch films produced from fossil-based raw materials. After the end of the useful life of these films, toxic chemicals (especially microplastics) are released into the soil and consequently into groundwater. These flows can diffuse into clean water sources nearby, such as lakes, resulting in higher toxin concentrations. Because of this, the fish diversity in that lake decreases. If the aim is to understand the regional environmental impacts, a midpoint category indicator such as freshwater ecotoxicity could be selected. On the other hand, if the aim is to assess biodiversity loss, an endpoint category score related to the ecosystem should be considered, which is also relevant beyond the local-regional dimension.

Among others, the land use change indicator is worth significant attention for the bioeconomy sector in terms of the cultivation of food versus biomass feedstock. Land use change is a process by which human activities transform the natural landscape, referring to how the land has been used, usually emphasising the functional role of land for economic activities. In the bioeconomy, direct land use change occurs when agriculture or forest land is converted to feedstock cultivation, as a raw material for the above-mentioned bio-based mulch film. Several issues can arise from such conversion, for example, competition with food production, community displacement, loss of carbon sinks, or biodiversity (Box 7.1). On the other hand, indirect land use

---

[1] European Commission-Joint Research Centre – Institute for Environment and Sustainability: International Reference Life Cycle Data System (ILCD) Handbook- Recommendations for Life Cycle Impact Assessment in the European context. First edition November 2011. EUR 24571 EN. Luxemburg. Publications Office of the European Union; 2011.

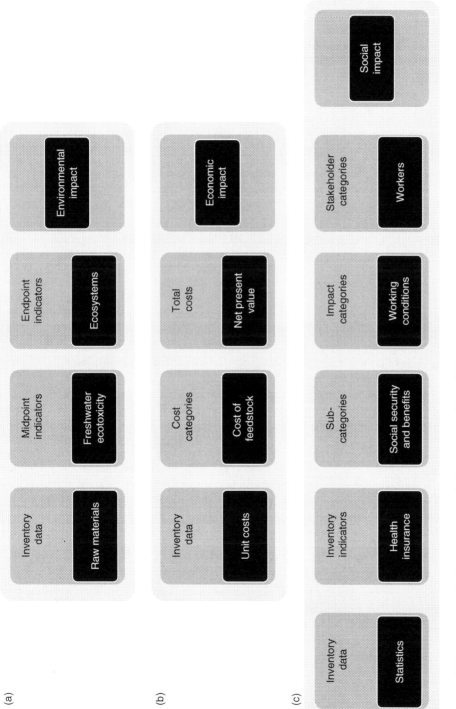

Figure 7.3 Life cycle stages for (a) environmental, (b) economic, (c) social impact assessment.

Table 7.1 Impact and damage categories commonly used in life cycle assessment

Impact assessment	Indicator	Description
Impact category	Climate change	Climate change is related to emissions of greenhouse gases into the air and can result in adverse effects on ecosystem health, human health, and material welfare.
	Acidification	Acidification describes the fate and deposition of acidifying substances mainly due to their high sulphur content
	Eutrophication	Eutrophication (also known as nutrification) includes all impacts due to excessive levels of macronutrients in the environment caused by emissions of nutrients to air, water, and soil.
	Freshwater aquatic ecotoxicity	The impact on freshwater ecosystems, due to the emissions of toxic substances into the air, water, and soil.
	Land use	The amount of land transformed or occupied for a certain time.
Damage category	Human health	The number of years of life lost and the number of years lived disabled. These two parameters are combined to get a single score defined as disability-adjusted life years.
	Ecosystems	The loss of species during a certain time, over a certain area.
	Resources surplus costs	The surplus costs of future resource production over an infinitive timeframe with the assumption of constant annual production and a 3% discount rate.

Box 7.1 Assessing the Net Climate Impacts of the Forest-Based Bioeconomy in Finland

Box authored by Elias Hurmekoski, Academy research fellow, University of Helsinki

The forest industry forms the cornerstone of the bioeconomy in Finland, a country characterised by more than 70 per cent of forest land cover. The utilisation rate of forests has continuously increased since the 1960s, with the increased forest growth driven by intensive forest management. Despite the increased level of harvest, the land use sector has remained a significant net sink of GHGs in the past decades (Statistics Finland 2021), in line with the principles of sustainable forest management. However, this perspective does not consider whether alternative management practices would have resulted in greater net removals of GHGs. In other words, statistics only portray occurred emissions, but they do not help to answer the question, of how forests should be managed to maximise climate benefits. Assessing the additional climate change mitigation potential requires comparing one or more scenarios to the baseline situation (also termed counterfactual scenario), that is, what would have happened in the absence of mitigation activities. The methodological approach builds on consequential LCA: the objective is to define the net GHG impacts of mitigation activities on the atmosphere across different time frames. The net climate impact is typically approximated by the net GHG emissions comprised of biogenic carbon stock changes in forests, soil, and harvested wood products, as well as the avoided fossil emissions attributed to changes in wood use (substitution impacts). The methods for calculating the net impact typically include forest simulation, material flow analysis, and spreadsheet models based on primary or secondary (attributional) LCA and life cycle inventory data.

In Finland, studies show that any increase in the level of the harvest would result in an increase in atmospheric GHG concentration at least until the end of the century, compared to no increase in the level of harvest (e.g. Heinonen et al. 2017; Hurmekoski et al. 2020; Soimakallio et al. 2016). This is because the net increase in the amount of carbon stored in the harvested wood products coupled with the emissions avoided from substituting fossil-based products remain magnitudes lower than the unrealised increase in the amount of carbon stored in standing forests had the level of harvest not increased. The potential climate mitigation impact of bio-based products is expected to lessen further, due to the decarbonisation of the economy, because the reduction of overall fossil emissions across all sectors reduces the future ability to avoid fossil emissions through wood use.

The trade-off between short-term and long-term benefits of wood use creates a strong motive to pursue alternative climate change mitigation strategies unrelated to the level of harvest. In terms of wood use, this could imply shifts in wood uses, as opposed to merely increasing all existing wood uses. For example, Roundwood use could be shifted from paper to textiles, and by-product use could be shifted from direct energy use to chemicals. Such strategies could increase the substitution impacts of wood use without increasing the level of harvest. Also, increased cascading (reuse, recycling, and downcycling) and resource efficiency could alleviate the need for harvesting primary woody biomass. By adopting such measures, it would be possible to simultaneously continue wood use and gain both short-term and long-term climate benefits. If the new wood uses were in higher value applications, the plausible extra profit could be used to fund further climate change mitigation measures.

It should be stressed that the conclusions on climate change mitigation potentials remain contingent on the counterfactual scenario and the definition of the system boundary, that is, the extent that affecting factors have been considered and accurately quantified. For example, an increase in natural disturbances in forests would result in larger net emissions in the baseline, depending on the extent and success of adaptation measures, which makes the interpretation of additional mitigation potential challenging. Also, there may be indirect price-mediated consequences, such as international, intersectoral, or intertemporal carbon leakages, which could prevent achieving the desired mitigation outcomes. It is extremely challenging to quantify all direct and indirect impacts of mitigation scenarios and to foresee how the world will develop by the end of the century, which is why such assessments should be interpreted with caution.

Climate change mitigation scenario analyses are performed to support decision-making within the forest sector, that is, how forests should be managed and how wood should be used to improve the impact on climate compared to the current state. However, in the future, when targeting climate neutrality within the next few decades, it will be necessary to track absolute emissions and removals in all sectors simultaneously to trace realistic low-emission pathways for the overall economy.

change (iLUC) can also occur, comprising the cascading changes in land use outside a biomass production area that are nonetheless induced by the newly established bio-economy activity (e.g. the biomass production for mulch film). For example, crops previously produced in the biomass production area are being produced elsewhere to meet demand, resulting in additional land being converted to agricultural land. As the demand for bio-based products increases, different evaluation models regarding the iLUC indicator have emerged (Marazza et al. 2020). Additional land use impacts can also be calculated, such as water consumption for biomass cultivation, the potential loss of biodiversity, soil carbon depletion, soil erosion, deforestation, as well as greenhouse gas (GHG) emissions from iLUC.

7.2.4   Interpretation

The last phase of an LCA study is the *interpretation* when findings of either the inventory analysis or the impact assessment, or both, are combined consistently with the defined goal and scope to reach conclusions and recommendations. During this phase, completeness, consistency, sensitivity, and hotspot checks are performed; limitations are addressed; and any improvements are portrayed. If applicable, alternative scenarios could also be simulated.

Further developments have also been reported to extend the scope of LCA studies to measuring and assessing the circularity under new standards (e.g. ISO/CD 59004 Circular Economy) regarding the bioeconomy aiming to assist, for example, in the application of policy settings, product design, and material circularity.

Despite being a useful tool for assessing the environmental impact of products, the LCA method is not without some limitations. A comprehensive sustainability assessment approach would require the evaluation of all societal and economic practices, values, and attitudes that result from or lead to technological, social, ecological, and political innovations. Additionally, even if a product's environmental performance (i.e. eco-efficiency) is improved, this may not always generate greater environmental sustainability, that is, greater sustainability of products or production systems does not always correspond to greater social inclusion (e.g. human rights, gender equality, fair trade). Hence, holistic approaches to innovations are required in various areas, including the bioeconomy sector such as the assessment of economic and social performance along with the environmental impacts (Morone & Yilan 2020).

7.3   Life Cycle Costing (LCC)

The economic performance of a product, process, or system is referred to as *economic sustainability*. Economic assessments usually employ diverse methods and metrics such as return on investment, payback period, net present value, and internal rate of return, while the method adopting a life cycle thinking approach is known as *Life Cycle Costing* (Vance et al. 2022). Life cycle costing has been used in many sectors, including the levelised cost of energy (LCOE) calculations, which determine the average cost of energy produced by different technologies by dividing the total lifetime costs by the total lifetime energy production (Yilan et al. 2020).

In fact, Life Cycle Costing is the oldest of the three life cycle techniques that are covered in this chapter. However, it has recently been linked to a framework that is consistent with the LCA applications and renamed *environmental life cycle costing* (Swarr et al. 2011). An environmental life cycle costing should assess costs occurring throughout the life cycle of a product and directly covered by one or more actors in the product life cycle, while conventional life cycle costing usually focuses on real and internal costs covered by the main producer or user (Hunkeler et al. 2008). This means that while conventional Life Cycle Costing mainly focuses on the product, service, or investment life span, potentially excluding upstream and downstream segments or processes, environmental life cycle costing focuses on the life cycle in its LCA-related meaning, thus including all stages from feedstock supply to consumption and/or end of life (Miah et al. 2017). Therefore, an environmental life cycle costing should have the same product system as LCA, as defined by ISO 14040/44 (Swarr et al. 2011). Besides this basic difference, an environmental life cycle costing could also include externalities, and the associated compensation policies, discussed in Chapter 4, and including CO_2 taxes, and all relevant subsidies and taxes (Hunkeler et al. 2008).

For these reasons, an environmental life cycle costing is thought to be carried out together or after an LCA. Results can be plotted to identify, among others, win–win scenarios, compare costs of different environmental measures, and analyse cost hotspots along the supply chain. Similar to the LCA framework, environmental life cycle costing[2] has four successive stages (Figure 7.2) determined by ISO 14040: goal and scope definition, inventory costs analysis, aggregation of costs, and interpretation (Hunkeler et al. 2008).

7.3.1   Goal and Scope Definition

During the first stage of LCC, the goal of the study, the functional unit, system boundaries, allocation procedures, and discount rates are defined. It is also important to state the viewpoint of the life cycle actor (whether supplier, manufacturer, user, or consumer) during this phase. At this stage, a cost breakdown structure should also be developed to facilitate the consistent collection of data along the full life cycle, which can also be aggregated along the life cycle (UNEP/SETAC 2011).

The goals and scope have to be properly defined, and data inventory issues, including allocation, must be considered. If LCC is carried out in combination with LCA, costs should be directly matched or attributed to input flows identified in LCA, which means using the same functional unit and the same system boundaries. It is important to note that the selection of alternatives must also be consistent with the functional unit

---

[2] Hereafter, LCC is used to refer to environmental life cycle costing throughout the chapter for practical reasons.

as defined in LCA (ISO 2006a, 2006b) even if the LCC perspective could include or exclude one or more actors or stakeholders and have a different goal and scope. Some examples of goal and scope are also listed: identify total costs for an actor, assess competitiveness (of cost of ownership), company management, marketing, trade-offs or win–win with environmental measures or between different costs, and optimisation of maintenance. The scope should present information not only on function and its unit but also on the product/service under study, system boundaries, allocation, methods of interpretation, data sources and quality, and value choices (Hunkeler et al. 2008; Swarr et al. 2011).

The use of a discount rate can also be important – especially for durable goods with cost flows in the future. In principle, the motivation for applying a discount rate seems valid for converting future costs into a present value for current decision-making. However, there is no consensus on criteria about which discount rate should be applied for an LCC. Therefore, a sensitivity analysis for different discount rates is recommended (UNEP/SETAC 2011).

7.3.2   Inventory Costs Analysis

Similar to LCA, the second stage is the *collection of information*. In LCC, data requirements are strongly dependent on the goal and scope of the study, and cost differences, rather than absolute figures, are the main concern. This also implies that different studies of the same object, with various goals and scopes, are usually not directly comparable to each other, as is the case for LCA studies. In addition, cost information is much more variable over time than life cycle inventory data; therefore, static databases are often not very useful for LCC, while the contrary is the case for flow data of life cycle inventory unit processes. However, in cases in which specific data are lacking or where only a generic LCC analysis is the goal, prices from databases can be employed. These data sources provide default price ranges for materials as well as manufacturing process costs, or relative costs. Furthermore, the field of cost estimation is quite developed and could be used to provide supplemental data to LCC. If LCC is applied regularly within an organisation, it is advisable to build and maintain an internal database for the most relevant cost categories of the processes, materials, and energy carriers under study. For the latter case, an internal data format should be established, which should also address issues of currency conversions, fluctuations over time (ranges of prices), and geographical price differences (Hunkeler et al. 2008).

One problem in data gathering is related to allocating costs to products that are produced together with co-products or by-products. In LCC, the costs of personnel and capital and acquired goods and services are to be allocated to the different outputs involved, based on their market prices. The same challenge also applies to the bioeconomy sector since usually multiple products are produced in the biorefineries. Thus, costs from a single shared process should be appropriately divided and allocated to the various products.

7.3.3   Aggregation of Costs by Cost Categories

The third stage of an LCC is the *aggregation of inventory costs* into cost categories while it is not needed to consider any impact assessment through characterisation models (as done in LCA) since the estimations have the same unit in monetary terms. However, an appropriate indicator should be selected along with a discount rate. It is also critical to determine how the total costs should be expressed, for example, over the life of the functional unit, or in terms of a normalised cost such as annual cost. Specifically, the normalised cost approach is preferred when a comparison is made across two alternatives with different lifetimes or end-of-life scenarios.

The definition of cost categories and the aggregation of costs are not a straightforward practice since most of the time more than one product is produced and allocation of cost to each product is required. Even so, we can list a number of cost categories which are mainly used such as costs of development, materials, energy, machines, labour, waste management, emission controls, transport, maintenance and repair, liability, taxes, and subsidies (Figure 7.3).

Furthermore, while LCC frameworks are typically applied considering a single stakeholder perspective, the life cycles of bio-based products typically involve multiple stakeholders with conflicting economic interests. For example, in a simplified case of biomass supply to a biorefinery, the stakeholders involved could be the producer of biomass (farmer) and the biomass processor (biorefinery operator). While the farmer has a more profitable enterprise at a higher selling price for the produced biomass, the biorefinery operator has a more profitable enterprise at a lower biomass price. For these reasons, LCCs are typically case- or industry-specific, leading to the development of various divergent LCC frameworks (Vance et al. 2022).

7.3.4   Interpretation

Finally, the last stage of an LCC is the *interpretation* which, by nature, is very specific to the case study selected. As mentioned for LCA, the evaluation of results from the previous stages as well as the checks of completeness, consistency, and sensitivity (ISO 14040/44 2006) are performed during the interpretation stage of an LCC. It is also possible to identify the hotspots as a result of a sensitivity analysis during this stage.

Connections between uncertain parameters used in LCC (e.g. project life, included life cycle costs and revenues, sales volume, and/or discount rates) and calculated outputs (e.g. net present value) should be revealed by a sensitivity analysis. The key question is how sensitive the outputs are to given deviations in the input parameters. In the sensitivity analysis, the uncertain input parameters are varied *ceteris paribus* by a certain percentage and their effects on the output parameters are noted. Thus, it is possible to determine how outputs vary for given variations in inputs. Sensitivity analysis also provides insights into the limits of conclusions related to different options concerning varying input values. Hence, the sensitivity analysis should be the basis for the final discussion and the development of recommendations.

Even if the LCC provides vital economic information to help decision-makers understand the life cycle costs and benefits involved in the short to long term, it bears some limitations. For example, LCC studies are time- and space-sensitive, meaning that an identical product might have a completely different cost across two different countries with different material costs, labour costs, interest rates, etc. Additional criticisms of using traditional economic assessments in sustainability assessments revolve around the utilisation of an individual business' profit potential as the sole metric for assessing the economic performance of a system, which neglects both non-monetary costs to the business and monetary and non-monetary costs shifted to employees, other businesses, and society (Vance et al. 2022).

Finally, the results of an LCC study should be analysed with the results of the parallel LCA study to identify environmental-economic win–win situations or trade-offs. The combined results of LCA and LCC can also be used for further analyses in the context of sustainability. Nevertheless, there are several challenges in combining LCA with LCC, such as harmonising the goals and the scope, when the goals of the interested public may be different. Therefore, the context in which the combination of both assessments is relevant must be stated. Such context may be concerned with public decisions in which the environmental impact of a new product must be complemented by its costs to the whole community, including owner cost, user cost, and external cost. Fair information to consumers is another relevant context. Another challenge is avoiding double-counting or inconsistent assessment. For instance, economic allocation in the case of LCA requires the use of cost allocation factors, whereas external costs in the case of LCC require internalising the environmental impacts. Another issue that impacts the integration is discrepancies between temporal considerations, that is, conventional LCA assumes a steady state, aggregated over a lifetime, while LCC considers discounted money values and is thus temporal by default (Gnansounou & Pandey 2016). After all, fully adapting to these requirements along with the life cycle is challenging.

7.4   Social Life Cycle Assessment (S-LCA)

As stated before, a product with good environmental performance (eco-efficiency) might not always necessarily be produced in a socially responsible way and thus requires comprehensive social analysis. The assessment of the social dimension of sustainability is the most recently developed as there is a strong recognition in the LCA community of the need to further integrate social criteria (Dahiya et al. 2020). Consistent with the environmental and economic assessment frameworks adopting the life cycle thinking perspective, the guidelines on S-LCA have been developed by UNEP (Benoît et al. 2009) and then updated (UNEP 2020).

S-LCA is referred to as a 'method that can be used to assess the social and sociological aspects of products, their actual and potential positive as well as negative impacts along the life cycle'. *Social impacts* are consequences of social relations (interactions) weaved in the context of activity (production, consumption, or disposal) and/or engendered by it and/or by preventive or reinforcing actions taken by stake-holders (e.g. enforcing safety measures in a facility). Social impacts are often per-ceived as being complex, but indeed, they are a function of many aspects including but not limited to politics, economy, ethics, psychology, legal issues, culture, etc. After all, S-LCA aims at estimating these social impacts by (in)direct effects of the stakeholders at local, national, and global levels.

S-LCA assesses the social and socio-economic impacts of all life cycle stages from cradle to grave, considering the complete life cycle of a product, including resource extraction, processing, manufacturing, assembly, marketing, sale, use, recy-cling, and disposal. Each of these life cycle stages (and their unit processes) can be associated with geographic locations, where one or more of these processes are carried out (mines, factories, roads, rails, harbours, shops, offices, recycling firms, disposal sites). At each of these geographic locations, social and socio-economic impacts may be observed in stakeholder categories that are deemed to be the main group categories potentially impacted by the life cycle of a product and are expected to have shared interests due to their similar relationship to the investigated prod-uct systems. The six main *stakeholder categories* taken into consideration for this assessment are (i) workers/employees; (ii) local community; (iii) society (national and global); (iv) consumers (covering end-consumers as well as the consumers who are part of each step of the supply chain), (v) value chain actors, and (vi) children[3] (UNEP 2020).

In accordance with the LCA, the S-LCA framework also has four phases (ISO 2006a): goal and scope definition, inventory analysis, impact assessment, and inter-pretation (Figure 7.2). On the other hand, stakeholder involvement is of crucial impor-tance in S-LCA methodology and is included in all four stages (Popovic & Kraslawski 2015). It is also reported that S-LCA studies are highly sensitive to changing geo-graphical locations due to the local and regional nature of social issues and so the geographical context should also be included in each stage (Fauzi et al. 2019).

7.4.1   Goal and Scope Definition

The S-LCA starts with defining the goal, scope, and functional unit. The aim, in this case, is to highlight the social impacts associated with a product or activity. The scope of an S-LCA study is of utmost importance since it can significantly affect the results according to the stakeholders and the types of impacts to be considered. Regarding the functional unit, the social impacts are not easily expressed per unit of process output as LCA results are done since semi-quantitative or qualitative data is used in this case. For this reason, the functional unit should be selected carefully for a combined assess-ment, including environmental and social aspects. Apart from the LCA applications, S-LCA encourages stakeholder involvement within the assessment itself considering each of the processes and the type of critical review required.

---

[3] A recently added stakeholder category during the revision of the S-LCA methodology.

When conducting the goal and scope phase of a study, one may refer to a stakeholder classification and classify the subcategories based on this. While the stakeholder categories provide a comprehensive basis for the articulation of the subcategories, the subcategories represent the basis for an S-LCA. The purpose of the classification of subcategories according to stakeholder groups is to make sure that the S-LCA matches the goal and scope and is assessing the full picture. A detailed definition of subcategories associated with stakeholder categories and inventory indicators is provided in Section 7.4.3.

7.4.2   Inventory Analysis

The second stage of an S-LCA is the data collection for prioritisation, hotspot assessment, site-specific evaluation, and impact assessment (characterisation). The data are aligned with the functional unit and aggregated if necessary. The most time-consuming step in this stage is collecting the necessary data to verify how organisations related to the production chain perform on social and socio-economic aspects according to the subcategories (see Section 7.4.3).

Selection of subcategories is challenging due to the high number of categories. To overcome this problem, social hotspots analysis can be performed to select the most relevant subcategories (and also indicators). *Social hotspots* are unit processes located in a region (e.g. a country) where a situation occurs that may be considered a problem, a risk, or an opportunity, in relation to a social issue that is threatening social well-being or that may contribute to its further development. Since the data collection is guided by the subcategories selected, it is also essential to have a good understanding of what information is needed, on which subjects, and what is the best way to access it to develop questionnaires, search for data on the Web, and conduct interviews. Inventory indicators can then be chosen and strategies for data collection can finally be developed.

In S-LCA, the activity variables data are collected and used more often compared to LCA while activity variables are used when data about impacts are not available in LCA. *Activity variables* reflect the relevance of social impact subcategories related to the process output (Norris 2006). For example, the most common activity variable is 'working hours', which refers to the number of hours spent to produce 1 USD output of the considered product system (Bouillass et al. 2021). Furthermore, the balance between quantitative, qualitative, and semi-quantitative data is generally different across methods. In S-LCA, less quantitative data are available compared to LCA and LCC.

7.4.3   Impact Assessment

Impact assessment is the third phase of an S-LCA, which aims to provide a combination of (a) the selection of the impact categories and subcategories, and the characterisation methods and models; (b) classification to relate the inventory data to particular S-LCA subcategories and impact categories; and (c) characterisation to determine and/or calculate the results for the subcategory indicators.

Impact categories are logical groupings of S-LCA results, related to social issues of interest to stakeholders and decision-makers. For the time being, stakeholder categories and subcategories are the basis on which to build the analysis. For example, the working conditions impact category can be evaluated under the stakeholder category workers.

By definition, two social and socio-economic impact categories can be identified. Type I impact categories aggregate the results for the subcategories within a theme of interest to a stakeholder, for example, human rights. On the other hand, Type II impact categories model the results for the subcategories that have a causal relationship defined by the criteria, and they correspond to a model of the social impact pathways to the endpoints such as human capital, cultural heritage, and human well-being. To do so, starting from subcategory results to impact categories on human well-being, with or without aggregating the information at the impact category level is required.

Subcategories aim to represent impacts within an impact category and are socially relevant characteristics or attributes to be assessed (i.e. fair salary, working hours). Subcategories of an impact category seek to describe the overall meaning of the indicators used to represent this subcategory. For example, considering the working conditions impact category, a relevant subcategory can be selected as social security and benefits. Under the selected subcategory, the following inventory indicators can be listed (i) health insurance, (ii) retirement insurance, (iii) paid maternity and paternity leave, and (iv) legal contracts. Hence, there may be two weighting/aggregation steps. The first one allows going from inventory indicator results to a subcategory result, and the second one allows reaching an impact category result from subcategory results (Figure 7.3).

Social and socio-economic mechanisms can take different forms, and so can the indicators. Because some social and socio-economic impacts might be best captured through qualitative indicators. Accordingly, it is possible to choose quantitative, semi-quantitative, and qualitative indicators depending on the goal and scope of the study. A *quantitative indicator* is a description of the issue assessed using numbers, for example, the number of accidents by the unit process. *Qualitative indicators* describe an issue using words. They are nominative, with text describing the social acceptance of a new bio-based product. *Semi-quantitative indicators* are categorisations of qualitative indicators into a yes/no form or a scale (scoring system), for example, the presence of child labour (yes–no). Quantitative indicators can be directly related to the unit process output as is the case in LCA. Although semi-quantitative in licators cannot be directly expressed per unit of the output process, it is possible to assess, in quantitative terms, the relative importance of each unit process in relation to the functional unit. This allows aggregation of final category results comprehensively and logically.

In S-LCA, the subcategories are classified by both stakeholder categories and impact categories, while they are classified only by impact categories in LCA. Whereas both LCA and S-LCA impact assessment methods may be sensitive to location, LCA impact assessment methods are not site-specific and use categories of location types that depend on physical factors such as geography type or population density. S-LCA, however, may require site-specific impact assessment in some cases and may also need information about political attributes, such as the country and its laws. S-LCA encounters both positive and negative impacts in the product life cycle because beneficial impacts are often of importance, and it encourages performance beyond compliance (with laws, international agreements, certification standards, etc.). In comparison, beneficial impacts in LCA seldom occur, and although examples exist (such as CO_2 uptake in the growth of plants), in general, what is desired from an environmental point of view is not having an impact.

7.4.4   Interpretation

Life cycle interpretation is the process of assessing S-LCA results to draw conclusions (Baumann & Tillman 2004). In accordance with the goal and scope of the study, this phase has several objectives including (i) the identification of the significant issues; (ii) the evaluation of the study (which includes considerations of completeness and consistency); (iii) the level of engagement with stakeholders; (iv) conclusions, recommendations, and reporting.

During this stage, significant issues are highlighted in terms of important social findings and critical methodological choices. They include the identification of key concerns, limitations, and assumptions made during the study and resulting from the study. Some key requirements regarding the evaluation process include the performance of a critical review, the documentation of the evaluation process, the actions taken to ensure transparency, and the verifiability of results. Conclusions have to be drawn and a recommendation made, based on the goal and scope of the study. It may be best to start with preliminary conclusions and verify if they are consistent with the requirements set out for the study. If these are not consistent, it may be necessary to return to previous steps to address the inconsistencies. If the preliminary conclusions are consistent, then the reporting of the results may proceed. The reporting should be fully transparent, implying that all assumptions, rationales, and choices are identified. Results may be presented differently depending on the intended audience and the ability to support a conclusion. It is also important to report on the participation and involvement of stakeholders in the study, particularly in case-specific studies (Imbert & Falcone 2020). The extension of the scope of S-LCA to an organisational level is another developing line of research, a more streamlined approach called social organisational life cycle assessment (SO-LCA) (Martinez-Blanco et al. 2015).

7.5   Combined Sustainability Assessments

After the introduction of impact evaluation methods for each sustainability sphere, it is also worth mentioning the need to combine these methods to reach an overall assessment result to support the decision-making process. In such cases with high complexity and uncertainty that also include a variety of stakeholders, the decision-making process becomes significantly critical (de Luca et al. 2017). For this aim, a wide range of methodologies exist, such as hybridised metrics (Lokesh et al. 2020), novel integrated assessment tools (Ladu & Morone 2021) (Box 7.2) or relatively more standardised tools, including LCSA, and MCDA as the best-known ones. The following sections will focus on the latter methods and their applications to the bioeconomy sector.

Box 7.2 Selection of LCA Impact Categories for Bio-Based Products

Box authored by Dr Luana Ladu, Researcher at the Technological University of Berlin.

Here we provide an overview of selected impact categories that should be considered in conducting a sustainability LCA of bio-based products. The categories have been proposed in the Integrated Sustainability Assessment Tool (Ladu & Morone 2021). As shown in the table given later, eleven impact categories are considered for the environmental dimension, covering various stages of the product life cycle: biomass production, production of bio-based products/materials, and use and end of life.

Two indicators are specific only to the biomass production life cycle stage and aim to protect soil quality and productivity (soil erosion) and to promote positive and reduce negative impacts on ecosystems and biodiversity. The other nine impact categories are related to the entire life cycle of the product. These impact categories are directed to mitigate climate change and promote good air quality; to conserve and protect water resources; to promote the efficient use of energy resources, and to prevent the depletion of non-renewable resources, to minimise the impacts on human health.

Environmental indicators used in the integrated assessment	Biomass production	Bio-based products/ material production	Use and end of life
Depletion of non-renewable (fossil) energy resources	X	X	X
Erosion risk associated with the biomass production for the product, in terms of the amount of specific soil loss (soil erosion)	X		
Global warming potential (GWP) of the product	X	X	X
Land use of the bio-based product (land use – soil quality index)	X	X	X
Particulate matter emissions (PM) of the product	X	X	X
Potential impacts on freshwater and terrestrial ecosystems for bio-based product (acidification terrestrial and freshwater)	X	X	X
Potential impacts on freshwater and terrestrial ecosystems for bio-based product (eutrophication freshwater)	X	X	X
Potential impacts on freshwater and terrestrial ecosystems for bio-based product (eutrophication terrestrial)	X	X	X
Potential impacts on human health for bio-based product (e.g. cancer human health effects)	X	X	X
Potentially affected species for bio-based product (potentially affected biodiversity)	X		
Water use of the bio-based product (water deprivation)	X	X	X

From a life cycle perspective, the proposed impact categories address the most relevant sustainability aspects, and they are directly associated with the following Sustainable Development Goals (SDG): SDG 2 (Zero Hunger), SDG3 (Good Health and Well-being), SDG6 (Clean Water and Sanitation), SDG7 (Affordable and Clean Energy), SDG8 (Decent Work and Economic Growth), SDG9 (Industry, Innovation and Infrastructure), SDG10 (Reduced Inequality), SDG12 (Responsible Consumption and Production), SDG13 (Climate Action), and SDG15 (Life on Land).

7.5.1   Life Cycle Sustainability Assessment (LCSA)

In recent years, life cycle assessment (LCA or E-LCA), LCC, and social life cycle assessment (S-LCA), from the theoretical framework of life cycle thinking, have emerged as tools that enable comprehensive sustainability evaluations introducing the innovative perspective of the whole life cycle of products or services to catch eventual burden shifts. Accordingly, the search for a shared methodological definition of LCSA has encouraged academicians to seek the best way to combine LCA, LCC, and S-LCA (de Luca et al. 2017).

LCSA is defined as 'the evaluation of all environmental, social and economic negative impacts and benefits in decision-making processes towards more sustainable products throughout their life cycle' (UNEP/SETAC 2011). To assess the overall sustainability of a bio-based system, the LCSA framework can be used, when quantitative results can be achieved. Common to all assessment methods, this can be performed in four stages starting with the definition of goal and scope, collection of inventory data, assessment of impacts, and finally interpretation.

There have been many studies considering the bioeconomy sector in different scopes and geographic contexts. For example, Martin et al. (2018) provide a list of sustainability indicators from a Swedish perspective. They identified the frequently used indicators in LCSA studies as being climate change, energy use, and acidification from the environmental assessments; investment cost and net present value from the economic assessment; and finally accidents/safety risks, economic development, and education from the social assessment. During the evaluation of all these indicators at once, a series of problems occur: trade-offs and conflicts of objectives, double-counting and problems of monetisation, Pareto-effects of high significance within cause–effect relations, contradictions between effects on different scales, allocation from effects to impact categories, coherence of functional units, and exogenous and endogenous weightings in accounting, rating, normative goal systems (Zeug et al. 2020).

It should also be underlined that in the first place, LCSA aimed to provide important information for managing the social responsibility of an organisation and its value chain – from the cradle to the grave– taking into account all dimensions of sustainable development. However, end-of-life activities hold a vital key to fully presenting the overall impacts extending the scope from cradle-to-grave to cradle-to-cradle. Covering end-of-life waste treatment allows for the investigation of a wide range of waste treatment scenarios and specifically addresses the question of whether biodegradability is an environmentally favourable property of bio-based materials. On the other hand, carbon cascading by using biomass first for material purposes and then recovering energy through incineration at the end of the product life cycle can maximise the GHG emissions savings of bio-based materials. Some LCA studies have also shown that composting can be more attractive than incineration (thus carbon cascading) if compost is used to replenish carbon stocks in agricultural soils (Weiss et al. 2012).

7.5.2   Multi-Criteria Decision Analysis (MCDA)

Decision-making in sustainability projects requires consideration of several aspects, including socio-political, environmental, and economic impacts and is often complicated by stakeholder views. MCDA is used as a formal methodology to handle available technical information and stakeholder values to support decisions in many fields and can be especially valuable in sustainable decision-making (Yilan et al. 2020). There is a variety of MCDA methods in the literature but Huang et al. (2011) suggest in their extensive review that even though the use of the specific methods and tools varies in different application areas and geographic regions, the recommended course of action does not vary significantly with the method applied.

MCDA is generally performed in four successive steps: (i) identification of the alternatives to be evaluated by the stakeholders; (ii) selection and valuation of the environmental, social, and economic sustainability criteria; and (iii) assigning criteria weights either subjectively or objectively, depending on the selected methodology; and (iv) ranking of the alternatives with a dimensionless score based on the selected sustainability criteria. Consequently, an MCDA including multiple stakeholder perspectives can be used to integrate data obtained from LCA, S-LCA, and LCC for comparative rankings (de Luca et al. 2017).

MCDA is widely appreciated for its ability to balance and integrate the tensions across three sustainability spheres, providing a holistic focus to decision-making processes in complex contexts, such as agriculture (Falcone et al. 2016), sustainable energy policies (Yilan et al. 2020), waste management (Yıldız-Geyhan et al. 2019), bioeconomy performance ranking of the European countries (D'Adamo et al. 2020), and policy implications regarding sustainability development goals (D'Adamo et al. 2022). Many scholars have combined the life cycle tools (individually or jointly) with different MCDA methods; indeed, as affirmed by Finkbeiner et al. (2010), life cycle evaluations can obtain additional insights from MCDA, for example, by addressing the scales of impact assessment, the selection of sustainability indicators, and the weighting and aggregation of indicator-specific results. Participatory approaches have been successfully developed and applied, alone or through MCDA tools, in life cycle evaluations of the bioeconomy sector (Mukherjee et al. 2020).

Take-Home Message

- Bio-based products are usually acknowledged as sustainable by definition, since they are derived from renewable raw materials instead of fossil origins. However, considering solely the raw materials is not enough to assess the sustainability performance of any product; overall life cycle impact scores of different product alternatives should be calculated to have a true idea about the actual impacts.
- Considering the environmental impacts, better scores might not necessarily mean better economic and social performance because trade-offs occur between sustainability dimensions. Hence, a holistic sustainability assessment with scientifically sound tools and methods should be performed to depict the full impacts on each dimension of sustainability.
- Life cycle assessment, life cycle costing, and social life cycle assessment are the most used methods for assessing, respectively, the environmental, economic, and social performance of products.
- A combination of these assessment methods is thus useful for evaluating the overall performance of the bioeconomy sector when aiming at providing insight to decision-makers such as businesses and policymakers.

Learning Exercises

1. Why is it necessary to embrace a life cycle thinking perspective?
2. What methods can be applied to assess the sustainability performance of bioeconomy products, processes, and activities?
3. What are the main stages of life cycle assessment methods for environmental, economic, and social performance?
4. What are the main strengths and limitations of each method?
5. Why are combined methods used for sustainability assessments?

Online Resources

Online course 'LCA (Life Cycle Assessment) Training Kit Material'. Available at: www.lifecycleinitiative.org/resources/training/lca-life-cycle-assessment-training-kit-material/

References

Antar, M., Lyu, D., Nazari, M., Shah, A., Zhou, X., & Smith, D. L. (2021). Biomass for a Sustainable Bioeconomy: An Overview of World Biomass Production and Utilization. *Renewable and Sustainable Energy Reviews*, **139**, 110691.

Baumann, H., & Tillman, A.-M. (2004). *The Hitch Hiker's Guide to LCA : An Orientation in Life Cycle Assessment Methodology and Application*. Lund: Studentlitteratur, Print.

Benoît, C., Andrews, E., Barthel, L., … Manhart, A. (2009). Guidelines for social life cycle assessment of products social and socio-economic LCA guidelines complementing environmental LCA and life cycle costing, contributing to the full assessment of goods and services within the context of sustainable development.

Bouillass, G., Blanc, I., & Perez-Lopez, P. (2021). Step-by-Step Social Life Cycle Assessment Framework: A Participatory Approach for the Identification and Prioritization of Impact Subcategories Applied to Mobility Scenarios. *The International Journal of Life Cycle Assessment*, **26**(12), 2408–2435.

Carus, M., & Dammer, L. (2018). The Circular Bioeconomy – Concepts, Opportunities, and Limitations. *Industrial Biotechnology*, **14**(2), 83–91.

D'Adamo, I., Falcone, P. M., & Morone, P. (2020). A New Socio-economic Indicator to Measure the Performance of Bioeconomy Sectors in Europe. *Ecological Economics*, **176**, 106724.

D'Adamo, I., Gastaldi, M., Ioppolo, G., & Morone, P. (2022). An Analysis of Sustainable Development Goals in Italian Cities: Performance Measurements and Policy Implications. *Land Use Policy*, **120**, 106278.

Dahiya, S., Katakojwala, R., Ramakrishna, S., & Mohan, S. V. (2020). Biobased Products and Life Cycle Assessment in the Context of Circular Economy and Sustainability. *Materials Circular Economy*, **2**(1), 7.

de Besi, M., & McCormick, K. (2015). Towards a Bioeconomy in Europe: National, Regional and Industrial Strategies. *Sustainability*, **7**(8), 10461–10478.

de Luca, A. I., Iofrida, N., Leskinen, P., … Gulisano, G. (2017). Life Cycle Tools Combined with Multi-Criteria and Participatory Methods for Agricultural Sustainability: Insights from a Systematic and Critical Review. *Science of The Total Environment*, **595**, 352–370.

EC. (2018). *A Sustainable Bioeconomy for Europe: Strengthening the Connection between Economy, Society and the Environment*. Brussels: European Commission. Retrieved from https://op.europa.eu/en/publication-detail/-/publication/edace3e3-e189-11e8-b690-01aa75ed71a1/language-en/format-PDF/source-149755478

Falcone, G., de Luca, A., Stillitano, T., Strano, A., Romeo, G., & Gulisano, G. (2016). Assessment of Environmental and Economic Impacts of Vine-Growing Combining Life Cycle Assessment, Life Cycle Costing and Multicriterial Analysis. *Sustainability*, **8**(8), 793.

Fauzi, R. T., Lavoie, P., Sorelli, L., Heidari, M. D., & Amor, B. (2019). Exploring the Current Challenges and Opportunities of Life Cycle Sustainability Assessment. *Sustainability*, **11**(3), 636.

Finkbeiner, M., Schau, E. M., Lehmann, A., & Traverso, M. (2010). Towards Life Cycle Sustainability Assessment. *Sustainability*, **2**(10), 3309–3322.

Gnansounou, E., & Pandey, A. (2016). *Life-Cycle Assessment of Biorefineries*, Elsevier.

Heinonen T, Pukkala T, Mehtätalo L, Asikainen A, Kangas J, Peltola H. (2017) Scenario Analyses for the Effects of Harvesting Intensity on Development of Forest Resources, Timber Supply, Carbon Balance and Biodiversity of Finnish Forestry. *Forest Policy and Economics*, **80,** 80–98.

Huang, I. B., Keisler, J., & Linkov, I. (2011). Multi-criteria Decision Analysis in Environmental Sciences: Ten Years of Applications and Trends. *Science of The Total Environment* **409**(19), 3578–3594.

Hunkeler, D., Lichtenvort, K., & Rebitzer, G. (2008). *Environmental Life Cycle Costing*, CRC press.

Hurmekoski, E., Myllyviita, T., Seppälä, J., Heinonen, T., Kilpeläinen, A., Pukkala, T., et al. (2020) Impact of Structural Changes in Wood-using Industries on Net Carbon Emissions in Finland. *Journal of Industrial Ecology*, **24**(4), 899–912.

Imbert, E., & Falcone, P. M. (2020). Chapter 6. Social Assessment, pp. 166–191.

ISO. Environmental management – Life cycle assessment – Principles and framework. ISO 14040., Pub. L. No. ISO 14040. (2006a).

ISO. Environmental management – Life cycle assessment – Requirements and guidelines. ISO 14044., Pub. L. No. ISO 14044. (2006b).

Ladu, L., & Morone, P. (2021). Holistic Approach in the Evaluation of the Sustainability of Bio-Based Products: An Integrated Assessment Tool. *Sustainable Production and Consumption*, **28**, 911–924e6.

Lokesh, K., Matharu, A. S., Kookos, I. K., … Clark, J. (2020). Hybridised Sustainability Metrics for Use in Life Cycle Assessment of Bio-based Products: Resource Efficiency and Circularity. *Green Chemistry*, **22**(3), 803–813.

Marazza, D., Merloni, E., & Balugani, E. (2020). Chapter 7. Indirect Land Use Change and Bio-based Products, pp. 192–222.

Martin, M., Røyne, F., Ekvall, T., & Moberg, Å. (2018). Life Cycle Sustainability Evaluations of Bio-based Value Chains: Reviewing the Indicators from A Swedish Perspective. *Sustainability*, **10**(2), 547.

Martínez-Blanco, J., Lehmann, A., Chang, Y. J., & Finkbeiner, M. (2015). Social Organizational LCA (SOLCA) – A New Approach for Implementing Social LCA. *The International Journal of Life Cycle Assessment*, **20**(11), 1586–1599.

Miah, J. H., Koh, S. C. L., & Stone, D. (2017). A Hybridised Framework Combining Integrated Methods for Environmental Life Cycle Assessment and Life Cycle Costing. *Journal of Cleaner Production*, **168**, 846–866.

Morone, P., & Yilan, G. (2020). A Paradigm Shift in Sustainability: From Lines to Circles. *Acta Innovations*, **(36)**, 5–16.

Mukherjee, S., Sharma, P. K., & Kumar, M. (2020). Bioeconomy and Environmental Sustainability. In *Current Developments in Biotechnology and Bioengineering*, Elsevier, pp. 373–397.

Norris, G. A. (2006). Social Impacts in Product Life Cycles – Towards Life Cycle Attribute Assessment. *The International Journal of Life Cycle Assessment*, **11**(S1), 97–104.

Popovic, T., & Kraslawski, A. (2015). Social Sustainability of Complex Systems, pp. 605–614.

Sijtsema, S. J., Onwezen, M. C., Reinders, M. J., Dagevos, H., Partanen, A., & Meeusen, M. (2016). Consumer Perception of Bio-Based Products – An Exploratory Study in 5 European Countries. *NJAS: Wageningen Journal of Life Sciences*, **77**(1), 61–69.

Soimakallio S, Saikku L, Valsta L, Pingoud K. (2016). Climate Change Mitigation Challenge for Wood Utilization: The Case of Finland. *Environmental Science & Technology*, **50**(10):5127–34.

Statistics Finland, 2021. Greenhouse gas emissions in Finland 1990 to 2019. National Inventory Report under the UNFCCC and the Kyoto Protocol. Submission to the European Union, p. 581.

Swarr, T. E., Hunkeler, D., Klöpffer, W., … Pagan, R. (2011). Environmental Life-Cycle Costing: A Code of Practice. *The International Journal of Life Cycle Assessment*, **16**(5), 389–391.

UNEP. (2020). Guidelines for Social Life Cycle Assessment of Products and Organizations. Retrieved from www.lifecycleinitiative.org/library/guidelines-for-social-life-cycle-assessment-of-products-and-organisations-2020/

UNEP/SETAC. (2011). Towards a Life Cycle Sustainability Assessment.

Vance, C., Sweeney, J., & Murphy, F. (2022). Space, Time, and Sustainability: The Status and Future of Life Cycle Assessment Frameworks for Novel Biorefinery Systems. *Renewable and Sustainable Energy Reviews*, **159**, 112259.

Vera, I., Wicke, B., Lamers, P., … van der Hilst, F. (2022). Land Use for Bioenergy: Synergies and Trade-offs Between Sustainable Development Goals. *Renewable and Sustainable Energy Reviews*, **161**, 112409.

Weiss, M., Haufe, J., Carus, M., … Patel, M. K. (2012). A Review of the Environmental Impacts of Biobased Materials. *Journal of Industrial Ecology*, **16**, S169–S181.

Yilan, G., Cordella, M., & Morone, P. (2023). Evaluating and Managing the Sustainability Performance of Investments in Green and Sustainable Chemistry: Development and Application of an Approach to Assess Bio-Based and Biodegradable Plastics. *Current Research in Green and Sustainable Chemistry*, **6**, 100353.

Yilan, G., Kadirgan, M. A. N., & Çiftçioğlu, G. A. (2020). Analysis of Electricity Generation Options for Sustainable Energy Decision Making: The Case of Turkey. *Renewable Energy*, **146**, 519–529.

Yıldız-Geyhan, E., Yılan, G., Altun-Çiftçioğlu, G. A., & Kadırgan, M. A. N. (2019). Environmental and Social Life Cycle Sustainability Assessment of Different Packaging Waste Collection Systems. *Resources, Conservation and Recycling*, **143**, 119–132.

Yu, D., Tan, H., & Ruan, Y. (2011). A Future Bamboo-Structure Residential Building Prototype in China: Life Cycle Assessment of Energy Use and Carbon Emission. *Energy and Buildings*, **43**(10), 2638–2646.

Zeug, W., Bezama, A., & Thrän, D. (2020). Towards a Holistic and Integrated Life Cycle Sustainability Assessment of the Bioeconomy: Background on Concepts, Visions and Measurements, UFZ Discussion Paper.

8 Innovation Systems and Global Value Chains in the Bioeconomy

---

Learning Objectives

To understand and be able to discuss critically:

- how actors and networks participate to the development of the bioeconomy.
- innovation systems and their relevance to the bioeconomy.
- global value chains and their relevance to the bioeconomy.

8.1   Introduction

Studying economic systems means assessing relationships between actors who participate in the dynamic development of the system. This chapter provides an introduction to two approaches which are relevant in understanding systems and their actors in the bioeconomy. Section 8.2 describes the innovation systems approach, which in opposition to a linear understanding of the development of innovation, envisions innovation as the iteration between multiple actors. Section 8.3 describes the global value chains (GVCs) approach, meaning the links between actors performing value co-creation at different stages, including the production, logistics, consumption, and recycling/disposal.

Both approaches, conceptualising respectively innovation systems and GVCs, share the idea that relationships between actors form the basic structure for studying a sustainable economic system.

Innovation systems have a horizontal perspective to production processes, while value-chains analysis adopts a vertical perspective. Yet, both approaches share the view that the transition to a sustainable bioeconomy system demands for innovation encompassing a variety of new technologies, production systems, and consumption behaviours, thus innovative socio-economic models. Innovation is generated as a result of interactive and dynamic learning processes, which are socially and territorially embedded and culturally and institutionally contextualised (Lundvall 1992). This emphasises the growing role of knowledge and networks in the emerging bioeconomy.

8.2   Innovation Systems

The innovation systems approach results from the observation that innovations do not appear isolated from their environment, as evolutionary perspectives to innovation have shown (Nelson & Winter 1982). Innovation is the product of interactions between competing firms, between customers and their suppliers, but also with communities of users and with public research organisations. Innovation systems are composed of networks of institutions and organisations. The innovation systems approach therefore consists of studying the interactions between institutions and organisations in order to study innovation processes.

The innovation systems approach emerged in the 1980s as a reaction to the linear model of innovation. The linear model of innovation is the result of the post–World War II consensus that recognised the key role of the state in organising and financing research. This publicly funded research was thought to be the source of discoveries that were to be industrialised. However, four findings about the characteristics of innovation have led to a move beyond this approach (Schot & Steinmueller 2018).

First, knowledge is not a global public good – the basis for the justification of state intervention for knowledge development in the post–World War II period – but has a strong tacit component. That is, this knowledge requires skills outside of the knowledge itself to be interpreted and used. Similarly, knowledge is 'sticky' (von Hippel 1994). This means that it does not circulate freely, again because of its idiosyncratic character, but also because it is attached to a cultural and institutional context.

Second, actors must have absorptive capacities to be able to take advantage of the knowledge circulating in innovation systems (Cohen & Levinthal 1990). These capacities depend on past experience. Thus, more recent work (Brusoni et al. 2001) has shown that firms know more than they incorporate into their production.

Third, absorption capacities are linked to the level of qualification of the actors, but also to their interpersonal networks and their insertion in networks promoting entrepreneurship.

Fourth, technical change is cumulative and path dependent. The cumulativity of technical change refers to the idea that new knowledge is always the product of old knowledge produced. New knowledge validates or invalidates old knowledge, especially through the combination of new knowledge. The accumulation of knowledge over the long term generates the absorption capacities mentioned above, generating lock-ins on technological trajectories (Arthur 1989).

The conjunction of these four stylised facts about innovation processes has led to them being considered to be a means of explaining the differences between national innovation systems.

8.2.1   The National Systems of Innovation

The first type of innovation system to be identified is at the national level. National innovation systems have described innovation processes by placing the analysis at the level of national institutions and organisations (Freeman 1995). In these models, the emphasis is on the role of innovation in the development of the competitiveness of states, in the context of neoliberal globalisation.

This model of approach is mainly concerned with *technology push* with a major role given to producers, although interactions with users can be taken into account. Work on national innovation systems has focused on the following dimensions of knowledge production (Limoges et al. 1994):

- The study of context in knowledge production
- The role of multi-disciplinarity in knowledge production
- The heterogeneity of innovation actors (SMEs, multinational companies, universities, technology transfer offices, etc.)
- The role of citizens in the production of knowledge
- The role of quality in innovation production processes

The focus on these dimensions has led to the formulation of public policies aimed at fostering the emergence of innovation networks and the interactions within these networks. This has led to a growing interest in the sub-national dimensions of network formation as a result of the emergence of these networks.

8.2.2 The Sectoral Systems of Innovation

The notion of sectoral innovation systems was put forward by Malerba (2002). They are defined as 'a set of new and established products for specific uses and the set of agents carrying out market and non-market interactions for the creation, production and sale of those products' (Malerba 2002, p. 248). A sectoral innovation system is characterised by the conjunction of a knowledge base, actors, and their networks and dedicated institutions.

The knowledge base of a sector is composed of knowledge from which the actors draw to produce new knowledge. This knowledge can be codified or non-codified. Codified knowledge corresponds to patents, academic publications, textbooks, or user manuals. Non-codified knowledge is all knowledge that results from acquired experience, etc. Knowledge is evaluated in light of its accessibility by the agents. Easily accessible knowledge leads to (1) limited concentration and (2) low appropriability of knowledge. The issue of appropriability is important because it affects the types of business models developed (Teece 2018). Thus, actors face a dilemma between fostering the adoption of their technologies to benefit from increasing returns to adoption, but this adoption can lead to the producer of the technology losing control of it. Depending on the sector, technology opportunities will vary. For example, technological opportunities in the biotech sector are strongly linked to the ability of start-ups to integrate existing production processes (see Chapter 2).

Similarly, the question of infrastructure is particularly important. In the case of the bioeconomy, the challenge of changes in scale (the transition from the laboratory to full-scale production) implies the development of pilot and demonstration plants (Hellsmark et al. 2016). The function of these units is to assist companies in identifying the conditions under which large-scale production of their products might be possible. However, this requires dedicated production units to carry out these tests, which must be shared across the sector because of their costs. Thus, an industry marked by (1) complex knowledge that is difficult to appropriate and (2) the need to have infrastructures that require significant investments will have the consequence of favouring large, concentrated, and already existing companies.

The actors and networks within a sectoral innovation system are heterogeneous. They can be individuals, firms, or non-firms (universities, financial institutions, government agencies, etc.) but also components of organisations (e.g. subsidiaries of a firm) or groups of organisations like industry associations. Agents are characterised by specific learning processes, absorptive capacities, expectations, and behaviours that are in interaction. These interactions consist of the exchange of knowledge through either market processes (e.g. markets for technology) or non-market processes (e.g. multi-actor research projects, interfirm alliances).

Firms are the key actors in the generation and diffusion of new technologies. These firms vary in size. As shown in Chapter 2, in the case of the bioeconomy, they are both multinational chemical or agribusiness companies and start-ups based on the promise of technological disruption. Nevertheless, these companies are, in relation to each other, within collective organisations or research projects. Consequently, the relevant level of analysis for studying sectoral innovation systems is not necessarily the firm. Indeed, depending on the case, it may be a sub-unit of the firm. For example, in the case of petrochemical firms, it is necessary to look at the functional units of the firm that are dedicated to biosourced activities. In the case of the study of start-ups, it may also be interesting to look at the level of individual trajectories of agents. In the case of the study of public research organisations or policymakers, it will be necessary to take into account the *rationales* guiding public policies. For example, until recently innovation policies in the bioeconomy have been linked to an imaginary of growth and competitiveness influenced by the biotechnology sector (Birch 2016). However, recent developments in bioeconomy innovation policies show that they are increasingly thought of as transformative innovation policies whose role is to enable the transformation of sectoral innovation systems (Mazzucato 2021).

Finally, sectoral innovation systems can be studied from the perspective of consumers. In the case of the bioeconomy, for the moment these consumers are mainly industrial consumers. Indeed, the molecules produced are located far up the value chains (Gereffi et al. 2005). The type of products offered (especially their complexity) will have a major impact on the relationships within the system.

Institutions, as defined above, are the rules and norms that organise the behaviour of actors. While institutions constrain actors (e.g. laws), they can also provide incentives or opportunities. Institutions can be formal (such as patents) or informal (such as traditions). Although many institutions are national, they have sectoral variations because of the different arrangements from one sector to another. In the case of the ecological transition, proponents of innovation systems approaches have been particularly interested in the role of public policies in fostering the development of environmental innovations (Oltra & Saint Jean 2009).

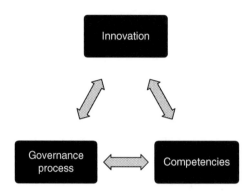

Figure 8.1 The three dimensions of regional innovation systems analysis.

A renewed understanding of innovation policies for transformative change invites to go beyond purely technological innovations *per se* in order to achieve a set of defined goals. In this perspective, the UN Sustainable Development Goals are now calling for greener production, social justice, inclusivity, etc. The evolution suggested by the SDGs and the transformative innovation policies orient innovation policies no longer towards sectors such as pharmaceuticals, biotechnologies, or chemistry but towards the social functions expected by the sectors. These policies, therefore, take into account the role of technological innovations by supporting technical change, while at the same time promoting organisational change characterised by the crossing of sectoral boundaries. Thus, transformation policies are based on the definition of missions in open-ended ways encouraging experimentation and diversity in new forms of engagement and networks. These networks involve public actors, firms, and actors of the social economy (such as associations and co-operatives).

8.2.3   The Regional Systems of Innovation

Along with a growing interest in the national and sectoral dimensions, research on innovation systems has focused on the regional dimension of these systems. The objective of these approaches is to study the economic situation of regions and to identify the strategies that would allow them to increase their prosperity through innovation strategies. To do this, regional innovation systems approaches (Cooke 2010) are based on the triptych shown in Figure 8.1, including innovation, competencies, and governance process.

Thus, regional innovation systems are particularly interested in the strategies that regions can put in place to respond to deindustrialisation or the fragmentation of value chains (see Section 8.3). Successful strategies combine disruptive innovation strategies organised through collective governance processes and require complementary skills. The governance process within regional innovation systems is studied from a network perspective. The performance of these networks is enhanced by the diversity of the actors in the network. The diversity within these networks helps to create a 'socio-cultural milieu' that favours the transfer of skills between actors thanks to mechanisms that encourage exchanges (events, etc.) (Bathelt & Cohendet 2014). Nevertheless, this process of forming communities within a milieu can contribute to locking actors into their development trajectory and hinder the renewal of the region by limiting creativity. In response to this risk, it appears that the SIRs have an interest in diversifying with external partners who have strategic advantages, and in particular positioning in global networks.

A major form of the regional innovation system in the bioeconomy is that of clusters. From this work, it emerges that *life sciences* clusters materialise innovation strategies thought to create prosperity for regions (Birch 2017). From this point of view, this perspective has largely been integrated into the European Commission's discourse on the bioeconomy (European Commission 2012) in its promise to create jobs in rural territories. Thus, the study of UK clusters of life sciences showed the regional anchoring role of dominant firms. These firms help to attract partnerships with universities, collaborations, and public funding. Nevertheless, the strong presence of large firms, because they have the skills in-house, reduces the need for them to develop exchanges within the cluster. To exist, these clusters need a strong regional knowledge base providing the region with the necessary skills to develop new activities.

Along with the innovation systems discussed so far in this chapter, there is the emerging notion of dedicated innovation systems. For a brief introduction, please see Box 8.1.

Box 8.1 Dedicated Innovation Systems

Box authored by Andreas Pyka, Professor of Innovation Economics, University of Hohenheim.

Since the late 1980s, innovation systems have enjoyed great popularity in economic research and economic policy (Dosi et al. 1988; Lundvall 1992, 1998; Nelson 1993). Without a doubt, the application of innovation systems theory in many economies, regions, and sectors has helped to constructively meet the major challenges of the time (high unemployment, transformation of former socialist economies, globalisation, and many more) and to provide for new economic dynamics and income growth. The old recipes of a Keynesian economic policy have lost their effect and have been replaced by supply-side approaches, especially from the field of Schumpeterian innovation systems. A particularly catchy description of innovation systems goes back to Gregersen and Johnson (1997): 'An innovation system can be thought of as a system which creates and distributes knowledge by introducing it into the economy in the form of innovations, diffuses it and transforms it into something valuable, for example, international economic competitiveness and economic growth.'

More than thirty years later, economies around the world are once again facing new challenges, especially with regard to achieving the sustainability goals that have since been agreed upon at the United Nations. There is no doubt that innovations play an outstanding role in achieving these goals, and yet it appears that the innovation systems approach is reaching its limits here in particular (Pyka &

Urmetzer 2023). The objectives of increasing international competitiveness and promoting further economic growth are far too one-dimensional to be able to meet the demands for restoring sustainability in the Anthropocene. To achieve sustainability goals, neither neoclassical 'more of the same' economic growth nor Schumpeterian innovation-driven structural change is sufficient. What is required is an irreversible transformation of all economic sectors, which includes the abandonment of the established business models that were so successful in the past as well as the overcoming of the cherished lifestyles of the second half of the twentieth century.

However, the theory of innovation systems can be retained as a promising approach in the future if it is freed from its retarding and disruption-hostile elements. This is what the *dedicated innovation systems theory* (Pyka 2017) aims to do, with its dedication anchored in the achievement of sustainability goals. The most important element of the dedicated innovation systems approach is the emphatic emphasis on a participatory innovation model in which the influence of established players is significantly reduced, as they regularly want to hold on too tightly to the economic successes of the past and therefore avoid major and, above all, genuinely uncertain changes as far as possible, as they fear that this will replace themselves (this is called the *not-invented-here syndrome* in management and the *replacement effect* in industrial economics). Instead, creative impulses come on the one hand from avant-garde consumers who design new sustainable lifestyles (Wilke et al. 2021), and on the other hand from entrepreneurs whose approaches to solutions are often incompatible with established economic practices and value networks. The table below shows the qualitative, sometimes disruptive changes in the orientations of economic actors that have to take place in a sustainability transformation on the institutional, supply, and demand side.

Orientations and implicit heuristics in decision-making	Established approaches	Sustainability-oriented approaches
Organisation of economies	Central	Regional/local
Production	linear fossil-energy intensive mass production resource intensive artificial obsolescence	circular renewable energies saving digitalisation, individualisation resource saving durable/sharing
Consumption	mass consumption waste intensive fast food, fast fashion	conscious consumption sustainable lifestyles vegan diets, etc.

A dedicated innovation system can now create the dynamics of the innovation process necessary to overcome the established economy if it succeeds in establishing a *circulos virtuosus* from the alliance between avant-garde consumers and sustainability-oriented entrepreneurs: new lifestyles create new economic niches for resourceful entrepreneurs. Both consumers and producers are encouraged to imitate and copy and to creatively develop new technologies and lifestyles. Above all, the latter ensures that a critical mass is built up; once this is reached, tipping points are crossed and the sustainable way of doing business can become irreversibly established (Pyka & Urmetzer 2023). The old orientations, which cannot be reconciled with comprehensive sustainability, are irrevocably replaced by the new orientations and patterns of action.

The bioeconomy plays an extremely important role in this process, as it embodies important new orientations of a sustainable way of doing business and provides important approaches for overcoming the lock-in in the age of fossil fuels and materials (Unruh 2000). However, it is not 'just' about substituting fossil-based with bio-based approaches but about completely changed value networks with new actors and new relationships between these actors. It is the mission of the theory of dedicated innovation systems not to lose sight of this.

8.3   Global Value Chains

Global value chain analysis emerged in response to the need to understand the deepening of the international division of labour. The basic principle of this type of analysis is to consider that value chains are constituted by lead firms and their suppliers where the former dominates the latter in the appropriation and control of the production of surplus value. The development of the knowledge economy – that is, the increase in the knowledge content of production – and the financialisation of firms' strategies from the 1980s onwards led to a deepening of the division of labour and to a transformation of industrial groups. In the case of the chemical industry, industrial groups had emerged at the end of World War I. These chemical companies included divisions specialising in fertilisers and pesticides, materials, and pharmaceuticals (Galambos et al. 2007). Because of the difference between low levels of profitability in the upstream part of the value chain for commodity chemicals and the high profitability of the fine chemicals and pharmaceuticals markets, the pharmaceuticals divisions have tended to become autonomous. Similarly, chemical companies have refocused on intermediate products with the highest added value (see Chapter 2 on the development of biotechnologies). This evolution of GVCs has been accompanied by an evolution in the geographical distribution of activities, notably because of relocation but also of the emergence of knowledge-intensive clusters. From then on, the GVC movement emerged to analyse the evolution of the international division of labour through two pillars: the governance of value chains and the upgrading of these strategies.

8.3.1   A Definition of Global Value Chains

A value chain describes all the activities to be implemented for the production of a product, from its initial design to its final consumption or even its recycling. These

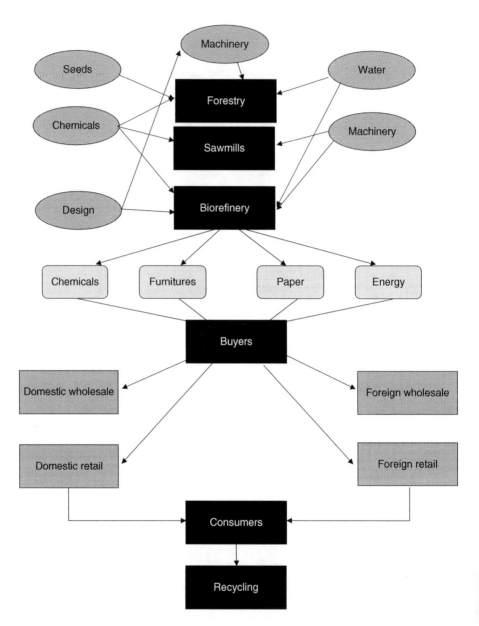

Figure 8.2 The wood-based biorefinery value chain.

activities are multiple and constitute successive stages involving both physical transformations by suppliers and service providers. A value chain is defined by the stages
of value creation and by the links established between the actors acting at different
stages of these value chains. For example, the diagram in Figure 8.2 describes the
complexity of the wood biorefinery chain.

The diagram in Figure 8.2 shows two essential elements for analysing the dynamics of value chains. On the one hand, a single company can be present in several value

chains. For example, petrochemical companies supply chemicals for the wood value chain but also for the production of agricultural fuels, pesticides, etc. Similarly, a company in the wood value chain may produce several products in the same chain. Similarly, a company in the wood value chain can produce several products from the same raw material, as illustrated by the example of the wood biorefinery. Nevertheless, as analyses of the cocoa or coffee issue show, the upstream part of certain value chains can be made up of many producers in the Global South, in relation to a limited number of intermediary processors, mastering a key stage in the production of value.

On the other hand, exchanges between actors constitute economic relationships that can take place either in highly competitive markets or through contractual relationships. This last point refers to the issue of value chain *governance*.

8.3.2   Governance of Global Value Chains

The analysis of the governance of a value chain makes it possible to study the power and co-ordination within a value chain. That is to say, it is a question of identifying which companies are in a position to impose their decisions. Gereffi (1994, p. 97) defines governance as the 'authority and power relationships that determine how financial, material and human resources are allocated and flow with a chain'. Thus, a value chain is made up of buyers and suppliers, both of which may have a role as lead firms (the dominant actor).

There are five types of value chain governance: markets, modular, relational, captive, and hierarchy (Gereffi et al. 2005). Table 8.1 presents them and gives examples of [corresponding product/value chain] types:

The models presented in this table are not exclusive and may evolve over time as a result of changes in institutional frameworks, power plays between actors, or the introduction of new technologies (see 8.3.3. on upgrading within GVCs). For example, Ponte (2014) describes how the global biofuel value chain has been constituted by localised actor decision-making in specific regions of the world with a form of governance essentially. Indeed, the policies of imposing minimum biofuel incorporation requirements in the European Union and in the United States, the Brazilian biofuel support programs of the 1970s–1980s as well as the mobilisation of advocacy groups seeking alternatives for non-fossil fuels, and agricultural lobbies created a favourable institutional context stimulating significant investments in Brazil, Europe, and Southeast Asia. The development of biofuels has generated strong criticism because of the problems of land grabbing, limited benefits for local communities, etc. Despite these strong criticisms, biofuels are still being used as an alternative to fossil fuels. Despite these strong criticisms, biofuels have been able to continue to develop both within national areas and at the global level.

In the case of Brazil, as in Europe, mandatory incorporation rates and subsidies have been put in place. Nevertheless, the development of biofuels in Brazil has been supported by the National Development Bank. The role of this bank is to promote the growth of ethanol production in Brazil by financing production and logistics infrastructures. In the case of the United States, even though production had already been going on for some time because of the development of chemurgy (see Chapter 1), biofuels have undergone significant new development as

Table 8.1 Types of governance and production in the global value chains of the bioeconomy

Type of governance	Definition	Examples
Markets	Market relationships emerge for relatively simple and standardised products that do not depend on specific consumer demands.	Biofuels
Modular value chains	Governance mode adopted for more complex products that must meet specifications that are easily codifiable and therefore transferable from the customer to the producer.	Bio-based parts of vehicles
Relational value chains	Governance adapted for very complex productions, not very codifiable, requiring numerous face-to-face interactions for the exchange of complex information. Requires the existence of complementary competencies between the client and the producer. Development of alliances between actors.	Innovative biotechnology processes
Captive value chains	High ability to codify but low ability of suppliers to control the production process. Lead firms control the relationship and seek to lock it down. Captive suppliers are dependent on the customer to provide designs, etc.	Agro-industrial co-operatives with their members
Hierarchy	When the products have a high level of complexity and whose specifications are weakly codifiable with strong stakes of intellectual property. Requires strategic management of close networks and access to specific resources.	Pilot and demonstration plants to organise the scale-up of processes

a result of their promotion within the various agricultural and energy policies of the early 2000s. Moreover, these policies have involved the major actors of the agro-industries. In the European case, biofuels have been included in the bioeconomy policies. Nevertheless, in reaction to the criticism of biofuels, the issue of sustainability indicators and the discourse on second-generation biofuels were included (see also Chapter 7).

If biofuels were first developed in national or European spaces, their expansion now involves the formation of relationships at the global level. For example, Brazilian biofuel producers have developed projects with African countries (Ghana, Angola) to transfer the Brazilian model or with the states of the American continent in a relational mode. The companies of agro-industries and biotechnologies have also been increasingly involved in the emergence of the biofuel GVC through the development of joint ventures and international collaborations. These collaborations aim at either developing crops, improving existing biofuels production technologies, or creating new ways to use biofuels (e.g. in the aircraft industry). This involvement in the development of innovation is evidence of evolution towards a form of hierarchical governance. Finally, the actors of the biofuel GVC take part in a series of global biofuels conferences during which the purpose is about legitimising and structuring a global discourse in favour of biofuels.

8.3.3 The Environmental Upgrading in Global Value Chains

The issue of upgrading is the second pillar of work using the GVC approach. Upgrading is defined as 'the process by which economic actors – nations, firms and workers – move from low-value to relatively high-value activities in global production networks' (Gereffi et al. 2005, p. 171). This line of research questions whether the strategies to be adopted by developing countries or dominated companies were able to overcome power asymmetries with developed countries and their lead firms. If the gains made by the growing integration into GVCs have indeed favoured economic development, the process of improving workers' rights and the quality of their employment is not automatic. In this sense, authors have studied social upgrading (Ponte 2019).

More recently, authors of GVCs have considered that the environmental improvement of products could be considered a form of upgrading in response to (1) a growing demand from consumers (whether or not they can afford sustainable products) and (2) a new dynamic of transformation of firms towards sustainability, which are increasingly sensitive to the reputational risk linked to the non-sustainability of their activities (Bolwig et al. 2010). Nevertheless, the spatial fragmentation of GVCs and the increasing independence of firms make the greening of GVCs more complex. Environmental upgrading is therefore the process by which firms follow to develop sustainable activities.

Three types of drivers are guiding the greening of GVCs (Marchi et al. 2013). First, the greening of GVCs is influenced by external factors such as pressures from (1) consumers or NGOs and (2) global goals defined by international institutions such as the Sustainable Development Goals. Second, the pressure to change can come from lead firms that have the ability, because of their power within value chains, to impose changes on their suppliers. Third, the drivers may be internal to the firm, implying an evolution of management systems to aim at a competitiveness objective based on the environmental features of products.

The three main processes for environmental upgrading (Marchi et al. 2013) refer to improvements at the process, product, and organisational levels (Table 8.2).

While these processes are analytically separated, process improvements and product improvements are very often linked. For example, the use of renewable materials for the production of plastics implies transforming processes to produce these new plastics. Nevertheless, as shown by the research on the role of eco-innovations in the transition to the bioeconomy, these innovations must also have a strong organisational dimension (Befort 2021; Pansera & Fressoli 2021). Indeed, still in the case of plastics, it is indeed possible to produce biodegradable and biosourced plastics like polylactic acids. Nevertheless, these plastics are now thought to be *drop-in* substitutes for petroleum-based plastics. That is to say, they must be single-use industrial products that are profitable, thanks to economies of

Table 8.2 The environmental upgrading processes in sustainable global value chains

Process improvements	Transformation of production by using a superior technology (high-tech or low-tech)
Product improvements	Environmentally friendly products using biomass and whose life cycle is considered from their conception
Organisational improvements	Transformation of the organisation of the firm to become sustainable in its internal management as well as in the production mode. Often oriented by the compliance with standards and certifications

scale. In the case of this type of substitution, there will be only two environmental upgrading processes that would be implemented. However, the work carried out since the 1980s (Lipinsky 1981; Lipinsky & Sinclair 1986) on these biodegradable plastics shows the difficulties that these products have to achieve drop-in strategies. On *the contrary*, it is possible to imagine functional strategies based on the abandonment of single-use plastics, biodegradable or not, and limit the use of these plastics for necessary uses (e.g. medical uses). This would be a complete transformation of the plastics value chain by combining the three processes described in Table 8.2. Finally, to evaluate the impact of these transformations, it is necessary to have monitoring tools (see Chapter 9).

The processes described above constitute the strategies on which firms can act to transform GVCs. To implement these strategies, firms have several tools in their hands. Work on environmental upgrading has shown that lead firms become sustainable under the effect of pressures that are essentially external (notably NGO campaigns) or intra-firm. Conversely, suppliers are generally forced to transform their practices because of changes in the strategy of lead firms. Increasingly, lead firms are imposing environmental standards to which firms must conform.

The first tool available to lead firms is standards and certifications. For example, firms can require their suppliers to obtain environmental certifications such as the organic or Rainforest Alliance labels. In the case of biomass value chains, lead firms can support and finance their suppliers to obtain these labels.

Beyond certification, lead firms can also impose specifications leading to a reduction in the consumption of resources (energy, chemicals, etc.) or to consider the end of life of products. Thus, de Marchi et al. (2013) have shown how producers such as IKEA have disseminated new types of packaging that reduce resource consumption.

The presentation of these tools shows that the issue of knowledge transfer between actors within the value chain is essential. That is to say that the adoption of new practices, organisational modes, or technologies can be very costly for the lead firms. By giving access to these environmental improvements to their suppliers, lead firms have a powerful lever to transform their value chains. It should be noted that by controlling the environmental transformation process, lead firms maintain their power within the value chains by organising governance that is at least relational if not hierarchical.

8.4   Conclusions

The key elements of innovation systems and GVCs discussed in this chapter can be reconciled in the circular bioeconomy transition perspective. Indeed, one of the main challenges for ensuring a successful transition to the circular bioeconomy is in the generation and diffusion of new knowledge to support economic, environmental, and societal shifts (e.g. qualified workforces with positive attitudes for acquiring new skills to exploit innovation paths and informed and empowered consumers and users).

Circular bioeconomy seen as an innovative interconnected network of countries and sectors needs a knowledge base able to integrate various types of knowledge and dimensions to exploit resources according to the re-framework – for example, reduce, reuse, recycle, recover, remanufacture, and refurbish. The knowledge base needed for a circular bioeconomy has to be broadened and continuously updated since the transition process has been envisaged but is yet to be achieved.

Much research (see, among others, Pauliuk 2018; The Ellen MacArthur Foundation 2015) concerning the circular bioeconomy has been focused on the circularity of resources and energy flows; however, little has been done to scrutinising the circularity of associated knowledge flows. Knowledge generation and diffusion patterns depend largely on the types of knowledge (e.g. formal or informal, technical, shift to circular business models) as well as on the properties of actors' networks (e.g. channels of knowledge generation and diffusion, policymaking processes, feedback mechanisms). Shifting from the current linear model to a circular model affects these patterns as new networks arise and other types of knowledge emerge and gain relevance in shaping the knowledge flows. In this regard, both vertical and horizontal linkages must operate simultaneously.

Take-Home Message

- The division of labour is vertical and horizontal.
- The development of innovation takes place at different scales.
- These different scales can be approached in terms of systems and relationships between actors.
- Depending on its product, a company must adopt a different positioning to succeed in innovating.

Learning Exercises

1. What are the benefits of each perspective described in this chapter for studying the bioeconomy? What are their main differences?
2. How can labels contribute to making global value chains more sustainable?
3. What types of global value chain make it possible to foster innovation?
4. What is the place of territories in the development of global value chains and innovation systems?

References

Arthur, W. B. (1989). Competing technologies, increasing returns, and lock-in by historical events. *The Economic Journal*, **99**(394), 116.

Bathelt, H., & Cohendet, P. (2014). The creation of knowledge: local building, global accessing and economic development – Toward an agenda. *Journal of Economic Geography*, **14**(5), 869–882.

Befort, N. (2021). The promises of drop-in vs. functional innovations: The case of bioplastics. *Ecological Economics*, **181**, 106886.

Birch, K. (2016). *Innovation, regional development and the life sciences: Beyond clusters*, Routledge.

Birch, K. (2017). *Innovation, regional development and the life sciences: Beyond clusters, First published*. ed, Regions and cities. London, New York: Routledge, Taylor & Francis Group.

Bolwig, S., Ponte, S., du Toit, A., Riisgaard, L., & Halberg, N. (2010). Integrating poverty and environmental concerns into value-chain analysis: A conceptual framework. *Development Policy Review*, **28**(2), 173–194.

Brusoni, S., Prencipe, A., & Pavitt, K. (2001). Knowledge specialization, organizational coupling, and the boundaries of the firm: Why do firms know more than they make? *Administrative Science Quarterly*, **46**(4), 597–621.

Cohen, W. M., & Levinthal, D. A. (1990). Absorptive capacity: A new perspective on learning and innovation. *Administrative Science Quarterly*, **35**(1), 128.

Cooke, P. (2010). Regional innovation systems: development opportunities from the 'green turn.' *Technology Analysis & Strategic Management*, **22**(7), 831–844.

Dosi, G., Freeman, C., Nelson, R., Silverberg, G., & Soete, L. (Eds.). (1988). *Technical change and economic theory*, London: Pinter.

European Commission. (2012). Innovating for Sustainable Growth: A Bioeconomy for Europe, Communication from the Commission to the European Parliament, the Council, the European Economic and Social Committee and the Committee of the Regions SWD(2012).

Freeman, C. (1995). The 'National System of Innovation' in historical perspective. *Cambridge Journal of Economics*. 19(1). doi:10.1093/oxfordjournals.cje.a035309

Galambos, L., Hikino, T., & Zamagni, V. (2007). *The global chemical industry in the age of the petrochemical revolution*, Cambridge University Press.

Gereffi, G. (1994). The organization of buyer-driven global commodity chains: How US retailers shape overseas production networks. *Commodity Chains and Global Capitalism*, 95–122.

Gereffi, G., Humphrey, J., & Sturgeon, T. (2005). The governance of global value chains. *Review of International Political Economy*, **12**(1), 78–104.

Gregersen, B., & Johnson, B. (1997). Learning economies, innovation systems and European integration. *Regional Studies,* **31**(5), 479–490.

Hellsmark, H., Frishammar, J., Söderholm, P., & Ylinenpää, H. (2016). The role of pilot and demonstration plants in technology development and innovation policy. *Research Policy*, **45**(9), 1743–1761.

Limoges, C., Scott, P., Schwartzman, S., Nowotny, H., & Gibbons, M. (1994). The new production of knowledge: The dynamics of science and research in contemporary societies. *The New Production of Knowledge*, 1–192. https://doi.org/10.4135/9781446221853

Lipinsky, E. S. (1981). Chemicals from biomass: Petrochemical substitution options. *Science*, **212**(4502), 1465–1471.

Lipinsky, E. S., & Sinclair, R. G. (1986). Is lactic acid a commodity chemical. *Chemical Engineering Progress*, **82**(8), 26–32.

Lundvall, B.-A. (1992). *National systems of innovation: Towards a theory of innovation and interactive learning*. London: Pinter Publishers.

Lundvall, B.-A. (1998). Why study national systems and national styles of innovation? *Technology Analysis & Strategic Management*, **10**(4), 403–422.

Malerba, F. (2002). Sectoral systems of innovation and production. *Research Policy*, **31**(2), 247–264.

Marchi, V. de, Maria, E. di, & Micelli, S. (2013). Environmental strategies, upgrading and competitive advantage in global value chains. *Business Strategy and the Environment*, **22**(1), 62–72.

Mazzucato, M. (2021). *Mission economy: A moonshot guide to changing capitalism*, Penguin UK.

Nelson, R. R., & Winter, S. G. (1982). An Evolutionary Theory of Economic Change.

Nelson, R. R. (1993). *National innovation systems: A comparative analysis*. Oxford: Oxford University Press.

Oltra, V., & Saint Jean, M. (2009). Variety of technological trajectories in low emission vehicles (LEVs): A patent data analysis. *Journal of Cleaner Production*, **17**(2), 201–213.

Pansera, M., & Fressoli, M. (2021). Innovation without growth: Frameworks for understanding technological change in a post-growth era. *Organization*, **28**(3), 380–404.

Pauliuk, S. (2018). Critical appraisal of the circular economy standard BS 8001: 2017 and a dashboard of quantitative system indicators for its implementation in organizations. *Resources, Conservation and Recycling*, **129**, 81–92.

Ponte, S. (2014). The evolutionary dynamics of biofuel value chains: From unipolar and government-driven to multipolar governance. *Environment and Planning A: Economy and Space*, **46**(2), 353–372.

Ponte, S. (2019). *Business, power and sustainability in a world of global value chains*, Bloomsbury Publishing.

Pyka, A. (2017), Dedicated innovation systems to support the transformation towards sustainability: Creating income opportunities and employment in the knowledge-based digital bioeconomy. *Journal of Open Innovation: Technology, Market, and Complexity*, **3**(4), 27.

Pyka, A., & Urmetzer, S. (2023). Transformation-analysis – Potentials and current limits of evolutionary economic. In K. Dopfer, ed., *Elgar Research Agenda for Evolutionary Economics*, Edward Elgar, Cheltenham, 2023.

Schot, J., & Steinmueller, W. E. (2018). Three frames for innovation policy: RD, systems of innovation and transformative change. *Research Policy*, **47**(9), 1554–1567.

Teece, D. J. (2018). Profiting from innovation in the digital economy: Enabling technologies, standards, and licensing models in the wireless world. *Research Policy*, **47**(8), 1367–1387.

The Ellen MacArthur Foundation. (2015). Towards a circular economy: Business rationale for an accelerated transition. Retrieved from https://ellenmacarthurfoundation.org/towards-a-circular-economy-business-rationale-for-an-accelerated-transition

Unruh, C. G. (2000). Understanding carbon lock-in. *Energy Policy*, **28**, 817–830.

von Hippel, E. (1994). "Sticky Information" and the locus of problem solving: Implications for innovation. *Management Science*, **40**(4), 429–439.

Wilke, U., Schlaile, M., Urmetzer, S., Müller, M., Bogner, K, & Pyka, A. (2021), Time to say 'Good Buy' to the passive consumer? A conceptual review of the consumer in the bioeconomy. *Journal of Agricultural and Environmental Ethics*, **34**, 20.

9   Monitoring Progress towards a Sustainable and Just Bioeconomy

---

> **Learning Objectives**
>
> To understand and be able to discuss critically:
>
> - the need to monitor progress towards a biodiverse and circular bioeconomy.
> - the tools and metrics available or under development to monitor such progress.
> - the limitations and way forward to monitoring systems for a sustainable and just economy and society.

9.1   Why Monitoring Progress towards a Biodiverse and Circular Bioeconomy

Typically, you cannot manage what you cannot measure. For this reason, there is a need to systematically evaluate and monitor the progress of the bioeconomy to define its contribution to economic development and its impacts (both positive and negative) on the environment and society (Figure 9.1) (Bracco et al. 2019; Calicioglu & Bogdanski 2021; Sikkema et al. 2017). To this purpose, indicators are needed to monitor progress towards a biodiverse and circular bioeconomy.

There is no single methodology for measuring the progress and sustainability of the bioeconomy; it depends on the context of reference and on what we want to evaluate (Kardung & Drabik 2021). In fact, one of the main problems related to this topic is the very definition of evaluation boundaries, their implications, and, before starting measuring, the need to know where the measurement will begin and end (Bracco et al. 2019). To assess the degree of sustainability, it is necessary to implement a multi-dimensional impact assessment that considers economic, environmental, and social dimensions (Kangas 2015; Karvonen et al. 2017). The economic dimension is the most intuitive to be understood and measured and concerns the ability of an economic system to produce income and work in a lasting way. On the other hand, the environmental component of sustainability refers to the impacts and changes caused in the environment that can affect human health and ecosystem stability. This dimension is connected to the concept of ecosystem services, which is the series of services that natural systems generate and that, directly or indirectly, influence and support human life and well-being. This concept helps in understanding the actual value of natural resources

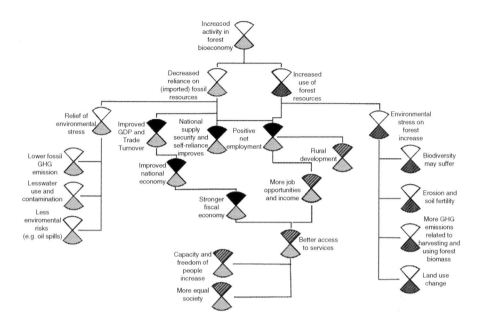

Figure 9.1 Pathways of impact in the forest bioeconomy at the national level. The upper and lower quarters of a circle represent respectively the sustainability dimensions expected to be impacted (white for environmental, black for economic and dark grey with white stripes for social) and the sign of the impact (grey for positive and dark grey with black stripes for negative).
Source: Karvonen et al. (2017)

and the compromises associated with their management (Karvonen et al. 2017; Villamagna et al. 2013). Finally, there is the social dimension of sustainability, which compared to the other two components is less studied and universally applicable, despite some attempts to develop universal social indicators (Jørgensen et al. 2008). Different authors, actually, state that social sustainability is more significant if evaluated on a national or regional scale since different social issues have different weights depending on the context of reference (Karvonen et al. 2017; Morales et al. 2015).

As mentioned earlier, to obtain an overall assessment of sustainability, it is important to use a multi-dimensional approach, not least because impacts on individual dimensions are interconnected and overlap. Indicators must thus be able to represent the three dimensions of sustainability, bearing information about the technical and biophysical issues associated with assessing the resource flows and cascading along the supply chain, as well as the potential environmental impacts; the social and human capital, including the level of rights, inclusion, and equality; and the economic issues such as turnover, added value, employment contribution, and labour productivity. In addition, indicators are also needed to evaluate the status and success of the governance process that supports the new economic model in public and private systems, this including public policies, subsidies, legislative frameworks, and other policy instruments, as well as the visions put in place and realm of influence exercised by private actors such as non-governmental agencies, sectors, companies and hybrid enterprises, think tanks, and other private sector entities (Figure 9.2).

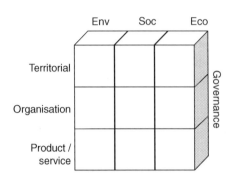

Env: technical and biophysical issues associated with assessing the resource flows and cascading along the bioeconomy, supply chain, as well as the potential environmental impacts; **Soc:** social and human capital in the bioeconomy, including also the level of rights, inclusion and equality; **Eco:** economic issues in the bioeconomy such as turnover, added value, employment contribution, labour productivity; **Territorial:** implementation of the bioeconomy at different territorial scales (local, regional, national or global); **Organisation:** implementation of the bioeconomy by companies or other actors; **Product:** implementation of the bioeconomy along the various stages of development and production for products and services; **Governance:** bioeconomy-related public policies coupled with visions and strategies by non-governmental agencies, sectors, companies and hybrid enterprises, think tanks, and other private sector entities.

Figure 9.2 Types of indicators needed to monitor just and sustainable progress towards new economic models such as the bioeconomy.

Additionally, in defining a monitoring and evaluation framework for new economic models, three levels are considered: the territory in which the model must be implemented, the organisations affected or involved, and the changes at product and service levels. The first level evaluates the implementation, in each specific territorial context, of the new economic model for the main purpose of guiding policymaking. Therefore, the aim of the evaluation is to monitor and measure the contribution of the bioeconomy to economic development and its environmental and social impacts at different territorial scales (local, regional, national, or global). In this case, the boundaries of the evaluation are wide and open and, often, the definition of an evaluation framework is complicated (Bracco et al. 2019). In fact, the driving factors that contribute to the transition process towards a sustainable bioeconomy vary between countries and territorial realities. Each territory has specific environmental, economic, and social characteristics, as well as different regulatory frameworks and policy mixes. For this reason, for example, the bioeconomy strategies implemented by the EU Member States vary in the objectives, measures, and actions identified, at both national and regional levels. Consequently, the indicators and tools used to measure the development, or the success of a strategy depends on these characteristics and are not applicable in any other country. However, to obtain data that allow the comparison between the various countries, it is necessary to create a common framework (Lier et al. 2018). Indicators at the organisation level assess the level of implementation of the new economic model in companies or other establishments. Here too, indicators should be able to capture the three dimensions of sustainability, as well as the governance processes in the organisation (e.g. agendas, leverage, and influence over the value chain). Regarding the analysis and monitoring at the product/service level, the objective is the evaluation of improvements along the various stages of development, production, retailing, and usage, again reflecting multiple sustainability and governance aspects, although in this case such perspectives are analysed within the more defined and enclosed boundaries of product/service lifecycle.

9.2 An Overview of Existing Monitoring Systems in the Bioeconomy, Green Economy, and Circular Economy

A portfolio of tools, metrics, and assessment frameworks have been or are being developed to support measuring the progress towards achieving the bioeconomy, the green economy, and the circular economy (Table 9.1). As mentioned in Section 9.1, these range from technical and biophysical types (e.g. resources and ecosystem services flows) to social and economic ones (e.g. financial flows, employment) to governance ones (e.g. public policies, subsidies, legislative frameworks, visions and tools of influence by private actors). Moreover, different indicators are suitable to address product, organisation, and/or regional, national, and global processes. In this section, we provide a number of examples which even if they are not exhaustive, are supposed to illustrate the diversity of indicators.

9.2.1 Measuring Progress in the Bioeconomy

There have been many independent efforts to develop indicators for the bioeconomy (Kardung et al. 2021). To synthesise the available information about useful indicators for monitoring and evaluation activities in the context of the bioeconomy,

Table 9.1 Examples of tools, metrics, and assessment frameworks for measuring progress towards the bioeconomy, the green economy, and the circular economy (mainly focusing on technical and biophysical aspects)

	Assessing bio-based content and fossil-biomass substitution share of economic activities	Assessing the contribution of abiotic resources and natural capital to economic activities	Assessing circularity of economic activities
Metrics/assessments at good/service level	e.g. bio-based carbon content (European standard EN 16785-1, European standards (2022))	e.g. product/consumption biodiversity footprint (PBF 2022)	e.g. Material Circularity Indicator (Ellen Mac Arthur Foundation 2022b)
Metrics/assessments at organisation level (e.g. company)	n/a	e.g. Natural capital protocol (Natural Capital Coalition 2016), Nature-related Financial Disclosures alliance (TNFD 2022)	e.g. Circulytics® (Ellen Mac Arthur Foundation 2022a)
Metrics/assessments at regional, national, and global levels	e.g. EU Bioeconomy Monitoring System (EC 2022)	e.g. Global Green Economy Index ™ (Dual Citizen 2022), Green Growth Indicators (OECD 2022), System of Environmental-Economic Accounting (SEEA 2022)	e.g. Global Circularity Metric (Circle economy 2018), EU Circularity rate, recycling rate (Eurostat 2022)

Note that the list is not meant to be comprehensive, but it just provides examples.

the Food and Agriculture Organization of the United Nations (FAO) established the International Sustainable Bioeconomy Working Group (ISBWG) as part of the project on guidelines for the sustainable bioeconomy. One of the activities conducted by the group was the creation of a list of aspirational principles and criteria which has the potential to provide a basis for building a unified monitoring framework by linking generic principles and criteria to context-specific indicators. These principles and criteria have made it possible to derive sixty-nine impact categories useful for linking the criteria to the indicators. In fact, each impact category has been associated with a series of indicators identified through a precise review of existing initiatives and approaches to monitoring the bioeconomy (Bracco et al. 2019). Specifically, geographical scope and sectoral variety were the key aspects considered for the definition of impact categories and indicators. The first aspect considered different territorial levels (global, regional, national, subnational), while the second considered different sectors (primary, secondary, tertiary, supply, support, regulation, and cultural), which allows the wide range of value chains and products involved in the bioeconomy to be encompassed. Through these approaches, two lists of indicators have been defined: one at the territorial level and one at the product/value chain level. In the definition of the first list, to address the impact categories, priority was given to the Sustainable Development Goals (SDGs), adopted in 2015 by the UN to promote its Agenda 2030. In the second list, priority was given to indicators for standards, labels, and certifications. The priority use of SDGs aims to minimise the risk of duplication and limits additional efforts and resources devoted to the monitoring and evaluation of the sustainable bioeconomy (Bracco et al. 2019).

The same FAO-appointed working group identified a total of 268 indicators for the monitoring of the various impact categories relating to biodiversity conservation, food security, and the resilience of biomass producers (Bracco et al. 2019). Other studies and projects have also attempted to synthetise information about indicators into coherent frameworks. For example, a report by Lier et al. (2018) offers an overview of bioeconomy strategies, policies, initiatives, and indicators in the context of EU Member States. The aim of BioMonitor, the Horizon 2020 research project, was to establish a monitoring framework for the EU bioeconomy of relevance to various societal stakeholders (Biomonitor 2022). The STAR-ProBio, also a Horizon 2020 project, defined an Integrated Assessment Tool (IAT) through a transdisciplinary process involving contributions from both industry and academia. The resulting tool consists of forty-eight sustainability indicators (at both the firm and product levels) with proposed metrics based on existing standards, methodologies, and best practices in sustainability assessment. Moreover, the tool proposed a scoring system that allows comparisons among bio-based products as well as comparisons against conventional products (for additional details, see Box 9.1).

9.2.2   Measuring Progress in the Green Economy

One form of monitoring for progress towards the green economy includes the accounting and internalisation of ecosystem services values in the current indicators

---

Box 9.1 Key Performance Indicators for the Evaluation of the Italian Bioeconomy

National-level performance indicators for the bioeconomy have been developed independently in several EU countries, as well as in Argentina, Australia, Malaysia, South Africa, and the United States (Kardung et al. 2021). In Italy, the assessment of the implementation of the bioeconomy is based on national data and statistics. The key performance indicators monitor a range of dimensions: innovation (e.g. intellectual property rights applications, patents, trademarks, designs), human skills (e.g. tertiary education, R&D employment), biomass availability (e.g. production and import of forest biomass), production and employment structures (e.g. innovative start-ups and employment in the bioeconomy sectors), investments (private and public spending on R&D), demographic, and market analyses (turnover, added value, exports, imports). An additional set of indicators have been selected to assess how the proposed measures affect social systems and the environment. The main objectives of this second set of indicators are to guarantee food safety, manage natural resources in a sustainable way, reduce dependence on non-renewable resources, cope with climate change, and strengthen economic growth (Fava et al. 2021; Intesa Sanpaolo & Assobiotec 2019).

---

of economic development and in private decision-making (Daily et al. 2009). Over the past few decades, an abundance of frameworks, tools, indicators, and data has been developed in the biophysical, socio-cultural, and monetary value of ecosystem services, including their synergies and trade-offs (Harrison et al. 2018).

Available environmental and socio-ecological data feed into regional and national accounting systems, such as the System of Environmental-Economic Accounting (SEEA 2022) adopted by the United Nations Statistical Commission to highlight the relationship between natural capital, the economy, and society. Provisioning services, such as food and fibres, are more easily accounted for compared to immaterial services. This is partly because materially tangible services are more easily quantifiable or are already sold in markets. Another example of a macro-level metric used for policy support is the Natural Capital Index, which is informative of biodiversity and ecological integrity at the regional or national level (ten Brink et al. 2012). Examples of national-level metrics more generally related to the overall green economy (as opposed to exclusively focused on natural capital and ecosystem services), including indicators of political, social, economic, and ecological progress, are the Global Green Economy Index promoted by private consultancy Dual Citizen (2022) and the Green Growth Indicators framework by the Organisation for Economic Co-operation and Development (OECD 2022).

In the private sector, several initiatives have been aimed at integrating ecosystem services into business sustainability. The Natural Capital Protocol (Natural Capital Coalition 2016) is a framework developed by the Capitals Coalition to support companies in assessing their impacts and dependencies on ecosystem services, with considerations extending to their supply-chain environment. The Taskforce on Nature-related Financial Disclosures (TNFD 2022) is a market-led global initiative aimed at developing a risk management and disclosure framework that is supposed to support organisations in reporting and responding to nature-related risks and opportunities. The ultimate goal is to redirect global financial flows towards nature-positive activities. An example of a product-level metric for the green economy is the Product Biodiversity Footprint (PBF) approach, developed as a public–private partnership involving I-Care & Consult and Sayari, funded by the French Environmental Protection Agency (ADEME), and the companies L'Oréal, Groupe Avril, and Keering. The approach integrates LCA and ecological knowledge to allow comparisons between product variants to support product sustainable design (Asselin et al. 2020).

9.2.3   Measuring Progress in the Circular Economy

The circularity of the global economy is estimated at about 9 per cent (de Wit et al. 2018). This represents the share of cycled materials against the total material inputs of the global economy each year. In the EU 27, the circularity rate has increased by 4.5 percentage points since 2004, up to almost 13 per cent in 2020 (Eurostat 2022). The circularity rate is an indication of the share of the secondary materials which are recovered and re-inserted into the economy. However, such a rate is lower than the recycling rate (in the EU 27, 55%), because circularity requires and combines additional solutions beyond recycling waste, such as improving the efficiency and longevity of processes/products. Both the circularity and recycling rates show large variations based on the type of material studied. In 2020, biomass in the EU 27 was circulated at a rate of 9.6 per cent, against 25.3 per cent for metal ores, but progress is expected (ibid.). According to Haas et al. (2015), there is a need for a focus shift from end-of-pipe solutions (such as recycling) to an overall reduction in the continuous growth of the societal stock. In particular, solutions should be aimed at increasing the longevity of products and infrastructures, reducing material requirements, and facilitating upgrades, repairs, remanufacturing, and reuse.

Examples of metrics at the product and organisation levels are those promoted by the Ellen MacArthur Foundation, a private sector organisation that promotes the development of the circular economy. The Circulytics framework includes several company-wide indicators, including aspects about the potential for transformation towards circularity (e.g. strategy, innovation, skills, supply-chain influence) and aspects about the actual circular economy outcomes (e.g. material and water flows, energy use, product design) (Ellen Mac Arthur Foundation 2022a). The Material Circularity Indicator (a score between 0 and 1, where 1 indicates the highest circularity level) crunches down product-level information about material reused/recycled, lifespan and durability, destination of use, and efficiency of recycling at product creation and at disposal phase (Ellen Mac Arthur Foundation 2022b).

Overall, evaluating progress in the circular economy presents challenges, even though indicators are based on well-established methodologies such as material flow analysis, life cycle analysis (LCA), and input–output analysis (see Box 9.1).

Limitations exist in accounting for certain aspects, such as the length of cycles or the increasing scarcity of resources, and in fully representing progress in regard to multi-dimensional aspects of social and ecological sustainability (Corona et al. 2019), which calls for multi-dimensional and multi-criteria approaches to evaluate the circular economy (Oliveira et al. 2021).

9.3   Challenges and Prospects for Monitoring Progress towards a Sustainable and Just Economy and Society

The bioeconomy includes the production and use of a wide variety of raw materials, products, and technologies. The future development of this meta-sector depends on the creation of new markets and the conversion of existing industries and markets. Moreover, there are many hybrid sectors for which no distinction is made between organic and non-organic-based products. On top of this, the development of policies and strategies for the bioeconomy is linked to the reference territory and other contextual aspects. All these characteristics affect the availability, quality, and consistency of data necessary to set up and apply a monitoring system. To assess the sustainability promises of the bioeconomy, it is necessary to adopt indicators that couple the territorial, organisational, and products/services perspectives.

The need for such indicators raises three issues. First, to measure change, different methodological tools can be used for putting indicators into practice (Box 9.1). However, indicators are also chosen based on the objectives set by policies or other decision-making agents. This means that an indicator is not neutral but reflects the broad framing of the decision-makers and the imaginaries guiding the decision-making process (Holmgren et al. 2020).

Second, linked to the previous issue, the results are not 'absolute'. An indicator only indicates what it has been designed for, as it happens for labels (see Chapter 8). It means that the indicators must be further contextualised by applying weights and priorities to each indicator. To this end, democratic participatory methods may allow to improve the social appropriation of transition policies and fit these policies for the needs of the citizens. The weighted values can and should be aggregated into summary indices to provide a picture of the general impacts of each alternative scenario evaluated (Karvonen et al. 2017).

Third, there is a major issue regarding data availability. This chapter showed the progress made during the past fifteen years regarding the monitoring of the bioeconomy (see also D'Adamo et al. (2020) and Giampietro & Renner (2021)), as well as of the circular and green economy. Despite major progress, the monitoring of the bioeconomy remains problematic due to the lack of data (Fava et al. 2021). Available data (e.g. from national statistics) have not been designed to evaluate the dynamic relationship between the economic, social, and sustainability dimensions. Despite this, multiple, complementary, and overlapping indicators for sustainability and sustainable development exist (see also Box 6.3 in Chapter 6). There are currently 231 indicators available for the United Nations Sustainable Development Goals, 1,600

World Bank global development indicators, and 367 statistical measures (of which 338 are different) relating to 138 indicators for monitoring the seventeen SDGs of the UN's 2030 Agenda for Sustainable Development (ISTAT 2022; Kardung et al. 2021; Kardung & Drabik 2021). While all efforts are important, the sheer number of potential indicators increases the complexity of the quest to assess sustainability transformations.

In conclusion, let us recall that there is a twofold debate on the bioeconomy. On the one hand, it is a question of determining what form the bioeconomy of the future should take. We showed in Chapter 2 and 3 that they can be very different from each other. On the other hand, the second debate concerns the strategies and actions needed for the transition to the bioeconomy. These will depend on the type of bioeconomy imagined and expected (Befort 2020). From this point of view, the debate on the design of indicators must be linked to the reflections on the transition paths towards a sustainable bioeconomy and the monitoring of the evolution of the bioeconomy across products, organisations, sectors, and regions (Kardung & Drabik 2021).

Take-Home Message

- Indicators should be able to capture the three sustainability dimensions of the bioeconomy on various scales (territorial, organisational, products/services), as well as information about the governance processes underpinning the implementation of the bioeconomy.
- A range of monitoring systems is underway, although these are largely being developed independently by nations or other actors.
- Metrics and tools are also available to assess how our society and economy can maintain natural capital and circularity of resources.
- Challenges remain in monitoring progress towards a sustainable and just society and economy.

Learning Exercises

1. What indicators are needed to measure progress in a (circular) bioeconomy, and why?
2. What monitoring systems are in place or being developed for assessing progress towards the bioeconomy at national, company, and product levels?
3. What tools and metrics/assessments are available or are being developed to measure aspects of the circular economy and the green economy at national, company, and product levels?
4. What are the limitations of monitoring systems, tools, metrics, and assessment frameworks which have been or are being developed to monitor progress towards a just and sustainable economy and society?
5. What is the way forward to develop multi-dimensional metrics which can capture progress towards a just and sustainable economy and society?

Online Resources

Lecture 'Circular, green and bioeconomy?' by Adj.Prof. D'Amato, University of Helsinki. Available at: www2.helsinki.fi/fi/unitube/video/4e981398-96fa-4ec8-aac6-81047267cff5

Lecture 'Ecosystem services: assessment and indicators' by Adj.Prof. D'Amato, University of Helsinki. Available at: www2.helsinki.fi/fi/unitube/video/e13f0893-77bc-41ce-a9a4-66490bb11504

Lecture 'Ecosystem services: valuation' by Adj.Prof. D'Amato, University of Helsinki. Available at: www2.helsinki.fi/fi/unitube/video/704f76ef-df44-472b-b94d-aec969d15f34

Resources and toolkits for the Material Circularity Indicator by Ellen Mac Arthur Foundation. Available at: https://ellenmacarthurfoundation.org/material-circularity-indicator

Resources and toolkits for Circulytics®. Available at: https://ellenmacarthurfoundation.org/resources/circulytics/resources#:~:text=The%20Material%20Circularity%20Indicator%20(MCI)&text=Measures%20the%20circularity%20of%20material,product%20design%20and%20material%20procurement

Resource from FAO on Indicators to monitor and evaluate the sustainability of bioeconomy www.fao.org/3/ca6048en/CA6048EN.pdf

References

Asselin, A., Rabaud, S., Catalan, C., … Neveux, G. (2020). Product biodiversity footprint – A novel approach to compare the impact of products on biodiversity combining life cycle assessment and ecology. *Journal of Cleaner Production*, **248**, 119262.

Befort, N. (2020). Going beyond definitions to understand tensions within the bioeconomy: The contribution of sociotechnical regimes to contested fields. *Technological Forecasting and Social Change*, **153**, 119923.

Biomonitor. (2022). Biomonitor Project. Retrieved from https://biomonitor.eu/

Bracco, S., Tani, A., Çalıcıoğlu, Ö., Gomez San Juan, M., & Bogdanski, A. (2019). *Indicators to Monitor and Evaluate the Sustainability of Bioeconomy: Overview and a Proposed Way Forward*, FAO.

Calicioglu, Ö., & Bogdanski, A. (2021). Linking the bioeconomy to the 2030 sustainable development agenda: Can SDG indicators be used to monitor progress towards a sustainable bioeconomy? *New Biotechnology*, **61**, 40–49.

Circle economy. (2018). The Circularity Gap Report 2018. Circle Economy.

Corona, B., Shen, L., Reike, D., Rosales Carreón, J., & Worrell, E. (2019). Towards sustainable development through the circular economy – A review and critical assessment on current circularity metrics. *Resources, Conservation and Recycling*, **151**, 104498.

D'Adamo, I., Falcone, P. M., & Morone, P. (2020). A new socio-economic indicator to measure the performance of bioeconomy sectors in Europe. *Ecological Economics*, **176**, 106724.

Daily, G. C., Polasky, S., Goldstein, J., … Shallenberger, R. (2009). Ecosystem services in decision making: Time to deliver. *Frontiers in Ecology and the Environment*, **7**(1), 21–28.

de Wit, M., Hoogzaad, J., & von Daniels, C. (2018). The Circularity gap report. *Circle Economy*.

Dual Citizen. (2022). Global Green Economy Index (GGEI). Retrieved from https://dualcitizeninc.com/global-green-economy-index/

EC. (2022). EU Bioeconomy Monitoring System. Retrieved from https://knowledge4policy.ec.europa.eu/bioeconomy/monitoring_en

Ellen Mac Arthur Foundation. (2022a). Resources and toolkits for Circulytics®. Retrieved from https://ellenmacarthurfoundation.org/resources/circulytics/resources#:~:text=The%20Material%20Circularity%20Indicator%20(MCI)&text=Measures%20the%20circularity%20of%20material,product%20design%20and%20material%20procurement

Ellen Mac Arthur Foundation. (2022b). Resources and toolkits for the Material Circularity Indicator. Retrieved from https://ellenmacarthurfoundation.org/material-circularity-indicator

European standards. DIN EN 16785-1 Bio-based products – Bio-based content – Part 1: Determination of the bio-based content using the radiocarbon analysis and elemental analysis. (2022). Retrieved from www.en-standard.eu/din-en-16785-1-bio-based-products-bio-based-content-part-1-determination-of-the-bio-based-content-using-the-radiocarbon-analysis-and-elemental-analysis/?gclid=CjwKCAjwve2TBhByEiwAaktM1EIYGW2nda20UtVE_VHghu4m_A3QZc4FWydtNrcHBSfbXGNOszC6xxoCkYAQAvD_BwE

Eurostat. (2022). Circular economy – Material flows. Retrieved from https://ec.europa.eu/eurostat/statistics-explained/index.php?title=Circular_economy_-_material_flows#-Sankey_diagram_of_material_flows

Fava, F., Gardossi, L., Brigidi, P., Morone, P., Carosi, D. A. R., & Lenzi, A. (2021). The bioeconomy in Italy and the new national strategy for a more competitive and sustainable country. *New Biotechnology*, **61**, 124–136.

Giampietro, M., & Renner, A. (2021). The Generation of Meaning and Preservation of Identity in Complex Adaptive Systems the LIPHE4 Criteria, pp. 29–46.

Haas, W., Krausmann, F., Wiedenhofer, D., & Heinz, M. (2015). How circular is the global economy?: An assessment of material flows, waste production, and recycling in the European Union and the world in 2005. *Journal of Industrial Ecology*, **19**(5), 765–777.

Harrison, P. A., Dunford, R., Barton, D. N., … Zulian, G. (2018). Selecting methods for ecosystem service assessment: A decision tree approach. *Ecosystem Services*, **29**, 481–498.

Holmgren, S., D'Amato, D., & Giurca, A. (2020). Bioeconomy imaginaries: A review of forest-related social science literature. *Ambio*, **49**(12), 1860–1877.

Intesa Sanpaolo & Assobiotec. (2019). 5th report on European Bioeconomy. Retrieved from https://group.intesasanpaolo.com/content/dam/portalgroup/repository-documenti/research/it/bioeconomia/La%20Bioeconomia%20in%20Europa_nr%205.pdf

ISTAT. (2022). Istat indicators for sustainable development goals. Retrieved from www.istat.it/it/benessere-e-sostenibilit%C3%A0/obiettivi-di-sviluppo-sostenibile/gli-indicatori-istat

Jørgensen, A., le Bocq, A., Nazarkina, L., & Hauschild, M. (2008). Methodologies for social life cycle assessment. *The International Journal of Life Cycle Assessment*, **13**(2), 96–103.

Kangas, A. (2015). Natural Resources Institute Finland – A foundation for the bioeconomy.

Kardung, M., Cingiz, K., Costenoble, O., … Zhu, B. X. (2021). Development of the circular bioeconomy: Drivers and indicators. *Sustainability*, **13**(1), 413.

Kardung, M., & Drabik, D. (2021). Framework for Assessing the Development of a Circular Bioeconomy: BioMonitor Policy Brief# 5.

Karvonen, J., Halder, P., Kangas, J., & Leskinen, P. (2017). Indicators and tools for assessing sustainability impacts of the forest bioeconomy. *Forest Ecosystems*, **4**(1), 2. https://doi.org/10.1016/j.jclepro.2019.07.039

Lier, M., Aarne, M., Kärkkäinen, L., Korhonen, K. T., Yli-Viikari, A., & Packalen, T. (2018). Synthesis on bioeconomy monitoring systems in the EU Member States.

Morales, M. R., Tirado, A. A., & Lobato-Calleros, O. (2015). Additional indicators to promote social sustainability within government programs: Equity and efficiency. *Sustainability (2071–1050)*, **7**(7).

Natural Capital Coalition. (2016). Natural Capital Protocol. Retrieved from www.natural capitalcoalition.org/protocol

OECD. (2022). Green growth indicators framework. Retrieved from www.oecd.org/green growth/green-growth-indicators/#:~:text=%E2%80%9CGreen%20growth%20is%20 about%20fostering,give%20rise%20to%20new%20economic

Oliveira, M., Miguel, M., van Langen, S. K., … Genovese, A. (2021). Circular economy and the transition to a sustainable society: Integrated assessment methods for a new paradigm. *Circular Economy and Sustainability*, **1**(1), 99–113.

PBF. (2022). Product Biodiversity Footprint. Retrieved from https://sayari.co/product-bio diversity-footprint#:~:text=The%20%E2%80%9CProduct%20Biodiversity%20 Footprint%E2%80%9D%20(,considering%20their%20impact%20on%20biodiversity.

SEEA. (2022). Green growth indicators. System of Environmental-Economic Accounting. Retrieved from https://seea.un.org/

Sikkema, R., Dallemand, J. F., Matos, C. T., van der Velde, M., & San-Miguel-Ayanz, J. (2017). How can the ambitious goals for the EU's future bioeconomy be supported by sustainable and efficient wood sourcing practices? *Scandinavian Journal of Forest Research*, **32**(7), 551–558.

ten Brink, P., Mazza, L., Badura, T., Kettunen, M., & Withana, S. (2012). Nature and its role in the transition to a green economy. *A TEEB Report.* www.Teebweb.org *and* www .Ieep.eu.

TNFD. (2022). Taskforce on Nature-related Financial Disclosures. Retrieved from https://tnfd .global/.

Villamagna, A. M., Angermeier, P. L., & Bennett, E. M. (2013). Capacity, pressure, demand, and flow: A conceptual framework for analyzing ecosystem service provision and delivery. *Ecological Complexity*, **15**, 114–121.

Index

Printed in the United States
by Baker & Taylor Publisher Services